MARSHALLS THEOLOGICAL LIBRARY

General Editor

PETER TOON, MA, M.TH, D.PHIL

Consultant Editor

RALPH P. MARTIN, MA, PH.D

MARSHALLS THEOLOGICAL LIBRARY

OLD TESTAMENT THEOLOGY:
A FRESH APPROACH
by R. E. Clements

EVANGELICAL THEOLOGY 1833–1856:
A RESPONSE TO TRACTARIANISM
by Peter Toon

NEW TESTAMENT PROPHECY
by David Hill

Other volumes in preparation

EVANGELICAL THEOLOGY

1833-1856

A Response to Tractarianism

PETER TOON

MARSHALL, MORGAN & SCOTT

LONDON

49532

2 83 · 4 2. ℬ .

MARSHALL, MORGAN & SCOTT
a member of the Pentos group
1 Bath Street, London EC1V 9LB

Copyright © Peter Toon 1979
First Published 1979

British Library CIP data
Toon, Peter
   Evangelical theology, 1833–1856 (Marshalls theological library).
   1. Evangelicalism–Church of England–History
   2. Oxford Movement–History
   3. Theological, Anglican–History
   I. Title
   230'.3   BX5098
ISBN 0-551-05582-0

Printed in Great Britain by Butler & Tanner Ltd
Frome and London.

*For Roger T. Beckwith
and James I. Packer
in thankfulness for their work in and
for Latimer House, Oxford*

CONTENTS

PREFACE

First of all I would like to express my thanks to the Council of Latimer House, Oxford, for employing me for three years in Oxford in order that I could write on the history of Evangelical theology. In those three years (1973–6) I produced with Michael Smout a biography of Bishop J. C. Ryle (published by James Clarke in the UK and Reiner Publications in the USA) and this book. It is a great privilege to live and work in Oxford.

It appears to me that a lot of Anglican Evangelical theology in the nineteenth century was produced in controversial situations. This book attempts to describe how the Evangelicals reacted to the appearance of Tractarian theology. A further book needs to be written showing how they reacted to the 'Liberal' theology – that is to new views about the Bible, revelation, creation, miracles and related subjects which gained popularity in England from about 1850.

I am very grateful to the Rev Dr Geoffrey Rowell, chaplain of Keble College, who read and criticised the manuscript when it was being written. Also to the Rev Dr E. Yarnold, S.J., the Rev R. T. Beckwith, and Canon Michael Hennell I am grateful for their comments on specific parts of the work. The late Fr Stephen Dessain, together with Dr John Walsh, Clyde Ervine, George Herring and Brian Stanley gave me help on specific points.

To the librarians of Pusey House, Oxford, and Lambeth Palace, London, together with the Keeper of Western Manuscripts at the Bodleian Library, Oxford, I am grateful for permission to use manuscripts.

My wife has made sacrifices so that I could complete this work and she deserves many thanks.

Oak Hill Theological College   PETER TOON
London N14
4 May 1977

INTRODUCTION

There has been no shortage of studies of John Henry Newman and the Tractarian Movement. Readers of this literature could perhaps be forgiven if they gained the impression that the only significant group in the Church of England between 1833 and 1845 was that surrounding Newman, Edward B. Pusey and John Keble.

In fact, of course, the Tractarians were only a minority in Oxford and though their developing teaching was widely read and appreciated it soon met the opposition of able men of different churchmanship. Academic, liberal thinkers quickly recognised the tendencies of the new theology. Dr T. Arnold of Rugby School published his famous article on 'The Oxford Malignants' in the Whig *Edinburgh Review* as early as 1836, while from Professors R. D. Hampden and Baden Powell came criticism of what appeared to them to be the elevation of Church Tradition above Holy Scripture.[1] Many of the older type of orthodox clergy, the 'high and dry' as they have been called, also soon became embarrassed by the novel doctrines of those whom they had at first regarded as friends. One of their number, Professor Godfrey Faussett, believed he was witnessing the 'Revival of Popery' and said so publicly in a sermon in 1838.[2] Another, Ashurst T. Gilbert, Principal of Brasenose and Vice-Chancellor, was made Bishop of Chichester by Sir Robert Peel because of his opposition to Tractarianism in the University. This opposition from High Churchmen, however, was never large and not always significant for the basic reason that Tractarianism often appeared only to be a variation or modification of traditional High Churchmanship.

Within Oxford there were only a few Evangelicals in prominent positions – John MacBride was Principal of Magdalen Hall (later Hertford College), Benjamin Symons was Warden of Wadham and Richard L. Cotton was Provost of Worcester. The Vice-Principal of St Edmund Hall was John Hill, while in several of the Colleges known Evangelicals held Fellowships. For example, for part of the period W. W. Champneys, afterwards Rector of Whitechapel, was Fellow of Brasenose, Charles A. Heurtley, afterwards Lady Margaret Professor, was Fellow of Corpus Christi, and E. A. Litton, author of several important theological text-books, was Fellow of Oriel. And James Garbett, Fellow of Brasenose from 1825 until 1836, became the Professor of Poetry in 1842. All these men played a part in opposing Tractarianism.[3]

Outside the University, as the Evangelical opposition to the new movement produced hundreds of tracts, pamphlets, printed sermons and books, the dangers of the new 'heresies' were constantly brought before the eyes of the Evangelical constituency through its weekly and monthly newsjournals and magazines. There was certainly quantity, if not quality, in the mass of material. Neither the growing liberal wing of the Church, the Broad Churchmen as they came to be called, nor the orthodox churchmen were able to match this tremendous output of literature by Evangelicals, supported as they were by publications from non-Anglican Evangelicals from England, Scotland and Switzerland.

In view of the size and theological commitment of Evangelicalism such a prolific response was predictable. The number of Evangelical clergy had grown consistently since the beginning of the nineteenth century. In the first decade they numbered about one-twentieth, by 1820 they had grown to one-tenth, in 1829 they were an eighth, in 1839 a fifth and in 1853, by one calculation, over a quarter of all clergy in England and Wales.[4] Lay strength was possibly even greater. So when the Tractarian Movement began the majority of English clergy were still of the orthodox type and were in a position to retain and renew their High Churchmanship (as many did), to move towards the Tractarians (as many did), to move towards the Evangelicals (as a few did) or to move in the direction of a Broad Churchmanship (as some did). But, though the Evangelical clergy increased in numbers and as a proportion of the whole, there was a general admission that their ministries did not in general have that spiritual quality and commitment which had characterised the men of the period of Scott, Milner, Venn and

Simeon. To assert this is not, however, to agree with one writer for whom the Evangelical Movement was 'already effete' by 1833, or with another who spoke of 'an exhausted teaching and a spent enthusiasm'.[5] It is possible to be a large, growing and powerful party in the Church without making significant achievements in the realms of personal or corporate holiness or theological enterprise. Further, it is well known that Evangelicals were very prominent in foreign missions before and after 1833.

In most of the books on the Oxford Movement there are references to, or hints concerning, the opposition of Evangelicals to the new doctrines. These are probably made in the most explicit way by Bishop E. A. Knox in his book, *The Tractarian Movement, 1833–1845* (1933). Newman, having had an Evangelical background as a schoolboy, was conscious of the reaction of 'the Peculiars' (as he called Evangelicals) and so he often referred to it in his letters and mentioned it in his *Apologia*.[6] But, as yet, no one appears to have made a serious attempt to write an account of the Evangelical response to Tractarianism. Thus the purpose of this work is twofold. First of all, it is to establish that there was a large and powerful Evangelical response to Tractarianism; and, secondly, it is to describe and evaluate this response. So the work is divided into two parts. In the first the origin and progress of the controversy between the Tractarians and Evangelicals is described and in the second three major areas of doctrine, which were at the heart of the battle of words, are studied. These are the Rule of Faith, Justification, and the Church, Ministry and Sacraments.

As to the limits of this study the year 1833 chooses itself as the *terminus a quo* since it was in the autumn of this year that the *Tracts for the Times* began to appear. The year 1856 is chosen as the *terminus ad quem* in order to include the Evangelical response to the final stage of the developing eucharistic doctrine as found in the writings of Archdeacons Denison and Wilberforce and Professor Pusey. However, this point in time is a useful termination for other reasons. By this time the face of at least part of the Tractarian Movement was changing and assuming the character of what became known as the Ritualist Movement.[7] And, on the other side of the fence, the Evangelicals were beginning to enjoy favours, in terms of preferment, from the patronage of the Prime Minister, Lord Palmerston, and these were, in the main, new experiences.[8]

In attempting to provide an historical account of the Evangelical response to Tractarianism a writer is faced with several difficulties. First of all, while there is an abundance of books, articles and monographs on the Tractarians, there is no comprehensive, scholarly study of the Evangelicals in the Church of England in this period when the *Tracts for the Times* were being written and circulated.[9] Of older works G. R. Balleine's *History of the Evangelical Party* is regrettably too sketchy to be of significant help. Of more recent studies Ford K. Brown's *Fathers of the Victorians*, even if some of its assumptions are questionable, certainly helps to set the scene in the period leading up to the birth of Tractarianism. John Reynold's *The Evangelicals at Oxford* provides a valuable list and analysis of Evangelicals educated at, and prominent in, Oxford, before, during and after the period of this study. Further, Ian Bradley's briskly written *The Call to Seriousness: the Evangelical Impact on the Victorians* provides a very useful, if popular, account of the Evangelical ethos and David Newsome's eminently readable *The Parting of Friends* highlights the loss to Evangelicalism of the children of the Wilberforce and Manning households. Useful and important as these books are, they do not provide, either singly or together, a unified, coherent account of the size, nature, impact and theology of the Evangelical party as it lived through the social, political and religious crises associated with the Emancipation Act, the Reform Act, the suppression of the Irish Bishoprics, *Tract 90*, the Maynooth Grant, the Papal Aggression and the impact of German biblical criticism on the Church.

Secondly, there is some difficulty in defining who were Evangelicals in this period. No one doubts that Lord Shaftesbury, Edward Bickersteth and Archbishop Sumner were Evangelicals but other churchmen are less easy instantly to categorise. Such were the intense religious feelings generated in this period that at times clergy and laity of the old orthodox school were drawn towards the Evangelicals (as the Evangelicals were drawn to them) as they jointly protested about some Tractarian innovation or on behalf of some truth of the Reformation. The term

'Evangelical High Churchmen' was coined both to distinguish
traditional High Churchmen from Tractarians and to emphasise
their commitment to the Reformation principles of the sole
authority of Holy Scripture and justification by grace through
faith. To distinguish an Evangelical High Churchman from
an Evangelical with a high doctrine of the visible, episcopally
governed, national Church is not easy and between about 1838
and 1848 perhaps impossible in some cases. At the other end
of the Evangelical spectrum were those who shared with Nonconformists and Scottish Presbyterians an admiration for the
Puritans of the seventeenth century as well as fairly low views
of the value of the historical episcopate. It was to this grouping
that the term 'Low Churchmen' was attached in the 1830s and
the term 'Recordite' later.[10] So to include at one end the Evangelical with a high view of episcopacy at the other the Evangelical with a low view, the following definition of an Evangelical
is proposed as a basis for including or excluding men and women
from this study:

> An Evangelical Anglican has a strong attachment to the
> Protestantism of the national Church with its Articles of
> Religion and Prayer Book. He believes that the Bible is
> authoritative in matters of faith and conduct and is to be
> read individually and in the home as well as in church. He
> emphasises the doctrine of justification by faith but with good
> works and a specific (holy) life-style as the proof of true faith.
> He claims to enjoy a personal relationship with God through
> Christ, the origins of which are usually traced not to sacra-
> mental grace but to a conversion experience. And he sees
> the primary task of the Church in terms of evangelism or
> missions and so emphasises preaching at home and abroad.

Under this umbrella many people, clerical and lay, male and
female, Arminian and Calvinist, millenarian and non-millen-
arian, sheltered from, and more often than not, challenged
the storms of life.

Thirdly, since the Evangelical criticism of Tractarian doctrines and practice was not planned by a committee in London,
Oxford or Cambridge, but was dependent in the main upon
individual initiative by editors of periodical publications,

academic and parochial clergy, and informed laity, it is not easy either to classify or to describe it for it is varied both in content and quality. Any organisational unity which Evangelicalism possessed was related to the machinery of support for the Church Missionary Society, the Church Pastoral-Aid Society and similar organisations. Only in 1865 did some Evangelicals form the Church Association with the specific aim of combating the Tractarian (Ritualist) Movement and preserving Protestant principles.[11] Between 1833 and 1856 a coherent, systematic criticism of Tractarianism can be looked for only in either a journal which was published throughout the period or the writings of a theologian who lived through these years and responded to the theological questions. In fact only one Evangelical responded to most of the major aspects of Tractarian doctrine and he was William Goode the younger, a Cambridge graduate and son of the well-known Evangelical who was a contemporary of John Newton and who succeeded William Romaine in Blackfriars, London, in 1795. Regrettably there is no modern study of either father or son. To look through the list of Goode's publications from 1838 to 1856 is to gain a good idea of what were the areas of conflict. As he was probably the most learned of the Evangelicals in terms of knowledge of historical theology and ecclesiastical history and law, his books will figure prominently as sources in the pages which follow. Significantly, he had also been one of the more learned opponents of the doctrines and practices of Edward Irving, Henry Drummond and their charismatic circle, with its interest in apocalyptic and eschatological speculation.

Of regular Evangelical publications only three were published right throughout the period and they were the *Christian Observer*, the *Christian Guardian* and the *Record*. Founded by the Clapham Sect the *Christian Observer* appeared monthly and represented those principles and commitments associated with Wilberforce and his colleagues. It was fully committed to the Liturgy of the Church and to the Threefold Ministry; it steered a middle way between Calvinism and Arminianism; it opposed 'enthusiasm' and commended 'vital Christianity'; it was a firm supporter of the British and Foreign Bible Society and the Church Missionary Society; and in a polite way it was opposed to Roman Catholicism and committed to a sincere, paternalistic, social involvement by Christians. The editor from 1816 to the middle of 1847 was Samuel Charles Wilks, who had attended St Edmund Hall when Daniel Wilson was the Vice-Principal. He was succeeded by William Goode who held the post only until the end of 1849 when John W. Cunningham of Harrow, author of the best-selling *The Velvet Cushion*, took over until 1859. In the pages of the *Christian Observer* it is perhaps possible to find materials for constructing a systematic response to Tractarianism but since the review articles are from different hands one does not always find coherence on all matters.

The *Christian Guardian*, originally known as *Zion's Trumpet* when it was published in 1798 by Thomas T. Biddulph and his colleagues of the Bristol Education Society, was printed and published in London from 1809 with George B. Mitchell as general editor.[12] Always dwarfed by the *Christian Observer* it merged for a time with the *District Visitors' and Sunday School Teachers' Magazine* but returned to being *The Christian Guardian and Churchman's Magazine* in 1850. Because of its changing fortunes and editorial policies, it is impossible to find in its pages a systematic criticism of Tractarianism.

The *Record*, which began its life in January 1828 as a weekly paper viewing the news about Church and State through moderate Evangelical eyes, ran into financial difficulties within a few months and was taken over by a group of laymen which included Alexander Haldane, son of James, and nephew of Robert Haldane, the Scottish, Calvinistic, aristocratic evangelists.[13] Haldane, a lawyer by profession, later wrote most of the editorials in the paper until his death in 1882.[14] These set forth an aggressive Calvinistic Evangelicalism, Tory in outlook, and strongly opposed to Roman Catholicism, Tractarianism, Latitudinarianism, Socialism and Chartism. Their tone often grieved some readers, but the success of the paper reveals that it was appreciated by both clergy and laity. On 30 March, 1843 it claimed that its circulation was greater than that of the *Globe* and only sixty less than the *Standard*. While there was a consistency of tone and content in the unveiling of Tractarian errors, it was the consistency of journalism and this does not easily lend itself to systematic presentation and is better conveyed and understood through appropriate quotations and summaries.

Several other magazines need to be mentioned, for they were not without influence in specific circles. Widely read in the Church of Ireland and by scattered individuals in England was the *Christian Examiner*. It was founded in 1824 to support the Protestant cause in the lively controversy with Roman Catholicism and became a mouthpiece for the Evangelicals. From 1838 it contained frequent critical reviews of Tractarian literature and commendations of books against Tractarianism. If it is true that 'contemporaneously with the appearance of the *Tracts* the Evangelical revival [in Ireland] was approaching its zenith in numbers, influence and scholarship', then the contents and circulation of the *Christian Examiner* were part of this revival.[15] One of its most learned contributors was James T. O'Brien of Trinity College, Dublin, who became Bishop of Ossory, and as such issued some powerful charges against Tractarianism.

Then there was the *Christian Lady's Magazine* which first appeared in 1834. Its editor was known to thousands as Charlotte Elizabeth, the writer of tracts and fiction. Daughter of a clergyman, Charlotte Elizabeth Browne had an unhappy marriage to a Captain George Phelan. After his death she married a Mr L. H. J. Tonna.[16] Converted to Evangelical Christianity through reading the Bible alone, she first wrote tracts for the Dublin Tract Society and progressed gradually to longer works. She had the honour, as she saw it, of having her writings anathematised in the Italian States by the Pope. In her writings on religion she took a firm, Protestant ('Recordite') position and even suspected a Jesuit plot behind the Tractarian Movement. Indeed, so pleased were the leaders of the Protestant Association with her attitude to Roman Catholicism and the Protestant cause that they invited her to edit the *Protestant Magazine* from 1840.[17]

Also worthy of mention is the *Churchman's Monthly Review* of which the first issue appeared in January 1841 and the last in December 1847. It was brought into being by the Evangelical House of Seeley and Burnside in order to review the large amount of material produced by the Tractarian controversy.

Consisting wholly of anonymous review-articles of such length as the individual case merited, it provides an excellent source of information as to Evangelical views.

The fourth difficulty which the writer faces is that this un-organised but powerful Evangelical response to Tractarianism was not a response to everything which the Tractarians wrote and did. It was a selective response which appears to have had as its selecting key whether any given teaching or action resembled medieval or Roman theology and ritual, or whether it departed from what was believed to be the teaching of the Reformers. So Evangelicals did not criticise Newman for his opposition to latitudinarianism even as they did not later criticise H. P. Liddon for his Bampton Lectures, *The Divinity of our Lord and Saviour Jesus Christ* (1866). But they did criticise Newman for his doctrine of justification even as they later criticised Liddon for his doctrine of the Eucharist.

One final comment. In this study little can be done to remedy the absence of a reliable history of the Evangelical party between 1830 and 1860; it is to be hoped that such a history will soon be written. But, in order to help set the scene and make the Evangelical response to Tractarianism the more meaningful, a brief survey of the development of the Tractarian Movement will be given at the beginning of the three historical chapters.

PART ONE

HISTORICAL

CHAPTER ONE

FROM SUSPICION TO HOSTILITY

1833–1841

The Tractarian Movement was born in a period of crisis for the United Church of England and Ireland. While churchmen were troubled about the nature and authority of the Church and her ministry, there came from a small group of Oxford men, who claimed to understand both the problem and its remedy, a call to the clergy to recover and restore to the Church her divine heritage.[1] At first this did not involve the printing and distribution of tracts.

Following a conference in July 1833 at Hadleigh, Suffolk, in the rectory of the High Churchman, Hugh James Rose, and attended by other High Churchmen including William Palmer, author of *Origines Liturgicae* and a Fellow of Worcester, it was decided that immediate action was needed to save the Church from spiritual disaster. One part of the remedy would be the formation of local associations of friends of the Church. Palmer was enthusiastic for these and set out their purpose as follows:

(i) To maintain pure and inviolate the doctrines, the services, and the discipline of the Church – that is, to withstand all change which involves the denial or suppression of doctrine, a departure from primitive practice in religious offices, or innovation upon the apostolical prerogative, orders and commission of bishops, priests and deacons.

(ii) To afford churchmen an opportunity of exchanging their sentiments and co-operating together on a large scale.[2]

Faithful churchmen were to combine for God against latitudinarianism, liberalism, scepticism and neology. However, this project did not succeed and in its place an address, composed by Palmer on similar principles, was circulated among the clergy before being sent at the close of 1833, with seven thousand signatures, to the Archbishop of Canterbury.

While Palmer toured the country during the autumn of 1833 in order to commend the idea of associations of friends, Newman began to write anonymous tracts. Though he had not been at the Hadleigh Conference he had corresponded with the participants, and the writing of tracts was his way of meeting the crisis. The first three appeared on 9 September, 1833 and by the end of 1834 forty-six were available. They covered such topics as the apostolic succession of Anglican bishops, the efficacy and centrality of the sacraments, and the Visible Church as the sphere of God's grace. Close friends helped Newman with the writing of the tracts and these men, with others, formed a close-knit group. They included John Keble, the Professor of Poetry; Richard Hurrell Froude and Charles Marriott, Fellows of Oriel; Isaac Williams, Fellow of Trinity; and Robert I. Wilberforce, son of William Wilberforce. To their number by 1835 was added Edward B. Pusey. As Palmer put it: 'His high religious character, his learning, and the station which he occupied in the University as Professor of Hebrew, together with his aristocratic connexion with the Earls of Radnor, rendered him an acquisition of the highest value.'[3]

The *Tracts for the Times* appeared regularly between 1833 and 1841, becoming longer after July 1835. The ones which seem to have caused the most comment and reaction were those on 'Baptism' (67–9) by Pusey, on 'Reserve in communicating Religious Knowledge' (80 and 87) by Williams, and on the 'Breviary' (75) and the 'Thirty-Nine Articles' (90) by Newman. Because Pusey had put his initials at the end of one of his tracts the anonymous writers were all called 'Puseyites' and their teaching 'Puseyism'. The early word 'Tractator' was soon replaced by 'Tractarian'.

Apart from writing tracts, Newman, the obvious leader of the new movement, was very active propagating his view of Catholic Christianity both in his preaching in St Mary's and in the writing of books. If the former activity primarily influenced young men in the University, then the latter made an impact throughout the nation. In *The Prophetical Office of the Church* (1837) he plotted a *via media* between popular Protestantism and Roman Catholicism as he criticised both systems. He looked to the ancient, primitive Church of the Fathers for true religion. In the *Doctrine of Justification* (1838) he set forth, on what he believed were biblical grounds, an approach to this controversial doctrine which fused the best insights of the Protestant and Roman teaching. The quality of these and other books commanded widespread attention. So also did the *Remains of R. H. Froude* (1838–9), edited by Newman and Keble; but Froude's declared hatred for the principles of the Protestant Reformation and his admiration of medieval Catholicism shocked many Victorian readers, lost the movement many possible friends, and turned mild critics into formidable opponents.

In 1836 'A Library of Fathers of the Holy Catholic Church' was announced under the editorship of Newman, Pusey and Keble, and to this was added later 'A Library of Anglo-Catholic Theology'. These two sets of volumes reflected the twin thrust of the movement as it searched for truth: it looked to the Bible as understood by the Fathers and the Caroline divines.

So by the year 1838 the Tractarians had gained the ear of many High Churchmen. Their stand in Oxford against latitudinarianism and for God's Church and truth had won for them much respect. Newman believed that the first seven years were years of prosperity. The emphases of the 'Oxford divines' were generally understood by supporters to be such principles as the importance of the apostolic succession for the Church of England and Ireland, the antiquity and value of the threefold ministry, the necessity of sacraments as definite vehicles of divine grace, the interpretation of the Scriptures by the teaching of the Fathers according to the rule, *quod semper, quod ubique, quod ab omnibus,* and opposition to liberalism in all its forms. Sections of the periodical press, the *British Magazine* and *British Critic,* as well as the *Times* newspaper gave support to the propagation of these 'Church Principles' (as they came to be called).

I. SUSPICION AND CO-OPERATION, 1833–6

The Evangelicals, being concerned about the welfare of the Church of Christ, showed interest in the associations of friends of the Church. In the Diary of John Hill of St Edmund Hall this entry occurs under the date, 19 October, 1833: 'Wrote a long letter to Dr Wilson in answer to his enquiry about a projected association of friends of the Church.'[4] Dr William Wilson was Vicar of Holy Rood, Southampton, and brother-in-law of the Bishops, J. B. and C. R. Sumner. Two weeks later Charles Girdlestone, Vicar of Sedgley in Staffordshire and a former Fellow of Balliol, received a letter from Newman, whom he had helped to find his first curacy at St Clement's Oxford, concerning the associations.[5] Referring to the civil government Newman claimed that churchmen 'groan under that heterogeneous un-ecclesiastical Parliament and will not submit to its dictation'. 'I do not know how far these sentiments will approve themselves to you,' he went on, adding, 'We shall be truly glad of your co-operation, as of one who really fears God and wishes to serve Him, but, if you will not, we will march past you.' Looking for other recruits he ended the letter with a question: 'Do you think there is any chance of Mr [William] Marsh of Birmingham joining us?'[6]

Girdlestone's reply was negative. He felt unable to participate in the venture since the objects of the proposed associations were indistinctly defined, the way to achieve them was not clear and the view of the times was exaggerated. 'Now this whole paper', he concluded, 'breathes a censorious querulous, discontented spirit, a spirit of defiance, unless I am much mistaken, to the party predominant at present in the State, a spirit which is the most likely of all others to bring the Church into contempt with that party and what is worse a spirit which is thoroughly opposite to the Christian rule of overcoming evil with good.' It seems that not only did he reject Newman's overtures but that he also wrote a letter of protest to the *Christian Observer*.[7] Through his friend Benjamin Harrison, chaplain to the Archbishop of Canterbury, Newman also had similar contacts with Dr William Dealtry, Canon of Winchester and former incumbent of Clapham.[8] But this time the topics were the *Tracts* and the Address to the Archbishop.

Newman also wrote to the *Record* choosing a subject which he knew would not be without some attraction to the Evangelicals. It was the lack of sound discipline within the Church, a reality which had been an underlying cause of several recent secessions from the Evangelical ministerial ranks.[9] Five letters were published between 28 October and 14 November and were signed 'A Churchman'.[10] The first letter set the context of discipline within the contemporary cries for Church reform and interpreted the troubles of Church and Nation in terms of God's judgments upon the national Church. It also argued in favour of retaining the Commination Service of the Book of Common Prayer as well as the excommunication in the Service of Holy Baptism. Conscious that the friends of the *Record* had campaigned against co-operation with Socinians in the British and Foreign Bible Society, he ended his letter by acknowledging that 'these honest men have begun a system of excommunication'. Scripture proofs for the exercise of discipline provided the content of the second, while the third emphasised the guilt of all churchmen in the lack and rejection of discipline within the Church, a rejection based on expediency. In the fifth letter Newman set the problem in the context of the alarming increase of Roman Catholics in England. He wrote:

> I do not think I am speaking too strongly when I say that there are a multitude of men who will follow the teacher that speaks loudest . . . Now Rome will be sure ultimately to suck these in by the pointed and determinate character of its pretensions unless another powerful body is given the opportunity of witnessing its creed as powerfully; and it is plain that nobody can do this with the influence which would attend the movements of a reformed English Church.

To achieve the latter would mean the appointment, to say the least, of a 'more spiritual class of bishops'. Interestingly, in none of the letters is there a reference either to the *Tracts* or to the associations of friends.

One correspondent, whose letter was published in the same

issue as Newman's fifth, revealed how many clergy felt about the question of reform:

> If we bestir ourselves and petition for efficient reform we are charged with seeking or aiding the destruction of the Church, in whose defence we should hardly count our lives dear. If we sit still we are subjected to the unfounded charge of desiring to prevent or retard that for which we most earnestly pray, and would labour, if we knew how.'

The brief editorial answer on 14 November gave little help to this clergyman.

The first reference in the *Record* to the setting up of local associations, as well as to the *Tracts* and the Address to the Archbishop, occurred on 2 December. It was stated that the *Tracts* were not published by an association of friends in Oxford but 'by some of the leading members of it, issuing from one press at Oxford, and which are freely circulated by those who are giving invitations to the clergy to enlist themselves under its banner'. Though there was no editorial comment, this did come three days later in the following way:

> We must confess the surprise was extreme and the sorrow poignant with which we read the tracts of the Apostolical Society at Oxford, extracts from which appeared in our last number. Had we not read them with our own eyes it would have been difficult to persuade us that such effusions could have escaped, at any time, from the pens of Protestant clergymen, more especially at such a time as the present, and with the professed object, and that most sincerely entertained, of defending the Church in her great peril. In time of need to go for spiritual weapons to the armoury of the 'Man of Sin' – to lay a foundation which, in fact, will not give solid support to that lapsed body, the *heretical* Church of England, but on which the only true apostolical Church of Rome has ever rested in imaginary security and triumph, alike in prosperity and adversity – deliberately, learnedly, zealously to pursue such a course as this would, if persevered in, be ominous of nothing less than destruction.

These were strong words, appearing to teach that the Church

of England lost the high doctrine of apostolic succession of the *Tracts* at the Reformation. It is not surprising to find that more editorial comments appear in later issues in December 1833. First of all, it was explained on 9 December that if the apostolic succession is a solid ground of support for the Church of England it is an even greater support for the Church of Rome. Further, it was argued that the apostolic succession had not prevented the Church of Rome from falling into error and that this emphasis on the succession of bishops had the effect of excluding orthodox Dissenters. So the hope was expressed that the men of Oxford would realise that 'this bed is shorter than that a man can stretch himself on and the covering narrower than that he can wrap himself in it'. On 12 December two letters were printed, one stating that the succession of bishops was a matter of history, and the other claiming that its author had been strengthened spiritually by the views expressed in the *Tracts*. Thus of apostolic succession the editor now felt obliged to state:

> We do not deny the possession of the apostolic succession by the Church of England; we only attach an inferior degree of importance to it to that expressed by our correspondents. It was only when taking into our mouths the argument by the Papal Church that we denied it; but immediately thereafter we asserted the denial only to be 'figment' of the Papacy.

He was also at pains to emphasise the validity of the ordinations in Lutheran, Reformed and other Protestant denominations. Newman saw some of these comments as reflecting a measure of repentance but he was sorry, as he told Hurrell Froude, that his sixth letter was rejected by the editor.[11] By 23 December the editor had again been assured that the association in Oxford was distinct from the *Tracts* and that it should be supported as should also other associations in other places. And there the matter rested for two years. Against the *Tracts* the proprietors of the *Record* were now opposed, but during 1834 and 1835 the paper remained silent concerning them as other pressing matters were reported. Virtual silence until 1838 was also the position adopted by the editor of the *Christian Guardian*.[12]

In the *Christian Observer* neither the Tracts nor the associations

were mentioned during the autumn of 1833, but when the
preface for the bound volume for 1833 came to be written in
December, the editor, C. S. Wilks, made the following comment (which followed reflections upon the lives of William
Wilberforce and Hannah More, both of whom had recently
died):

> We lament to hear the ominous notes of preparation for a
> party-spirited collision, the effects of which, unless wiser
> counsels prevail to check the evil, may be most injurious to
> our national Church and with it to the best interests of
> Christianity in the land. On the one side we see ranged a new
> and active sect, composed chiefly of Dissenters who agree
> with the Church of England in her leading doctrinal tenets,
> but avowing themselves her enemies as an established Church
> and combining with infidels, radicals and Socinians to raze
> her foundations. On the other side we see a Society formed
> at Oxford, the members of which, professing themselves to
> be the most orthodox upholders of the Church, have begun
> to scatter throughout the land publications which, for
> bigotry, Popery and intolerance surpass the writings even of
> Laud and Sacheverell.

Wilks here made the mistake which must have been a common
one in late 1833 of seeing the *Tracts* as publications of the
Oxford association. Nevertheless, Newman was obviously unhappy about the way the *Tracts* were regarded in the magazine
here and that which was to follow in 1834; two years later he
told the editor that 'the general conduct of your Magazine
towards the *Tracts* . . . has been an exception to its usual mild-
ness and urbanity'.[13]

During 1834 the *Christian Observer* contained a variety of
critical references to the *Tracts*. One letter to the editor, probably by Girdlestone, complained about the divisive tendency
of emphasising the doctrine of apostolic succession; and a
review of publications on Church reform declared that the
Oxford writers contended 'for the power of the keys to the
fullest range of the Roman Catholic priesthood'.[14] In 'Answers
to Correspondents' in the May issue the following was printed:

Two Oxford friends complain of our having used the expression 'the Oxford Tracts' in relation to certain papers which, though written by five or six Oxford men, are stated to be almost universally disapproved of by members of that University. Our reply is, that we only took the title for intelligibility as we found it in current use; it is the title by which the tracts are asked for and sold and, if we recollect rightly, advertised. We did not give the title, and grieved should we be to suppose that such bigotry and Popery were espoused by more than a very small fraction of the members, resident or non-resident, of either of our Universities, notwithstanding we have received letters, from some who take a warm interest in these tracts, assuring us that they have 'wonderfully conciliated the clergy throughout the kingdom, have furnished a basis for church union, as opposed to the Erastian notions of the age; and that we are quite mistaken in considering the sentiments contained in them as confined to a comparatively few individuals'.[15]

This reference to a warm reception among some of the readership of the magazine confirms the impression gained from other sources, which will now be noticed, that even if the majority of the leaders of Evangelical opinion were opposed by May 1834 to the teaching of the *Tracts*, there were those Evangelicals who were, to say the least, sympathetic to its seemingly spiritual character.[16]

It is worthy of note that according to Henry Wilberforce, Bishop Sumner of Winchester, who never disguised his Evangelicanism, heartily approved of the first numbers and as late as October 1835 had a happy encounter with Newman at Wilberforce's home.[17] However, he changed his mind later.

A second illustration of a sympathetic reception is contained in the correspondence which took place between Pusey and his friend, Mrs Anne Tyndale, wife of the incumbent of Holton, a parish in which Pusey often stayed since his mother had leased the manor house in Holton Park, five miles from Oxford. Mr and Mrs Thomas Tyndale were Evangelicals and regularly called on John Hill at St Edmund Hall, where his rooms were a meeting place for Evangelicals, especially for the famous

B

afternoon tea.[18] Only a few letters of Anne Tyndale are preserved, and none of Pusey's, for the years 1833 to 1835 but they
are sufficient to illustrate how one intelligent lady, who was
no stranger to Evangelical theology, responded to the teaching
of the *Tracts*, which were sent to her by Pusey himself.[19] She
read them sympathetically but not uncritically and then took
up with him such topics as apostolic succession, the nature of
the Church and regeneration.

On 11 November, 1833 she referred to Newman's *The
Gospel a Law of Liberty* (Tract 8) and then wrote: 'If I could
quite enter into the opinion with regard to the apostolical
succession, I should like to have hundreds of that paper on
"Gospel Liberty" to circulate; as it is, if you wish them to be
circulated and would entrust me with a few I think I know
some people who would value them much. The puzzle to my
mind with regard to the Apostolical succession is this. If it is the
only accredited means of conveying spiritual instruction to the
Church, in what a dreadful state of famine the Church must be
wherever a graceless man is appointed to a bishoprick or a
ministry.' Returning to this subject on 20 November she
declared that there were expressions in *Tracts 4 and 5* which
'upon a first reading would perhaps be better understood by
a Catholic than a Protestant' and then proceeded to supply
eight quotations to substantiate her point. Later in the same
letter she wrote: 'Shall I own to you also that I find it very
difficult indeed to believe that those ministers who care nothing
for God or Christ or Salvation are really ordained by the Holy
Ghost? The writing of it almost makes me shudder but I
believe them to be ordained by the imposition of hands to the
sacred office of ministering in the Church and therefore look
upon them as lawfully appointed and I cannot help also thinking that it is the Holy Spirit in the hearts of true believers that
makes them turn away from their ministrations in disgust and
disapprobation.' Replying not to Anne's letter but to one from
her husband Pusey stressed the serious nature of the call to the
ministry and its commission from Christ. 'You will not, I hope,
think me a bigot,' he wrote, 'but I do not think the nature of
our commission and its origin is a subject about which in these
days, especially, clergy ought to agree to differ, at least, not

without having taken pains to ascertain the truth for them-selves.'[20] He also offered to loan either *A Discourse of Church Government* (1707) by Archbishop J. Potter or some writings on the subject by William Jones of Nayland.

In a letter two months later Anne discussed the doctrine of the kingdom of God stating that it was usually described under four heads, celestial, ecclesiastical, political and spiritual. And then she went on, 'Is not the ecclesiastical kingdom that which the High Churchmen as a party are the most anxious to support, if we except a few individuals? Is not the spiritual kingdom that to which the attention of the Evangelical is chiefly directed? The only cause for division is perhaps that each takes a part instead of the whole. The Oxford writers are anxious to take both and in proportion as they do this, I expect to see the Evangelical party flock in to them.' To help Pusey the more she also supplied a careful definition of an Evangelical stressing the centrality of conversion. The only other letter which re-ferred to the *Tracts* was one of September 1835 which contained an appeciative, but very preliminary, comment on the first tract by Pusey on baptism, *Tract 67*.

During 1834–5 Evangelicals, High Churchmen and Tract-arians found a common cause and this was probably one factor among others which helped to delay any serious controversy between Evangelicals and Tractarians. The uniting cause was opposition to the admission of Dissenters into the University and to the removal of subscriptions to the Thirty-Nine Articles at matriculation. The Diary of John Hill has several references to meetings of the dons 'in the lodging of both Dr Burton and Mr Pusey at Christ Church' and also in Magdalen Common Room.[21] In May 1835 Convocation voted by a large majority to reject the proposal to abolish subscription but this was only a temporary holding back of the tide since it was abolished later in the century.

Pusey was a leader of those who opposed change and it was during 1835 that he committed himself to the Tractarian Movement. To quote Newman, his influence was 'felt at once. He saw that there ought to be more sobriety, more gravity, more careful pains, more sense of responsibility in the *Tracts* and in the whole Movement.'[22] From *Tract 67* they became longer and more scholarly. These more elaborate treatises were taken rather more seriously and so now the likelihood of elaborate replies became virtually inevitable. Controversy was, however, perhaps delayed because Evangelicals and Tractarians found themselves united once more in the University of Oxford against the appointment by the Crown of Dr R. D. Hampden as the Regius Professor. Hill noted in his Diary on 13 February, 1836 that 'this week has been marked by the general consternation occasioned by the information which reached Oxford on Monday that Dr Hampden ... was appointed Regius Professor of Divinity.' Then throughout February, March and April there are many references in the Diary to meetings Hill attended in efforts which proved ineffectual to prevent this appointment. Looking back to these events two years later the editor of the *Christian Observer* wrote:

> In point of fact it was not the Oxford Tract divines and their friends, active as they were, who formed the large majority against Dr Hampden: but clergymen and laymen of very different sentiments, great numbers of them went down to vote on the occasion from their extreme disapprobation of Dr Hampden's writings. Unhappily, however – and we greatly lamented it at the time – the local management of the opposition to Dr Hampden being very much under the influence of Dr Pusey and some of his friends, and the subtlety of the Tract poison not being then so generally discovered as now, the business was in public opinion too much identified with what had no real connexion with it.[23]

In other words, Wilks believed that the Tractarians received too much credit!

The *Record* was convinced that the appointment of Hampden would produce 'a more profound impression on the Church than any other individual act' of the Cabinet and was happy to quote on 24 March, 1836 in some detail from Pusey's *Propositions maintained in Dr Hampden's Works*. From 25 February to May there were frequent reports on the affair from an Oxford correspondent and on 2 May the Circular from the 'Corpus Committee', containing its reasons for continuing the proceedings against Hampden, was printed in full. During this period the position of the paper remained as baldly stated on 25 February:

> It is obvious that the Church is called upon seriously to consider what she is to do under the present extraordinary and alarming circumstances in which she is placed. How can a situation more anomalous, absurd and ruinous be conceived? The present O'Connell-ridden, Papist-ridden Cabinet, wielding in simple verity the powers of the temporal head of the Church! What but ruin can follow from its prolonged exercise of these powers.

However, not every reference in the paper to Hampden was critical. On 4 April in a review of his inaugural lecture it was admitted that much in it was 'of a sound character and evangelical complexion'. And later in his career, when Tractarians were bitterly opposed to his elevation to the episcopate, the *Record* often came to his defence.

2. OPPOSITION TO NOVEL VIEWS ON BAPTISM, TRADITION AND JUSTIFICATION, 1835–40

Having begun the year 1836 noting that High Church principles were on the increase, the *Record* gave prominence on 21 April to the *Pastoral Letter from his holiness the Pope to some members of the University of Oxford*, written anonymously by Dr Charles Dickinson, chaplain to Archbishop Whateley.

> Supposing the Pope had sent out a body of Jesuits into the country and they had assumed the garb of clergymen of the Church of England, we cannot suppose them to work more skilfully and more effectually for the return of England into the bosom of the Papacy, than by the promulgation of such unsound and unscriptural principles as are developed in these Oxford publications, and in some others of a similar description published in London.

One of the London publications was the *British Magazine*, articles from which were constantly criticised. Commenting on the poem, 'Samaria', in the August issue, which commended a high view of episcopacy, the *Record* declared on 8 August that 'in avoiding Latitudinarianism, it is not necessary that we

should sink into bigotry'. Much attention was given from
August to October to the exposure of High Church principles
which were defined on 3 October as 'those which would lodge
power and attribute properties to the visible Church and
especially to the sacraments as administered by her, beyond and
above those with which it is invested by the great Head of the
Church as unfolded in the Scriptures of Truth'. Articles on
baptism and baptismal regeneration were printed being provoked by Pusey's *Tracts on Baptism* and they led at least one
clergyman to write to Pusey and condemn his views. This
disturbed Pusey who discussed with Newman whether he
should write to the *Record*.[24]

Pusey's writings on baptism represent a new development in
the Tractarian Movement and a brief comment on them and
their reception is necessary. Perhaps it needs to be stated that
they belong to a period in Pusey's life when he was moving
quickly towards asceticism.[25] Thus not only is there in the
Tracts a strong doctrine of baptismal regeneration but also the
teaching that since baptism achieves the complete forgiveness
of sins, further sins after baptism are never wholly forgiven in
this life. Christians must live penitential lives to show God their
sorrow for sin. This novel teaching shocked F. D. Maurice and
he later spoke of the *Tracts* 'with a kind of shudder as it were of
an escape from a charmed dungeon' for they represented the
parting of the ways between him and the Tractarians. Even the
High Churchman, H. J. Rose, believed that too much was made
by Pusey of the effects of post-baptismal sin.[26] And the editor of
the *Christian Observer*, as will be seen, believed that Pusey's
doctrines qualified him to teach at Maynooth Roman Catholic
College in Ireland.

As criticism of the *Tracts* flowed from the pages of Evangelical
periodicals, leaders of the Evangelical party were beginning to
refer to them in their writings. For example, the highly respected Edward Bickersteth, known to thousands through his
work for the Church Missionary Society, wrote as follows in his
Remarks on the Progress of Popery (1836):

A highly respectable, learned and devout class of men has
arisen up at one of our Universities, the tendency of whose

writings is departure from Protestantism, and approach to papal doctrine. They publish 'tracts for the times' and while they oppose the most glaring part of popery, – the infallibility of the Pope, the worship of images, transubstantiation and the like, – yet, though the spirit of the times is marked by the opposite fault, the very principles of popery are brought forward by them, under deference to human authority, especially that of the Fathers: overvaluing the Christian ministry and sacraments and undervaluing justification by faith. With much learning and study of the Fathers, with great apparent and in some cases real devotion and a devotedness ascetic and peculiar, they seem ... to open another door to the land of darkness and shadow of death, where the Man of Sin reigns.

His biographer tells us that from the time this book was published, January 1836, he became a firm opponent of Tractarianism.[27] Even so, he was so pleased with the 'Library of the Fathers' that he wrote to congratulate Pusey on it.

Meanwhile, tension between Evangelical and Tractarian was restored by the preaching and then printing of a sermon by John Keble. The subject of Tradition and its relation to Scripture was very much in the thought of Keble and Newman at this time, as is seen, for example, in Newman's correspondence with the Abbé Jager.[28] Being asked to preach the Visitation Sermon in Winchester Cathedral on 27 September, 1836, Keble agreed, seeing in this providence the opportunity to sound once more the same note of urgency which had rung so clearly through his Assize Sermon of 1833, the sermon which Newman saw as the beginning of the Oxford Movement. This second sermon, *Primitive Tradition recognised in Holy Scripture*, began with a description of the perilous position in which the English Church was placed and then claimed that there was comfort to be found in the text, 2 Timothy 1.14, 'That good thing which was committed unto thee keep by the Holy Ghost which dwelleth in us.' He asserted that before the New Testament was written and collected, and then existing alongside it, was a primitive, apostolic tradition which was in harmony with it, containing the doctrine of the Apostles' Creed, the Threefold

Ministry, the Eucharist as a commemorative sacrifice, infant baptism, and the doctrine of the Holy Trinity. He gave the impression that if the ancient Fathers were carefully studied more traces of this apostolic tradition would be discovered. Contrary to usual Anglican exegesis which understood the 'good thing' in terms of the whole Gospel, Keble thought it referred to this primitive, apostolic tradition. His friends were quite excited by the sermon. Newman thought it was 'the boldest and most powerful composition' which they had yet printed, and George Cornish exclaimed to Keble, 'What a stir you are making in the world! Who would suppose that so quiet and orderly a body was the author of such combustion.'[29]

Dr William Wilson, correspondent of John Hill and holder since 1832 of the second stall in Winchester Cathedral, heard the sermon and carefully read it. His *A Brief Examination of Professor Keble's Visitation Sermon* appeared early in 1837. Its tone was set by two quotations on the title-page, one from Bishop Taylor and one from Bishop Tomline. The former read: 'To prove by Scripture that there are any traditions not written in Scripture is a trifling folly.' Wilson criticised Keble for an imprecise use of the word 'tradition', since he did not distinguish between *res tradita, modus tradendi,* and *actus tradendi.* He also criticised what he saw as a careless use of the Fathers, an incorrect exegesis of 2 Timothy 1.14 and the seeming abandonment of the principle of *sola scriptura.* In the copy of Wilson's pamphlet which belonged to Newman there is a marginal note reading, 'Fundamental mistake of Dr Wilson is thinking Keble would add essentials rather than insisting on a particular authority for them.' Perhaps so, but he was not the only one to think in this way.[30] Surprisingly the *Christian Observer* did not review Keble's sermon although Wilks did tell his readers later that he had made full notes on it for future use.[31]

The most important teaching on Tradition came from Newman. Following the correspondence with the Abbé Jager he published *Lectures on the Prophetical Office of the Church viewed relatively to Romanism and Popular Protestantism* (1837). Apart from material on Tradition, in which he distinguished between episcopal and prophetical tradition, he also had provocative comments on Private Judgment (the right of the individual to interpret Scripture for himself) and Romanism. The reviewer in the *Christian Observer* wrote:

> There is so much of zeal for the prosperity of that Church of which Mr Newman is himself a member and a minister that it is impossible not to lament the failure of his enterprise in its defence. The chief error, ingrained, interwoven, incorporated with his whole treatise is the deference to be paid to the authority of *human* writings and the disparagement of the *sacred* records. Far as this last may be from the intentions, and even from the contemplations of the author it meets us in every page of his volume, and unless we are greatly deceived, will prove noxious to his own spiritual health.[32]

A little later Evangelicals in the diocese of Chichester objected to the underlying assumptions of the printed Visitation Sermon, *The Rule of Faith* (1838), by the Tractarian Rector of Lavington, H. E. Manning. Here again the problem was the place given to Tradition as the interpreter of Scripture.[33]

In Chester John Bird Sumner warned his clergy of the 'specious pretence or deference to Antiquity and respect for primitive models', while in Calcutta Daniel Wilson charged his clergy to beware of the views of Keble and Newman and trust in the sure words of Scripture.[34] Leading Evangelical preachers also published sermons against the supposed Tractarian teaching that Tradition is as authoritative as Scripture. From Baptist W. Noel, minister of St John's Chapel, Bedford Row, London, came the brief but potent *The First Five Centuries, or the Early Fathers No Safe Guides* (1839) and from Josiah Pratt, Vicar of St Stephen's, Coleman Street, London, came *Perverted Tradition the Bane of the Church* (1839). Christopher Benson, Master of the Temple in London, who apparently coined the word 'Tractarian', published sermons he had preached in the Temple Church as *Discourses on Tradition and Episcopacy* (1839). Meanwhile, the Evangelical press welcomed *Not Tradition but Revelation* by Philip N. Shuttleworth (soon to become Bishop of Chichester), the *Revival of Popery* by Professor Faussett and *A Lecture on Tradition* by Professor Hampden.

The year 1839 also saw the first instalments of *Ancient Christianity*, a book which challenged the high claims often made in the Church of England for the ante-Nicene Church. W. A. Shirley, Archdeacon of Derby, told a friend that he 'dreaded these Oxford Tract views' to which this book was 'the best answer he had seen.[35] Charlotte Elizabeth was also very impressed with it. 'Everybody has heard of this book,' she wrote, 'as being a terrible thorn in the side of Puseyism: but everyone does not know the nature of the wound it inflicts in that quarter.' The wound was to show 'an awful scene of corruption' very soon after the apostolic period. She thought that the book was 'written with consummate ability; deep, close, cool; cutting with a calm steady hand through the very bones and marrow of the evil' with which it dealt.[36] Another Evangelical believed it was 'one of the most remarkable publications' of the age.[37] The *Record* reviewed each instalment as it appeared and its praise extended as the reviewer read more and learned that 'the religious and moral state of the Nicene Church was considerably *worse* than we had ever conceived it to have been'.[38] At this stage few knew that the author was Isaac Taylor, a layman who had been a Nonconformist before joining the Church of England and was best known for his *Natural History of Enthusiasm* (1829).

Estimates of the value of the writings of the Fathers varied in Evangelicalism. At one extreme the *Record* declared that 'a careful perusal even of the four octavo volumes of Hartwell Horne [the Biblical Commentator] would make a much more intelligent and sounder divine than the reading of all the Fathers from the first to the fifteenth century.'[39] At the other extreme was G. S. Faber of Durham in whose books on the doctrine of the Trinity, Regeneration and Justification the writings of the Fathers of the first five centuries were fully used. Edward Bickersteth took a mediating position in the preface to his edition of *The Christian Fathers of the First and Second Centuries* (1838). He argued that 'because they have been overvalued . . . we must not undervalue them as if they were of no use in assisting us to a fuller understanding of the sacred volume.'

Though Isaac Taylor chose to live an isolated life in Stanford Rivers, most Evangelical clergy tended to confirm each other's suspicions about Tractarianism before they launched into print on the subject. They met at their clerical meetings, the most important of which was probably that which was held in Islington Vicarage each January with Daniel Wilson the younger as host. Newman was aware of these meetings, which attracted ministers from up to sixty miles around London, and wrote to Pusey on 10 January, 1837: 'They have periodical meetings at Islington and we before now have been the subject of discussion. Mr Hill goes up to report progress. Mr Wilson is a regular don – a conceited self-sufficient man with eighteen clergymen dependent on him and looked up to as a Bishop.'[40] Certainly John Hill went nearly every year to the Islington Conference and his Diary has brief descriptions of what happened. For example on 4 January, 1837 he wrote in it:

> Goode next spoke chiefly (as several before luncheon had done) about the Tracts for the Times. I was then permitted to speak – wishing, while I acknowledged the evil of the doctrines alluded to, to impress the impropriety of identifying them with Oxford and endeavouring to describe the true character and state of Oxford.

William Dodsworth, a former Evangelical and now minister of Margaret Street Chapel, London, told Pusey on 6 January that 'there was a most violent and abusive attack on us at a meeting of clergy at Islington.'[41] And it is possible that it was at this same meeting that Walter Kerr Hamilton, an Oxford incumbent, began to move his theological position from Evangelicalism to Tractarianism. His biographer wrote that Hamilton connected his conversion 'with a meeting of Evangelical clergy that was held at Islington for the purpose of denouncing . . . the Oxford Tractarians'.[42]

The *Christian Observer* did not report the Islington Conference but on 7 January, 1837 Newman privately explained that he was 'getting into controversy with the *Christian Observer* in its own pages', and that he fervently hoped that he would be able 'to teaze them *usque ad necem, insaniam*, or something equally bad'.[43] This controversy arose from a challenge thrown out by Wilks. In a long editorial comment in December 1836 he had remarked that some of Pusey's views as expressed in his *Tracts on Baptism* were based 'upon the darkest ages of Popery when men had debased Christianity from a spiritual system . . .

to a system of forms and ceremonial rites'. Indeed, such were Pusey's views that 'the learned Professor ought to lecture at Maynooth or the Vatican and not in the chair of Oxford where he puts forth this Popish doctrine'. And he concluded by inviting a supporter of the *Tracts* to show how Pusey could truly remain a Church of England minister in holding views which were contrary to the Articles and Homilies. The supporter who accepted the challenge was Newman himself, which shows how much, even in January 1837, he still valued the Evangelical party and desired to persuade its members to join him.

Two letters from Newman were published in four instalments in the February to May issues of 1837. Soon afterwards they appeared as *Tract 82*. In his second letter, referring to his first, Newman rightly remarked that his own seven pages of large type had 'elicited' from the editor 'about sixty pages' of small type. 'I am not complaining of your so distending yourself,' he continued, 'I had rather be David with a sling and a stone than Goliath whose height was six cubits and a span.' Happily, editorial comment on the second letter amounted only to twenty-seven pages of small type while the letter took eighteen pages of larger type. In the first letter Newman dealt with baptismal regeneration, supporting Pusey in the contention that the patriarchs of the Old Testament were sanctified but not regenerated. In the second he defended the practice of giving the eucharistic elements to children, referred to Keble's sermon for a definition of apostolic tradition and explained how Tractarians reconciled their consciences to the Homilies and Articles.

The editorial comment in this exchange, the equivalent of about one hundred and forty pages of ordinary type, may be regarded as the first lengthy Evangelical attack upon the leading tenets of Tractarianism. Yet, due to the nature of its composition which was hasty, it was not well planned but rather a collection of random comments. Its character was set in the opening volley:

What we have intended, and still intend, in this discussion is to speak as God shall give us grace very plainly our view of the character and evils of the system inculcated in the

Oxford Tracts; which even weeping, we believe to be anti-Evangelical, anti-Protestant, and a snare of our ghostly enemy to impede the progress of the pure Gospel of Christ and to endanger the souls of men.

At its best, claimed Wilks, Tractarianism reflected the worst features of the theology of Laud and the Non-Jurors; at its worst it was Popery in disguise. All the subjects which were later to become the topics of controversy were raised in the comments, of which the last was a challenge to Newman clearly to set forth his doctrine of Justification.

Newman did not send a third letter but rather began a series of lectures in the University Church on the subject which he later published as *Lectures on the Doctrine of Justification* (1838). The veteran G. S. Faber of Durham, who had criticised as Romanist the views on Justification of the Irish layman, Alexander Knox, now entered into a correspondence with Newman and even visited him in the hope of persuading him of the error of his position.[44] It was in this friendly exchange that Faber came to realise that Newman had written a good number of the *Tracts* and this information came as a shock to him.

At the centre of the Evangelical Protestant position was the doctrine of Justification by grace through faith and to remove it from its pedestal or worse still to deny it was tantamount to Popery and so on 15 April, 1839 the *Record* lamented:

Who has read *Newman on Justification*, himself having been given of God to receive the doctrine in its Scriptural simplicity and fulness, without lamenting over the dark conceptions of the man, and being led afresh to confess that till God teaches, darkness broods over the human mind, whether Greek or barbarian, in relation to the essentials of Gospel truth.

The Evangelical press welcomed all attacks upon Newman's novel doctrine, which was equated with Roman teaching. Among the pieces commended were Dr Hampden's *The Lord our Righteousness* (1839) and Dr Shuttleworth's *Justification through Faith* (1840).

The greatest praise, however, was reserved for the book by Charles P. M'Ilvaine, Bishop of Ohio, who had visited Oxford and lodged with John Hill in April 1835. The book had the provocative title, *Oxford Divinity*. Charlotte Elizabeth told her middle-class ladies that 'as a spiritually-minded Christian, as a learned divine, as a truly Apostolic bishop' M'Ilvaine was 'known and read of all men during his sojourn in England'. With this book he had 'more than realized the highest opinion that we could form of him by a work, the value of which it is impossible to calculate, unless we can compute the worth of Christianity itself'.[45] The reviewer in the *Christian Observer* welcomed the contents but not the title and the orthodox *Churchman* declared that '*this* is a book which *must* be answered or the credit of the whole school of Tractarianism is gone for ever'.[46] M'Ilvaine's purpose was to show that the Tractarian doctrine was the same either as medieval teaching or Tridentine teaching and was thus erroneous in nature.

3. OPPOSITION TO INNOVATIONS IN WORSHIP, 1837–8

The matter to which attention must now be given, though only of minor importance in 1837–8, does provide a foretaste of how deeply and bitterly feelings were to burn concerning ritualism, fanned, as they were, by the appearance of such publications as *Tract 78* on the Roman Breviary. In the early summer of 1837, Peter Maurice, Chaplain of New College and All Souls', published *The Popery of Oxford Confronted, Disavowed and Repudiated*. Though brief, it touched on a variety of controversial issues and opened up a new one. The seventh chapter on 'ceremonies, services and vestments' claimed that in the University Church Newman knelt on a low cushion placed on the step of the chancel in front of the communion table, in which position he continued during the prayers. At the new chapel at Littlemore, of which Newman had the pastoral care, the same practice occurred, and, worse still, Maurice had seen there 'a plain naked cross, either of stone or a good imitation of it, rising up and projecting out of the wall, from the centre of the communion table, and forming the fulness of one of those arches which are so ornamentally arranged in sevenfold perfection within the rails'. Finally he claimed that a deacon's stole, on which was embroidered St Andrew's Cross, had been

worn not only in one of the Oxford churches but also in a
College chapel. Disgusted by the booklet, Pusey wrote that 'the
walls of Oxford have been placarded . . . with "Popery of
Oxford" and its citizens have been edified with the exhibition
of Newman's and my name as Papists.'[47]

The *Christian Observer* for August carried a heading – 'Un-
authorised Innovations . . . at Oxford'. This comprised a letter
from 'an afflicted spectator' containing long extracts from
Maurice's booklet and editorial comment which pointed out
that 'the present contest is not a war with communion tables or
crosses, or unusual emblematical medallions, but with anti-
Protestant principles'. The editor explained:

> We are not over-scrupulous about ecclesiastical ceremonies,
> provided all things be done decently and in order; but
> ceremonies unusual or unauthorized ought to be discounten-
> anced were it only upon the ground of irregularity; and the
> particular observances [described by Maurice] are peculiarly
> to be deprecated because they are part and parcel of a
> doctrinal and ecclesiastical system which tends to subvert the
> pure Gospel of Christ and the foundations of the Protestant
> Church. We cannot hear without just alarm of Fellows of
> Colleges crossing themselves at particular parts of the
> service, as if they were in a mass-house, instead of a Protestant
> academical chapel; of the ostentatious display, inside and
> outside of churches, of crosses, triangles, doves and other
> decorations, in a manner unusual in Protestant places of
> worship; . . . of side tables introduced into chancels for the
> attendants to place the bread and wine upon . . .; and even
> in the University Church itself . . . of Mr Newman's accom-
> panying the administration of the Lord's Supper with
> unprescribed bowings, approachings and retirings.

And not only the editor was worried about St Mary's in Oxford.
Bishop John Sumner had advised his nephew in May 1837
not to go to the University Church.[48]

A further dimension was added to this controversy when
George Townsend, Master Keeper of the Peculiar of Allerton
in Durham, told the clergy in his *Charge* of August 1837 that he
had 'heard with surprise and grief that several of our brethren

in the South, believing themselves to be justified by the custom
of primitive antiquity, have lately made several alterations,
which must to the people of their congregations be regarded as
innovations'. Hearing of this, or perhaps reading a report of it,
Pusey wrote to Townsend providing an explanation of the supposed innovations. The latter seemed satisfied by the explana-
tions and told Pusey of this. Pusey then had printed in the
British Magazine his letter to Townsend and a summary of the
latter's reply.[49] Seeing this summary, which included the
assertion that Townsend had been misled by the *Christian
Observer*, Wilks wrote to Townsend and then printed part of
the reply he received in the January 1838 issue. Townsend
stated that the only particular on which the magazine had
misled him was on the extent of the proceedings in question. In
the February and March issues Pusey's explanation of the
innovations was subjected to examination and found to be
unsatisfactory. Had the innovations been those of an unknown
country curate, argued Wilks, there would have been nothing
to write about, but in that they were being advanced by men
who professed 'to be the only sound expositors of Anglican
doctrine and discipline' they had to be seen in relation to this
supposition. This meant that Maurice's cry of 'Popery at
Oxford' was not wrong.

In the *Record* of this same period is to be found continuing
criticism of what is now openly called 'Puseyism'. Such comments as the following on 7 August, 1837 reflect the general line
which was taken:

> The Church is set up as the object of worship; not the Church
> mystical composed of the living members of the body of
> Christ throughout the world: but the outward visible Church,
> the largest section of which is apostate Rome, the smaller the
> Church of England, to which are added any other Episcopal
> Bodies which glory in the true episcopal succession.
>
> The abettors of Puseyism, like the Jewish teachers in the
> days of our Lord, . . . dare not stand on the Word of God, but
> after the manner of the corrupters of the ancient faith, rest the
> opinions they promulgate in a great degree on tradition.

The use of the term 'Puseyites' was justified on the basis of the use by St John in Revelation 2.6 of the term 'Nicolaitans'. In the autumn of 1837 readers were entertained by an exchange of views on the relationship of the Church of England and the Church of Rome. Representing the Tractarian interest was Arthur P. Perceval, author of *Tracts 35 and 36*, and challenging him was 'W.C.', a Protestant of the Protestants. The latter also wrote at some length in the paper on 20 November on the doctrine of baptism in the *Tracts*.

Controversy over the sacraments also took place in specific local situations, in Leeds, for example. In the minds of many Evangelicals, W. F. Hook, 'one of the most dangerous individuals with whom the Church is afflicted', was closely identified with the Tractarian interest. He had been appointed Vicar of Leeds in 1837 while the Evangelical candidate, Hugh Stowell of Salford, had been rejected. It is therefore not surprising that accusations concerning Hook's supposed errors should enter the columns of a local newspaper, the *Leeds Intelligencer* in February 1838.[50] Miles Jackson, incumbent of St Paul's, Leeds, led the Evangelical attack criticising Tractarian views on tradition, baptism, the Lord's Supper, and the nature of the priesthood. When the paper refused to print his second letter he printed it with other material as *The Oxford Tracts Unmasked*, a pamphlet of forty pages which received favourable mention in the *Christian Observer* of 1838. The controversy continued as George A. Poole and Richard Ward wrote pamphlets in defence of Hook, and Jackson defended the position he had adopted. One complaint of the Evangelicals was that Hook had changed the way in which Holy Communion was administered, being influenced by Tractarian ritualism.

Apart from the sacraments and their administration, Evangelicals were also worried by the Tractarian doctrine of Reserve in the communication of Christian truth. The source of their consternation was *Tracts 80 and 87* by Isaac Williams, although the doctrine had already been taught by Newman and Keble in less obvious ways.[51] *Tract 80* contained a veiled attack upon the way in which the Atonement of Christ was presented in Evangelicalism:

The prevailing notion of bringing forward the Atonement

explicitly and *prominently* on all occasions is evidently quite opposed to what we consider the teaching of Scripture, nor do we find any sanction for it in the Gospels. If the Epistles of St Paul appear to favour it it is only at first sight.

The point being made was that self-denial is also a part of the preaching of the Cross – 'if any man will come after me, let him deny himself and take up his cross.'

The comments on Evangelical preaching moved George Townsend once more into action and he devoted a major part of his *Charge* of 15 August, 1838 to a condemnation of the teaching of *Tract 80*. He saw the doctrine of Reserve as 'the perversion of the simplicity of Christian teaching' and stated that 'our brethren at Oxford are continuing to revive the obsolete, to recommend the foundations of the old and unendurable pretensions on which all the power of Rome was founded; and to render, therefore, the Reformation, which is nothing but the re-establishment amongst us of spiritual and scriptural Christianity, as a by-word and reproach'.[52] Two months later, and two hundred miles away in Berkshire, C. S. Bird wrote a long letter on the subject of Reserve which his friend, Henry Budd of White Roding in Essex, urged him to publish believing it to be 'the most powerful blow' that Newman and his associates had yet received. He did publish it and it was the first of several important books against Tractarianism from his pen.[53] In a delayed comment, an editorial in the *Record* on *Tracts 80 and 87* claimed on 27 August, 1840 that

> the character of these tracts is mysticism rendered plausible by metaphysical and sophistical reasoning. The temper and spirit is Gnostic and superstitious. Everything is mysterious and almost too sacred to be handled. The reverence expressed is morbid, quite alien from the healthful spirit of the Scriptures but in harmony with that of the ascetics and contemplative devotees.

Isaac Taylor likewise criticised the doctrine by utilising the teaching of certain patristic sources which did not advocate Reserve against others which did; from Hugh Stowell came a defence of Evangelical preaching and criticism of Reserve in holding back the whole counsel of God. From G. S. Faber, who had previously studied the subject, came short but pungent criticism, and five years later Bishop O'Brien added his weighty attack.[54]

4. IN DEFENCE OF THE REFORMED CHURCH OF ENGLAND, 1838–41

The low estimate of the character and teaching of the English Reformers of the sixteenth century and their denigration in the *Remains* of Froude,[55] the first part of which appeared in 1838, served to unite churchmen in loyalty to the founding fathers of the English (and Irish) Protestant Church and thereby to prepare the way for the erection of a Memorial to the Oxford Martyrs of 1555–6 as well as to assist the sale of the writings of the Reformers. The initial impulse within Oxford itself towards the erection of a Memorial near the place where the martyred Bishops died seems to have come from Charles P. Golightly, who sought to follow the teaching of the judicious Richard Hooker and was friendly with both traditional High Churchmen and Evangelicals. With Newman, however, he had crossed swords and had become a resolute and determined opponent of Tractarianism; so much so that he refused the offer of the Principalship of Chichester Theological College in order to remain in Oxford.[56] Before Golightly moved into action a brief correspondence appeared in the *Record* on 24 and 27 April, 1837 in which a call was made for the erection of memorials to the Protestant martyrs in the various places in Britain in which they had suffered under Mary. The *Christian Observer* had a piece entitled 'Martyrological Antiquities of Oxford' in 1837, the same year in which the new edition of Foxe's *Acts and Monuments* in eight volumes began to appear.[57] In this context of new interest in the Reformers the publication of Froude's *Remains*, with its criticism of them, was regarded by Pusey as the primary stimulation which led to meetings in Golightly's house, attended by R. L. Cotton of Worcester College and others, at which there was discussion as to what would be the most appropriate memorial to the martyred bishops.[58]

Following several private meetings a public meeting was called in Oxford for 17 November, 1838 where it was decided to erect 'an Oxford Memorial of Cranmer, Latymer and Ridley'. Cotton and Golightly were appointed secretaries of the Management Committee of thirty-four which was set up at the meeting. Evangelical interest was represented by the Principal of Magdalene Hall (John MacBride), John Hill, Sir R. H. Inglis, the MP for the University, and R. L. Cotton. On the 19th a prospectus was issued to solicit support and declare the aims of the Committee. Part of it read:

> It was resolved at the meeting that the best mode of testifying a grateful admiration of these pious Martyrs would be the erection of a Monumental Structure in which Architecture and Sculpture should combine to record the fact of their preferring the endurance of a most cruel death to sacrifice of principle.

Also a letter was sent to the Bishop of Oxford, Richard Bagot, asking for his support. Though he and other bishops did give their financial support, Bagot was unable to persuade Pusey, Newman and Keble to give theirs, a fact which appeared to most observers to confirm the worst fears of opponents of Tractarianism.[59] Definite opposition to the Memorial came from A. Welby Pugin, Professor of Ecclesiastical Antiquities at St Mary's College, Oscott, and a convert to Roman Catholicism from the Church of England. He addressed a *Letter* to the Committee and subscribers in which he attempted to denigrate the characters of the three martyred bishops. His *Letter* was answered by Thomas Lathbury, Curate of the Abbey Church, Bath, and best known as the historian of Convocation, in *The Protestant Memorial: Strictures on a Letter* (1839).

As Hill's Diary testifies the Committee met often and the subscriptions flowed in, reaching £7,302 by 1 June, 1842.[40] The decision to erect both a Memorial and a new aisle in St Mary Magdalene's Church was taken at a public meeting on 5 March, 1840, reversing a decision of 31 January, 1839 to build a church dedicated to the martyrs. The foundation stone of the Memorial was laid on 19 May, 1841 and the aisle was dedicated on 19 May, 1842. The Memorial was chiefly designed by Sir G. G. Scott, grandson of the famous Evangelical, Thomas Scott, and the stonemason was Mr Henry Weekes.[61] At the request of the

Committee the design was modelled on the crosses erected by Edward I to the memory of Queen Eleanor, and specifically the one at Waltham. The stone came all the way from Mansfield Woodhouse. It stands today reminding those who study it not only of the martyred bishops but also of the strong Protestant feeling in Oxford in the early years of the reign of Queen Victoria.

Apart from uniting to defend the honour of Cranmer, Ridley and Latimer some moderate Evangelicals and High Churchmen were beginning to unite in defence of the central doctrinal emphases of the English Reformation. The evidence for this assertion is found in the editorial policy of the *Church of England Quarterly Review* from 1840 to 1843, in the policy of the enlarged *Churchman* during the same period and in the management and editorship of the Parker Society.[62]

The first number of the *C. of E. Quarterly Review* in January 1837 declared that it would fight the 'triple alliance of infidelity, liberalism and papistry' on old High Church principles. These principles meant opposition to Tractarianism, for writing in January 1839 the editor declared that 'it is to Tradition . . . that a party in Oxford would in these days direct the Church as to a rival of the Word of God! They would hew out for us a broken cistern which can hold no water and little by little lead us back to all the corruptions of Popery.' In January 1840 a new editor took over and a new title appeared to join others of recent creation, 'Puseyite' and 'Tractarian' for example. It was 'Evangelical High Churchman' and was invented by Henry Christmas, the new editor, who was soon to become Librarian of Sion College, London. He claimed that only Evangelical High Churchmen, who looked to Scripture, the Fathers and the Reformers could give a satisfactory answer to Tractarians. Then in January 1841, in a review of G. S. Faber's *The Primitive Doctrine of Regeneration* (1840) published by the Evangelical House of Seeley and Burnside, Christmas wrote of following the example of Faber and of 'the full possibility of preaching a doctrine gloriously Evangelical whilst holding a discipline nobly apostolic'. Nine months later he claimed that 'one by one the sounder-minded are drawing together: the *Record* on the one hand and the *Tracts for the Times* on the other are losing their adherents.'[63] This was wishful thinking rather than objective reporting. Commenting on the term 'Evangelical High Churchmen' the *Record* of 24 August, 1840 could not believe that there were such beings. 'Evangelical Churchmen we know there are, and many, too, we are glad to say. But of such an heterogeneous race as Evangelical *High*-Churchmen we know nothing: nor can we believe that such do really exist.'

Henry Christmas was also closely connected with the new and enlarged series of the *Churchman* from January 1841. G. S. Faber was a regular contributor, sending a series of 'Provincial Letters' from Durham which were later published under the same title. In a letter of 6 March, 1841 to C. P. Golightly, Faber explained why he was writing for the new magazine:[64]

> Their views correspond with my own, or rather, which is much better, with the Church of England; that is to say, holding a just medium between Tractarianism and what for want of a better name I have been wont to call Ultra-Protestantism. If I wished to designate our principle perhaps I could not do it better than by the name of Evangelical High Churchmanship; though I will fairly confess that my own High Churchmanship stops with a full historical conviction of the aboriginal appointment of Episcopal Ecclesiastical Polity, but yet without samarianising every Reformed Church which from its local infelicity was organised unepiscopally.

The Chairman of the Committee of Management of the *Churchman* was F. P. Walesby, the Professor of Anglo-Saxon at Oxford, and on the committees associated with this were both High Churchmen (e.g. J. W. Whittaker, Vicar of Blackburn) and Evangelicals (e.g. W. Champneys, Vicar of Whitechapel). The list of contributors as printed in 1841 included such Evangelicals as Edward Bickersteth, T. R. Birks and T. H. Horne. In December 1841 Christmas took over as sole editor and declared that the views expounded in the magazine would be:

> Those of the Church of England – not as expounded by the 'Tracts for the Times' – still less as understood by the

Calvinistic divines who still remain in the communion of our
Church; but as taught in her own Liturgy – as elucidated by
Hooker and Bramhall and Hammond and Hall and Sander-
son . . . and Waterland . . .; in a word, our views are those of
Evangelical High Churchmen. We acknowledge the supremacy
of Scripture, the great doctrines of the Atonement and of
Justification by Faith only; while we hold the personal
Episcopal Apostolic Succession, the truth of our Baptismal,
Visitation and Burial Services and the right of the Church to
decree rites and ceremonies and to decide in controversies of
Faith.

It is perhaps worthy of note that William Goode republished in
1843 treatises on the doctrine of the Church by Bishop Sanderson and Dr Thomas Jackson, two High Church divines.

The names of Christmas, Bickersteth and Horne appear
again in the history of the Parker Society. While the origin of
this Society, named after Matthew Parker the first Elizabethan
Archbishop of Canterbury, is to be traced to the zeal for the
writings of the Reformers of Henry Budd, Edward Bickersteth
and John Ayre (son-in-law of Legh Richmond), it only became
a reality with the arrival of the Penny Post in 1840, with the
support of both High Churchmen and Evangelicals throughout
the country, and with the employment in the editorial team of
men of differing churchmanship. Like the Martyrs' Memorial it
was a protest in favour of the Reformation and against the
teaching of the Tractarians.

Following the great success of the subscribers' edition of
Foxe's *Acts and Monuments* (1837–41) and by the untiring efforts
of George Stokes, an active member of the Committee of the
Religious Tract Society, Henry Budd's suggestion first made in
1827 to form a society whose object would be the reprinting of
the works of the English Reformers was realised by the forma-
tion of the Parker Society in 1840 under the presidency of Lord
Ashley.[65] The Council, though dominated by Evangelicals, also
contained other churchmen – John Jackson, later Bishop of
Lincoln, George E. Corrie, Master of Jesus College, Cambridge,
Alfred Ollivant, Bishop of Llandaff and G. F. W. Mortimer,
Headmaster of the City of London School.

Utilising the penny post Stokes sent out thousands of circulars and by the summer of 1841 over 4,000 subscribers were enrolled. Meanwhile, editors were being chosen and commissioned and they included not only Christmas but such High Churchmen as C. H. Hartshorne, Curate of Cogenhoe and J. J. S. Perowne, Fellow of Corpus Christi, Cambridge. The Evangelical stalwarts, William Goode, Prebendary T. H. Horne, and Dr Hastings Robinson, Rector of Great Warley, were also editors. By 1855 fifty-four volumes had been published and the Society, having completed its task, was disbanded.

At least half of the Evangelical books to which reference has been made in this chapter came from the House of Seeley and Burnside, which with the House of Hatchard produced most of the books, tracts and pamphlets written by Evangelical Anglicans. A senior partner in Seeley and Burnside was Robert Benton Seeley, an active Anglican layman who was a founding member of the Church Pastoral-Aid Society. His reputation has been eclipsed by that of his third son, Sir Robert Seeley, the historian and essayist. In 1834 R. B. Seeley published anonymously *Essays on the Church* as a defence of an Established Church against the criticisms of Nonconformists. Each year until 1840 he brought out a new edition of the book, making major changes in 1838, 1839 and 1840 in order to meet the challenge from Tractarianism. Of the volume for 1838 Charlotte Elizabeth was full of praise and told her ladies:

> The *Essays on the Church* and that noble Christian journal, *The Record*, stand foremost in this extraordinary combat. They are first-rate in the service and our poor, weak, little bark, however incompetent to wage war like them, follows their track, hoisting the same colours and not shrinking from consequences. We love the Church of England as our own soul; we deprecate separation from her communion, because we believe her to be accordant with the Word of God in all vital, all essential points; but if such doctrines as those we have been exposing ever come to pervade her again, as they did previous to the Reformation, we would cast her off as an abominable branch. If captious Dissent is an error, approximation to Popery is a sin: man may justly denounce the

former as schism: God himself has branded the latter as apostasy.[66]

Pusey was far from pleased with the accusations of the 'Layman', with whom Charlotte Elizabeth so heartily agreed, and so he penned *A Letter ... to ... the Lord Bishop of Oxford* (1839), defending his colleagues and calling the 'Layman' and his friends, 'Ultra-Protestants'. Pusey's *Letter* quickly brought replies from C. P. Golightly in a further *Letter* to the Bishop and from Dr George Miller of Armagh in a *Letter* to Pusey himself.[67] From Seeley also came a long 'Letter to the Bishop of Oxford' printed at the front of his *Essays* for 1840. Of this new edition the *Record* commented on 21 May: 'We hesitate not to say that these *Essays* contain the best, the most judicious and the soundest apology for the Church of England both against Dissent and Puseyism, as well as against Popery, that has been published in this country recently.'

Another lay member of the Church who was competent to understand and write upon the theological issues of this controversy was Caroline Fry, better known to her contemporaries as 'the Listener', whose books, *Christ our Example* (1832) and *Christ our Law* (1838) were widely read. She visited Oxford in 1840 in order 'to listen' to what was being said and then she wrote her book, *The Listener in Oxford* (1840). She dealt with the use of Tradition, the doctrine of the Church, and the Sacraments. It was her firm conviction that 'the glory of God, the work of Christ, the ministration of the Spirit, the essential doctrines of revealed truth and every just ground of hope and promise of eternal life is assailed by these new teachers and betrayed by those who give them entertainment'.[68]

Caroline Fry articulated what most Evangelicals were thinking about the Tractarian publications by 1840. Suspicion, or in some cases half-hearted approval, had now turned to definite opposition. Not only the *Record* and the strong Protestant interest it represented but also the *Christian Observer* and the cultured Evangelicalism it represented were joined together to fight the same battle, the battle for the preservation of Protestantism in the Church, the battle for the Gospel. And it was to be a long battle.

CHAPTER TWO

CONTINUING OPPOSITION

1841–1845

The story of Tractarianism between 1841 and 1845 is one of humiliation in Oxford and increasing influence throughout the country. Within the University there were a series of setbacks beginning with the condemnation of Newman's *Tract 90* by the Heads of Houses on 15 March, 1841. Dean Church wrote:

> The proceedings about No. 90 were a declaration of war on the part of Oxford authorities against the Tractarian party. The suspicions, alarms, antipathies, jealousies, which had long been smouldering among those in power, had at last taken shape in a definite act. And it was a turning point in the history of the movement. After this it never was exactly what it had been hitherto.[1]

Newman himself was never the same again – at least as regards his Anglicanism. Soon he was to retire to Littlemore in order to meditate, to pray and to translate the writings of Athanasius. In 1845 he was to enter the Church of Rome.

Meanwhile in January 1842, by appointing James Garbett as the new Professor of Poetry, Convocation administered a defeat to Isaac Williams, the Tractarian candidate. The next setback was engineered by Dr Hampden, who, in his capacity as Regius Professor, made it impossible for the young disciple of Newman, R. G. Macmullen of Corpus Christi, to take his BD degree unless he sacrificed his 'Tractarian' conscience; but Macmullen did not give in easily and he took the matter to the University courts through which eventually he was given permission to proceed to his degree. However, the controversy contributed to the growing rift between the authorities and the Tractarians. The next person to run into trouble was Pusey. Following his sermon before the University on 24 May, 1843 the Lady Margaret Professor 'delated' it to the Vice-Chancellor as containing heretical views of the Lord's Supper. According to statute six Doctors of Divinity were brought in as assessors and they condemned the sermon as containing doctrine contrary to that of the Church of England. Then, somewhat arbitrarily, the Vice-Chancellor suspended Pusey from preaching to the University for two years. The final blow came in 1844 following an unsuccessful attempt by Tractarians to prevent the Evangelical Dr Symons, Warden of Wadham, from replacing Dr Wynter as Vice-Chancellor. W. G. Ward, a Fellow of Balliol, had published *The Ideal of the Christian Church*, which contained material offensive to the Protestant character of the Church. His teaching was condemned by Convocation and he was removed from his degrees. Not long afterwards he became a Roman Catholic.

By this time a complementary movement had been born in the University of Cambridge. It was in 1839 that the Cambridge Camden Society was formed by John Mason Neale, Benjamin Webb and others.[2] Like the Camden Society (founded in 1838 by antiquaries and later amalgamated with the Royal Historical Society) it was named after William Camden (1551–1623), the famous historian. While the object of the Cambridge Society, and other local architectural societies modelled upon it, was ostensibly 'to promote the study of Ecclesiastical Architecture and Antiquities and the restoration of mutilated Architectural remains', in practice it was often a commitment to the restoration for the contemporary Church of a particular type of Gothic architecture – the Decorated or Edwardian style of the period 1260 to 1360. From 1841 the *Ecclesiologist* began to appear and in its pages such controversial topics as 'the connection of Architecture with Ritual, the science of Symbolism and the principle of Church Arrangement' were discussed. In 1845, following some alarm caused by the expression of extreme views in this magazine, and by the resignation of various patrons, the Society was reorganised and named 'the Ecclesiological Society'. As such it made an important impact on the Church of England. A. G. Lough suggests that the three primary ecclesiological principles of the Camdenians (as they were called) were the importance of the chancel as a necessary part of a parish church, the evil of pews, with the associated pew rents which often made it difficult for the poor to sit in church, and the placing of the baptismal font near the West door.[3]

While the principles of the Camdenians were being adopted by architects throughout the British Empire, the theological emphases of the Tractarian *Via Media* were likewise making their way into the ethos and teaching of the worldwide Anglican Communion. For example, the Scottish Episcopal Church, with its particular history of Non-Juror influence, readily received the teaching from Oxford.[4] The *Tracts* were reprinted and supplemented by a varied literature. Pusey published several important *Letters* addressed to Bishops, the weekly *English Churchman* began on 5 January, 1843, the *British Critic* appeared until 1844 when the less volatile, monthly *Christian Remembrancer* took its place; the Library of the Fathers and the Library of Anglo-Catholic Divinity continued to grow, and in published sermons, pamphlets, poetry and fiction the teaching reached a large and interested public.[5] It also penetrated the two basically High Church societies – the Society for the Propagation of the Gospel and the National Society[6] – and was one important factor in the renewal of the principles and spirituality of many High Churchmen who were not Tractarians.

Very few revival or renewal movements are able to hold together within themselves, after their initial success, the constituent but divergent groups. Some wish to proceed slowly, others more quickly and yet others very quickly. The Oxford Movement was no exception to this phenomenon and several groupings appeared in its ranks.[7] One, surrounding Pusey, Marriott and Keble, looked to the Fathers and the Caroline divines for inspiration to interpret and develop the Catholicity of the English Church; the Church of Rome had no particular attraction for them. Another, composed of younger men, inspired by Hurrell Froude with his attachment to Medievalism and the Non-Jurors, certainly looked to the Fathers and selected Anglican divines; but also these men looked to the Medieval Church and, in the case of W. G. Ward, to the Tridentine Church of Rome for guidance. Not surprisingly from this latter group which looked to Newman as its leader and was utilitarian in outlook came the majority of the secessions to Rome.

One result of the great emphasis made by both the Oxford

and Cambridge Movements on the Visible Church as the channel of God's grace to men was a concern to understand, interpret and obey the Canons of the Church published in 1604, some of which had fallen in disuse, and also to obey the Rubrics of the Book of Common Prayer. So bishops in this period felt the necessity to give their judgments as to the meaning of the Canons and Rubrics but, regrettably, the judgments given were seldom in agreement with each other. So the lack of any definite common agreement allowed extremists of the right or the left to justify their practices and thus to contribute to the confusion of the times. Inspired by medieval precedent the ritualism of the extreme Tractarians developed in this confusion.

I. CONDEMNATION OF TRACTARIANISM IN OXFORD, 1841–5

Before 1841 the University of Oxford had no occasion officially to condemn the teaching of the Tractarians, even though a majority of the senior members had been alarmed by it, especially since the appearance of Froude's *Remains*. But, as was noted above, between 1841 and 1845 the situation changed and official action was taken concerning the views of Newman, Pusey and W. G. Ward. Evangelicals played their part in these condemnations, as they did also in the election of the new Professor of Poetry.

Newman did not write *Tract 90*, the last and most famous of the *Tracts*, primarily to broaden or change the minds of Protestant churchmen. Rather he aimed to show, especially to some of his enthusiastic followers, how it was possible to hold 'Catholic' views and still assent to the Confession of Faith of the Church of England.[8] In his introduction he wrote:

> While our Prayer-Book is acknowledged on all hands to be of Catholic origin, our Articles also, the offspring of an uncatholic age, are through God's good providence, to say the least, not uncatholic, and may be subscribed by those who aim at being Catholic in heart and doctrine.

In Dean Church's view, the effect of this publication 'was like that produced on ordinary minds by the refinements of a subtle advocate, or by the judicial interpretation of an Act of Parliament which the judges do not like', for he was aware that 'some of the interpretations undoubtedly seemed far-fetched and artificial'.[9] Inside and outside Oxford *Tract 90* was condemned as containing false history and erroneous doctrine and the author was charged with dishonesty.[10]

Following a meeting, probably called by C. P. Golightly who was now at the centre of all opposition to Tractarianism in Oxford, there appeared on 8 March, some ten days after the appearance of *Tract 90*, the *Letter of the Four Tutors*. Two of the latter, H. B. Wilson of St John's and A. C. Tait of Balliol, were to become known as Broad Churchmen, while the other two, T. T. Churton of Brasenose and John Griffiths of Wadham, were Evangelicals. They called upon the anonymous author to declare himself (which he did) and they pointed out 'a highly dangerous tendency' in the *Tract* to suggest that certain important errors, such as the doctrine of purgatory and the adoration of images and relics were not condemned by the Articles of Religion. Though criticised for his action, John Griffiths, for one, remained unrepentant for his part in producing the Letter and justified his position in a published letter dated 5 April, 1841.[11] Pressed by Golightly, the Vice-Chancellor brought the matter to the Hebdomadal Council on 10 March; two days later the Heads of Houses censured the *Tract* by a majority of nineteen to two, the Evangelicals, Cotton, MacBride and Symons voting with the majority.[12] In the published statement from the Council it was declared that the argument of the *Tract* was incompatible with commitment to the Articles required by the Statutes of the University.

Meanwhile, as Newman wrote an explanatory *Letter to Dr Jelf*, the respected Canon of Christ Church, a host of pamphlets, defending or attacking the position of Newman, or defending or attacking the action of the Heads of Houses, also came from the Oxford and London presses. Among the Evangelical reaction was a tract from Charlotte Elizabeth, the female champion of Protestantism, and a booklet from John Jordan, Vicar of Enstone, Oxfordshire.[13] For Charlotte Elizabeth *Tract 90* contained 'the development of that foul conspiracy against our

Church, our Bible and our souls'. After taking her lady readers through the argument of this 'notorious tract' she concluded:

> Much has been said of the talent, the learning, the piety of those who have been engaged for some years in putting forth these tracts. Talent and learning they undoubtedly possess; but while they put them to such a use as this we must needs question the reality of their piety in the sense that their eulogists attach to the word. Surely Elymas possessed learning for he was a sorcerer; and talent, for he relied on his powers to turn aside the Deputy from the faith; but what said the Holy Ghost to him, speaking by the mouth of Paul. 'O full of all subtlety and all mischief, thou child of the Devil, thou enemy of all righteousness, will thou not cease to pervert the right ways of the Lord'.[14]

These were strong words and were matched by the *Record*, a paper of which Charlotte Elizabeth felt the need to affirm 'that the Church of England does not possess a firmer friend or Christianity a more powerful advocate'.[15] However, the only serious historical and theological examination of the claims made in *Tract 90* came four years later from William Goode in a work entitled *Tract XC Historically Refuted*, which was, in fact, not a direct reply to *Tract 90* but to a work of Francis Oakeley written in defence of *Tract 90*.[16] In opening his refutation Goode apologised for the delay in answering the historical claims of Newman and Oakeley and explained that no such 'Catholic' claims would ever have gained ground had the knowledge of Church history and historical theology not been so poor in England:

> The fact is, that (speaking generally) for the last hundred years and more both in the Universities and the Church, ecclesiastical learning has been not only neglected, but practically discountenanced, and heathen and secular literature (important in its place) substituted for it; and the Church is now reaping the legitimate and necessary fruits of such a state of things.[17]

Goode marshalled evidence to show how false was the basic

position of Oakeley – that the Articles were intentionally drawn up so that they who held all Roman doctrine (except perhaps that concerning the Papal jurisdiction) could subscribe them, and that Romanists did not quit the communion of the Church of England or its ministry until political regulations compelled them to do so. Because of his extreme views, Oakley was prosecuted by the Bishop of London in the Court of Arches, where he was found guilty of maintaining doctrines contrary to those of the Church of England.

On the basis of the agitation over *Tract 90* came further bitter controversy over the choice of the new Professor of Poetry to replace John Keble, whose statutable period of office came to an end in 1841. It appears that W. Simcox Bricknell, an Oxford City Lecturer at Carfax Church and Incumbent of Grove, Berkshire, was the first to alert members of Convocation to the forthcoming election. In view of the intention of the Tractarians to appoint a man of their persuasion, he urged all Evangelical Protestants, in words taken from the inscription on the Martyrs' Memorial, to rally around the Protestant Faith and to prevent this.[18] The candidate whom Bricknell felt must be opposed was Isaac Williams, author of the famous *Tract 80*. In a letter to Pusey he wrote: 'I firmly believe that, with the exception perhaps of your own views upon the subject of "Sin after Baptism", no publication which has emanated from the party to which Mr Williams belongs has tended more to *disturb* the minds of men that the *Tract* upon "Reserve".'[19] Of the poetry of Williams one writer claimed that it was 'dreamy, mystical, far-fetched and often unintelligible'. The same writer believed that there were two good reasons why Williams ought not to be elected. First of all he could render powerful service to the Tractarian cause from his professorial chair, and secondly, and probably more importantly, his very election would show that the University itself did not approve the action taken by the Heads of Houses in condemning *Tract 90*.[20]

James Garbett, formerly Fellow of Brasenose, whose claim was perhaps more as a critic of poetry than as a poet, was the candidate in opposition, with the Principal of Brasenose, Dr Gilbert, leading his election committee. As a champion of the non-resident members of Convocation who favoured Garbett there emerged Lord Ashley, already unpopular with the Tractarians for his activity in the creation of the Jerusalem Bishopric. Ashley asserted that 'no power on earth' would induce him to assist in elevating the author of *Tract 80* 'to the station of a public teacher'.[21] One group of non-residents did their best to stop the election proceeding as a contest between two parties; W. E. Gladstone and about two hundred and fifty others tried without success to persuade both candidates to withdraw. In the event Garbett's committee agreed to the proposal from Williams' committee that there be a comparison of promises made for both candidates. Meanwhile Bricknell, who highly admired the character and work of C. P. Golightly, gave solid support to Garbett by attacking the views of both Williams and his major supporter, Pusey, in further pamphlets.[22] At St Edmund Hall, John Hill, assisted by his daughters as well as his wife, wrote forty-five letters on 15 and 16 November to members of Convocation from the Hall and was able to record in his Diary that he had thirty-seven absolute promises for Garbett and four conditional ones.[23] When all the promises were counted it became clear that Garbett had 921 supporters and Williams had 623 which meant that Williams withdrew and Garbett was duly elected. On 24 January the *Record* interpreted this as a token of the mercy of God.

Garbett celebrated his elevation to the professorial chair by giving the Bampton Lectures for 1842 on *Christ as Prophet, Priest and King* which he saw as a vindication of the Church of England from the novelties of the Tractarians. The chairman of his election committee was made Bishop of Chichester, an event interpreted as a reward for his opposition to Puseyism.[24] Though Garbett was sympathetic to the emphasis on the Visible Church as the sphere of God's grace, he was convinced that their system of theology was basically Romanism. He closed his lectures as follows:

The system is Romanism; not partially, but essentially; not *yet* Romanism, indeed, as historical recollections have expressed it, or as the conclusions of reason have demonstrated it to be; not Romanism in *all* its palpable and revolting incongruities to the heart and understanding. But –

c

Romanism, as it has, in all ages, represented itself to the young and to the devout – Romanism, as it is when purified by elevated feelings, and minds originally trained in Scripture truth – Romanism, as it combines with itself all that is grand and beautiful in art, specious in reason and seductive in sentiment – Romanism, which may be safe in those scripturally-trained minds who have presented it to themselves and to the world in this beautified shape – but Romanism, still perverting the truth of the Gospel while it decorates it – Romanism, which though it looks paternally and benignly in the amiable spirits of its present advocates, involves principles ever fatal to human liberty and progression – Romanism, with the establishment of whose theory the Articles of the Church of England cannot co-exist, and whose unseen and unavowed operations in *practice* will paralyse her spiritual power and destroy the Church of Christ, by substituting human forms for her Prophet, Priest and King.

He believed that the key to Tractarianism was to be sought in *Tract 90* and the unfolding of the system in the *British Critic*.[25]

One resident Master of Arts who had thoroughly supported Garbett was Golightly, who often entertained both Evangelicals and High Churchmen in his rooms in Holywell Street. Though he did not specifically call himself an Evangelical Golightly was certainly regarded by Evangelicals as a defender of the true Protestant Faith. Later in life he described himself as 'neither a High Churchman nor a Low Churchman but simply a Protestant and true son of the Church of England'.[26] In this period he toiled unceasingly in Oxford acquainting members of the University with the latest Tractarian error or innovation. Also he engaged in a massive correspondence, telling friends, acquaintances and even strangers of the latest Tractarian exploits. Among these correspondents were such leading Evangelicals as Edward Bickersteth, Bishop O'Brien, Charles S. Bird, Archdeacon J. H. Browne, George S. Faber, Charles A. Heurtley and William Goode and such prominent Churchmen as Bishop Blomfield and Archdeacon Samuel Wilberforce.[27] Occasionally Golightly also sent letters to the national newspapers, usually signed by a 'Master of Arts' of Oxford and disclosing the more sinister aspects of Tractarianism. The *Record* usually printed all his letters and regarded them as primary evidence. Thus from Golightly readers of the *Record* on 17 February, 1842 learned that about one quarter of resident members of Convocation were favourable to Newman, the very man who was responsible for 'the grand engine of mischief ... the parish pulpit of St Mary's'. They also learned of the disclosures made by Golightly in two letters to the *Standard* newspaper in November 1842. His accusation that W. G. Ward of Balliol and J. Bloxam of Magdalen were fraternising with Roman Catholics as a direct result of their Tractarian beliefs led to a minor controversy in Oxford, involving William Palmer of Magdalen, who came forward in defence of Ward and Bloxam.[28]

As his private correspondence with Golightly shows, Pusey was well aware that his words and actions were under constant scrutiny.[29] But confident of what was his duty he went ahead and preached what Liddon called 'the most important sermon of his life'.[30] Delivered on 14 May, 1843 in Christ Church it was printed as *The Holy Eucharist, a Comfort to the Penitent* (1843). Pusey offered to the baptised who were troubled by post-baptismal sin the Eucharist as an ordained means of grace to the penitent heart, but his doctrine of the Eucharist pleased only some of his hearers. Dr Faussett laid a complaint before the Vice-Chancellor who, according to statute, had to set up a Board to study the sermon in order to enquire whether or not it was in harmony with the doctrinal teaching of the Church. Oi the six members of the Board one, Dr B. P. Symons, the Warden of Wadham, was described in a pamphlet as belonging to what 'is commonly called the Evangelical or Low Church School'; but the *Record* thought that Symons, Jenkyns and Hawkins were 'unquestionably High Churchmen'.[31] Whatever their churchmanship the members of the Board judged that Pusey had seriously erred and so the Vice-Chancellor, without allowing Pusey much scope to defend himself and following proceedings which were unsatisfactory in method, ruled that he should not preach again in the University for two years.

Meanwhile the *Record* had welcomed the condemnation and

Golightly had been busy describing events to various clergy.
As a result Edward Bickersteth wrote to him on 5 June to state:

> I thank God that at length there has been an authoritative
> condemnation of Dr Pusey's heresy. It was due to the whole
> Church; it was due to Oxford; it was due to Pusey himself.
> No act of love to an heretic is more deep and true than an
> open condemnation of his heresy. God Almighty grant him
> repentance unto life that he may hereafter preach the faith
> he has sought to destroy.[32]

On 29 May William Goode expressed his gratitude that 'the
authorities in the University of Oxford have at least called one
of the leaders of the Tractarian party to account' and affirmed
his earnest hope 'that no fear of any threats will prevent their
acting decisively in this matter'.[33] Thirteen years later in his
The Nature of Christ's Presence in the Eucharist Goode was to deal
exhaustively with the quotations from the Fathers and other
sources which Pusey cited in defence of his position.

In the Evangelical magazines welcome reviews were given to
at least five booklets which attempted to expose the false
doctrine of the presence of Christ in the sacrament as taught by
Pusey. Of these one came from an Oxford Baptist preacher and
another from the Professor of Poetry.[34] Garbett also published
Dr Pusey and the University of Oxford: A Letter to the Vice-Chancellor,
dated 24 August, 1843. Its purpose was to defend the University
authorities against allegations of unjust action in an Address to
Dr Wynter from friends of Pusey who included W. E. Gladstone
and Lord Dungannon. Garbett rejoiced that the 'University
pulpit, that most powerful organ of public instruction' had
been preserved from error for two years by the suspension of
Pusey.

Protestant laity could not wholly join Garbett in his rejoicing
for they feared that the spiritual welfare and eternal salvation
of the young scholars of Oxford, who were open to the influence
of Tractarian teachers, was in danger. So, urged on by regular
editorials in the *Record*, laymen signed an Address to the Chancellor, Vice-Chancellor and Heads of Houses. Bearing thousands
of signatures, headed by those of five dukes, three marquises,
thirteen earls, ten viscounts and five barons, the Address was

presented in December 1843. It called upon the authorities to 'take such steps ... open to them for protecting youth committed to their care from the dangerous influence of Tractarianism ... and for securing to them, for the future, only such tuition as is in strict accordance with the principles of the Protestant Church and Constitution of these realms'.[35] Though much activity had surrounded the collection of signatures the receipt of the tactful and neutral reply of the University was only briefly noticed in the *Record* of 1 February, 1844.

If Protestants could accuse Tractarians of heresy then Tractarians could do the same concerning Evangelicals. Their opportunity came in May 1844 when Garbett preached before the University. His sermon on 12 May was printed as *Is Unauthorized Teaching always Schismatical?* and was a strong protest against 'Church Princples' which outlawed good, non-episcopalian Christians from the 'covenant mercies of God'. Charles Marriott attempted to delate the sermon to the Vice-Chancellor but he failed. One report of the incident stated that 'the Tractarians were much annoyed with this sermon and endeavoured to get it condemned by the Vice-Chancellor as heretical. They not only failed in their attempts but they have excited an attention to the sermon which will increase its circulation and usefulness.'[36] Other Tractarian attempts to obstruct or discredit Evangelicals achieved little. For example, the Principal of St Edmund Hall had to defer taking his BD degree 'in consequence of the prevailing cavillings and determination of the Tractarian party to put up every hindrance they can ... especially in reference to Divinity degrees', thereby, presumably, taking their revenge for the treatment of Macmullen, whom Hampden had prevented from proceeding to his degree.[37]

The major Tractarian move to discredit opponents came at the beginning of the Michaelmas Term, 1844. The period of office of Dr Wynter as Vice-Chancellor expired and it was expected that he would be succeeded by Dr Symons. But a letter had appeared in the *English Churchman* on 29 August accusing Symons of being 'one of that body who did their best to set the mark of the beast on the Church of England'. Five weeks later the *Christian Remembrancer* followed this apocalyptic

allusion with an article warning of the possible threats to
Catholic truth with Symons at the helm of the University. Also
the *Times* newspaper, still friendly to the Tractarian interest,
questioned by implication the integrity of Symons. All this led
John Griffiths, the deputy of Symons at Wadham, to publish
certain letters written during September and October to him
and by him which, he believed, vindicated the character of his
senior colleague.[38] Yet, despite these letters and despite the
repeated warnings in the *Record*, the opponents of Symons took
the matter to Convocation where they hoped by the popular
vote to nullify the proposal that Symons be the next Vice-
Chancellor. Hill noted in his Diary that *placets* were 882 and
non-placets 183 making a majority for Symons of 699, achieved
once more by the arrival of non-resident members.[39] The
Record, which had repeatedly called upon Oxford men to go and
vote, saw the large majority as a victory for Protestantism and
commented on 19 October, 1844: 'The Tractarians made a
great blunder in the battlefield they chose. They fought at a
great disadvantage. Many of those who are substantially with
them refused to go to Oxford on an expedition of contumacy
and rebellion.' Newman told Pusey that 'the country parsons
are of unfathomable strength; they and the Conservative feeling
which moved with them turned out Sir Robert Peel in 1829;
brought in the Duke of Wellington in 1834; censured Hampden
in 1836; and made Symons Vice-Chancellor in 1844'.[40]

With Symons now the president of the Hebdomadal Board
the University was immediately faced with the problem of what
to do with W. G. Ward and his book *The Ideal of a Christian
Church* (1844). The ideal he appeared to have in mind was that
of the Roman Catholic Church. Even Dr Hook believed that
Ward 'maligned the English Church for the purpose of eulo-
gizing that of Rome'.[41] One Evangelical reviewer sarcastically
commented:

> The author does not know himself to be dishonest. No, he
> thinks himself a noble witness for Catholic truth, an intel-
> lectual Hercules, who can look down, with the calmness of
> superior wisdom, not only on the despised Evangelicals, but
> on halting High-Churchmen and lukewarm and timorous

Tractarians. He is the Moses who stands in the gap against the Protestant apostasy, or the Elijah who is to restore our spiritual desolations.[42]

Ward appeared before the Vice-Chancellor on 30 November and 3 December following which it was announced that three propositions would be submitted to Convocation on 13 February. These were that parts of the *Ideal* were contrary to the Thirty-Nine Articles, that Ward should be degraded from his degrees and that a 'test be imposed on all persons, lay or clerical, who might hereafter be suspected of unsound opinions, in place of simple subscription'. The last proposition proved to be extremely controversial and for a time diverted attention from Ward and his *Ideal*. It was opposed by different types of churchmen for a variety of reasons. Evangelicals were divided in their views. The Archdeacon of Derby, W. A. Shirley, wrote to his friend Dr Symons on New Year's Day giving six reasons why he could not vote for the proposal.[43] The editor of the *Christian Observer* looked into the history of the University and argued that 'A Judgment and Decree of the University . . . passed in Convocation, July 21, 1683, against certain pernicious books' made the need for a new statute and test unnecessary, for by this old statute it was already declared that those who take an oath of adherence to the Thirty-Nine Articles do so according to the intended sense of those who framed them.[44] The *Record* supported Symons and so did Garbett who in *The University, the Church and the New Test* (1844) argued that the only way to prevent an uncontrollable comprehensiveness of interpretation, either in a Tractarian or Liberal direction, was to have such a test as Symons proposed. In the event the proposal was withdrawn and another put in its place.

Golightly, Bricknell and others in Oxford decided that to condemn the *Ideal* without condemning the interpretation of the Articles given in *Tract 90* was unsatisfactory. So Bricknell wrote a long tract, *Oxford, Tract 90 and Ward's 'Ideal'* which went through five editions in two months and was highly praised in the *Record*. Further a memorial was signed by 474 members of Convocation requesting that on 13 February the Convocation be asked to repudiate the pernicious system of interpretation of the Articles favoured by the Tractarians.[45] The Heads of Houses allowed this new proposal to go before Convocation; but, while Ward was degraded from his degree and his book censured, no action could be taken about *Tract 90* because the Proctors exercised their statutable right to forbid proceedings which, in their view, were inexpedient for the University. 'After the announcement of the third measure, the proposed decree of censure on *Tract 90*', wrote Hill, 'the Senior Proctor said "Nobis Procuratoribus non placet".'[46] In fact the proposal was never voted on in any later Convocation since the University dropped the matter at the request of the Archbishop of Canterbury.

The excitement surrounding the condemnation of Pusey's sermon and Ward's book was not allowed by Charles P. Heurtley, Rector of Fenny Compton, Warwickshire, completely to turn Oxford minds from the doctrine of Justification. He preached his Bampton Lecture: in 1845 on this doctrine setting forth a moderate and learned Evangelical Protestant position. Soon afterwards, to show his concern at the progress of Tractarianism he withdrew from the panel of translators for the Library of the Fathers.[47]

With Newman and Ward lost to the cause by 1845 the strength of Tractarianism was reduced in Oxford. Henceforth its greatest support, like that of Evangelicalism, would be outside the ancient University.

2. OPPOSITION TO TRACTARIANISM OUTSIDE OXFORD, 1841–5

To understand the national outcry against Tractarianism it is necessary to be aware that the determination to be faithful to the Protestant Reformation and thus to oppose Roman Catholicism (or anything which appeared to approximate to it) was a powerful factor in English religion in the 1840s as it had been in previous decades. The *Protestant Magazine*, organ of the militant Protestant Association founded in 1836 to call for legislation based on the Word of God, began circulation in 1839; the Parker Society made available several works of the Reformers each year from 1841; the Calvin Translation Society began to publish the works of the Genevan Reformer from 1843; and from the stolid British Reformation Society came the magazine, *British Protestant*, in 1845 and the reprinting soon afterwards of Bishop Gibson's classic *Preservative Against Popery* in eighteen red volumes. The great anti-Maynooth Committee of 1845 joined together Anglicans and Dissenters in opposition to government aid for Maynooth College, and the interdenominational Evangelical Alliance, which in part grew out of this Committee, saw opposition both to Popery and, at first, Puseyism, as a major unifying factor.[48]

In this context, not merely the teaching but news of the steady stream of Tractarian secessions to Rome (the names of seceders were regularly published in the *Record*) served to make Evangelical Protestants exceedingly suspicious of all that the Tractarians wrote or did. This suspicion lay behind the Lay Address to Oxford University mentioned above. It also lay behind the Addresses to Bishops in various parts of the country. For example, Bishop Sumner of Chester received a petition from 'the Protestants of Blackburn' in which they declared:

> We feel ourselves bound by the ties both of duty and of gratitude to acknowledge our lasting obligations to your Lordship for your firm, consistent and uncompromising resistance to the system of those Tractarian divines, who true to their self-assumed title of 'Ecclesiastical agitators' declare their determination 'to intrude upon the peace of the contented and raise doubts in the minds of the uncomplaining; vex the Church with controversy; alarm serious men, and interrupt the established order of things; set the father against the son and the mother against the daughter'.

In reply, somewhat predictably, the Bishop told his flock that he rejoiced in the proof afforded by the Address 'that the principles established by our Reformers are so dear to many hearts'.[49]

This great fear of Romanism also helped to feed the conviction of many that these times were times of crisis, so serious perhaps, that the battles of the Reformation would need to be fought all over again. The Evangelicals, who in general viewed the Book of Revelation as containing a chart of Western religious history, saw the battle being fought within and without the national Church as a contest for the Gospel, long predicted in the apocalyptic symbolism of that book. This view was adopted by the longest, if not the greatest Evangelical commentary on the Apocalypse of St John, that of Edward B. Elliott, whose *Horae Apocalypticae* (1844) went through five editions in thirty years.[50]

Elliott dedicated his book to Lord Ashley, whose commitment to predictive prophecy was such an important motivating force in his untiring efforts in 1841 to see the establishment of the Anglican Bishopric of Jerusalem in preparation for the 'restoration of the Jews' to their ancient homeland.[51] The scheme for the Bishopric, primarily Evangelical in origin, was 'contemplated with great satisfaction' by the *Record*.[52] When made public it was bitterly opposed by Tractarians. However, this opposition only caused Ashley, Bickersteth and others to increase their determination to see the scheme through to a successful completion. It was negotiated between Prussia and Britain in the summer of 1841 when academics were away from Oxford and politicians away from London. When the Universities resumed and Parliament reassembled heated discussion began. Critics claimed that it was Erastian in nature and a plain denial of the branch theory of the Church, Jerusalem being a part of the territory of the Eastern Church. The 'Puseyite world', as Lord Ashley termed it, protested loudly, with the *Times* attacking the scheme on 19 October. Both Newman and Pusey wrote to the Archbishop of Canterbury and talked of Lutheranism as a 'heresy'. This assertion stirred the Protestant soul of Ashley to tell his cousin, E. B. Pusey:

You talk . . . of 'the grave injury of countenancing heresy'; this is the necessary language, the inevitable issue of your principles; thus you class with the Gnostics, Cerinthians &c. of old, with the Munster Anabaptists and Socinians of modern days, the whole mass of the Protestant Churches of Europe, except England and Sweden. Everyone, however deep his piety, however holy his belief, however prostrate his heart in faith and fear before God and his Saviour, however simple and perfect his reliance on the merits of his Redeemer is consigned by you, if he be not episcopally ruled, to the outward darkness of the children of the Devil; while in the same breath you designate the Church of Rome as the sweet spouse of Christ and hide all her abominable idolatries under the mantle of her Bishops. This is to my mind absolutely dreadful.[53]

W. E. Gladstone 'stripped himself of a part of his Puseyite garments' and wished the Bishop-elect, Michael Solomon Alexander, well. On 7 November he was duly consecrated in the Chapel of Lambeth Palace as the Evangelicals blessed God for his mercies and as Newman's worries about the Church of England increased.

Not only did Pusey write privately to the Archbishop, he also published *A Letter to the Archbishop . . . on some circumstances connected with the present crisis in the Church* (1842). Even as his *Letter* to the Bishop of Oxford had elicited replies from Golightly and Miller, so this *Letter*, which was a respectful but passionate plea against the language used by some Bishops, J. B. Sumner for example, against Tractarianism, likewise brought replies from aggrieved parties.[54] In *The Case as it is* (1842) Goode claimed that Pusey had 'endeavoured with considerable skill to envelope the field of battle in a mist, in order, apparently, that those whom he apprehends to be about to interfere may be so blinded as to the real positions of the combatants, so unable to discern the parties engaged, so perplexed, in a word, by the inability clearly to distinguish what is going on, as to fear to move, lest in the confusion they should wound alike friend and foe'. Thus the need to state the true case, which was that on no less than twenty major points, from the Rule of Faith to clerical celibacy, the Tractarians had advocated erroneous teaching. The policy of Pusey and his friends was to introduce 'Catholic truths' which had already been rejected by the Reformers; they wished to undo the Reformation. Following this reply to Pusey, Goode also addressed a *Letter* to the Bishop of Oxford, whose recent *Charge* had caused a stir in Oxford, not least for its lack of a clear condemnation of Tractarianism. Goode challenged Bagot's claim that the views of the Tractarians were in accord with those Anglican divines 'who resisted the puritanical temper of the sixteenth and seventeenth centuries'. He did this by comparing the views of Newman and Pusey with those of Hooker on four doctrines – the Rule of Faith, the Apostolic Succession, the Eucharistic Sacrifice and Justification. His conclusion was that there were major differences between Tractarian and early seventeenth-century divinity.

The year 1842 also witnessed the publication of Goode's greatest book, *The Divine Rule of Faith and Practice*. He aimed to show that even for the early Fathers the Bible alone was the source of Church doctrine. The cynical dismissal of it by a writer in the *British Critic* probably shows that he had felt the force of the book's argument. Admitting that the volumes were a 'lasting monument' to the writer's industry he affirmed nevertheless that it had 'as little a place in modern controversy as the millstones and landmarks which the Homeric warriors used in an extremity to heave against one another would be in the warfare of these days'.[55] The *Record* took a different line asserting on 14 May, 1842 that the book was 'a work which leaves the most eminent leaders of the Puseyite heresy with no other alternative but the confession of ignorance or dishonesty'.

A valuable testimony to the impact of the writings of both Goode and Taylor on Tradition is found in the recollections of Roundell Palmer, the first Earl of Selbourne, who had been very friendly with the Tractarians in his Oxford days. He wrote:

My father once said to my brother William – repeating, unless I am mistaken, some works of Bishop Horsley, who knew the Fathers well – that 'the Fathers must be read with caution'. When Isaac Taylor in his *Ancient Christianity* collected out of the Fathers many things tending to disturb the ideal conception of a golden, primitive age of pure faith and practice; and when William Goode . . . in his *Divine Rule* . . . called the Fathers themselves as witnesses in favour of the direct use of Scripture for the decision of controversy, some of those who placed confidence in the Oxford divines, but were ignorant of the Fathers, waited anxiously for answers which never came. I remember a reply once made to myself when I asked whether anybody was going to answer Isaac Taylor, whose work I perceived to be producing in some quarters a considerable effect. I was told that in a little time he would answer himself, which he never did. It seemed plain that, although the advocates of Patristic authority might be powerful in attack they were weak in defence.[56]

William Palmer, Roundell's elder brother, seceded to the Church of Rome but Roundell himself remained a High Churchman.

Despite the hesitance of Bishop Bagot to condemn Tractarianism this was the period of strongly worded censures of Tractarian theology by archdeacons, chancellors and bishops. Two Evangelicals made edited collections of some of these *Charges*. Henry Hughes, Perpetual Curate of All Saints, Gordon Square, London, published *The Voice of the Anglican Church* (1843). This was brief and made the point that the very bishops whom the Tractarians claimed to honour were against them on many points of doctrine. A much longer compilation appeared two years later from the hand of W. S. Bricknell and was entitled, *The Judgment of the Bishops upon Tractarian Theology* (1845). Among the *Charges* quoted were two of the more important statements of Evangelical bishops, those of James Thomas O'Brien, Bishop of Ossory, Ferns and Leighlin, and Daniel Wilson, Bishop of Calcutta and Metropolitan of India, both delivered in 1842.

After referring to matters relative to India, Wilson urged his clergy to take a firm grasp of the Gospel, to honour and love the Church and willingly follow her godly order and discipline, to exercise proper pastoral care and always to be students of good theological literature. An example of the latter was Merle D'Aubigné's *History of the Reformation*. He reminded them that 'a momentous struggle' had arisen 'between the Bible on the one hand and tradition on the other; between primitive Christianity and the Christianity of the fourth and fifth centuries ... between the Gospel according to God and the Gospel according to man'. Tractarianism was not merely a revival of High Churchmanship; rather it was a new system of theology which had dangerous similarities with Roman Catholicism. So he concluded:

I entreat you as a Father, nay I enjoin you as a Bishop and

Metropolitan to be on your guard. Keep at the greatest distance, I pray you, in your several stations from the whole system as a system.

O'Brien did not do things by halves and his *Charge* took nearly three hours to deliver and over two hundred pages in print. 'Ours', he told the clergy, 'are no ordinary times. We live in times when the design of unprotestantising the national Church has been openly avowed as the great aim of the most active party in the Church.' He proceeded to attack two 'deadly errors' which if they prevailed would quench 'the light which the Church was intended to hold up in the midst of a fallen world'. The errors were the doctrine of Reserve and the doctrine of post-baptismal sin and its remedy.[57] Then, after offering his views on the origin and development of the Tractarian party, he commented critically on their distinctive doctrines of the Rule of Faith, the Eucharist, Justification, and Roman Catholicism. In the *Christian Lady's Magazine* the *Charge* was greeted with much enthusiasm.[58]

From the discussion of the old theological topics of a threatened Protestantism, we turn to the subject of ecclesiastical architecture which, with the growing influence of the Cambridge Camden Society, was becoming by 1842 a source of discussion and friction within the Evangelical press. On 6 January, 1842 the *Record* commented that 'the Society might have promoted an improved construction in churches and chapels, with regard to hearing, seeing, ventilation, light, warmth, economy, and general convenience and comfort, as taken in connexion with the character of our climate and our domestic habits'; but, instead, 'hitherto the principal writer, under an apparent zeal for brasses, painted windows, crosses and other trumpery has made the building of chancels and the substitution of ALTARS for TABLES the apparent desideratum of the Society'. On 20 June it was reported that the Cambridge Society appeared to have gained 'a most unwholesome ascendency in the Incorporated Society for the building of Churches and Chapels', for it was assumed by the Society that churches must have a chancel, that the 'altar' should be the focal point of the church and at the East end, while the entrance must be at the West end. Later in 1842 on 15 September it was claimed that 'the Cambridge Tracts for the Times (the *Ecclesiologist*) are growing even worse than their defunct Oxford predecessors'. A year later a reviewer in the *Churchman's Monthly Review* reported 'a great and important change . . . in the management of the Church Building Society within the last three years'.[59] There was some truth in this claim and that of the *Record* for the Church Building Society, incorporated in 1828, had received a memorial on the design of churches from the Camdenians and as a result amended *Suggestions and Instructions* were issued on 2 May, 1842 to architects.[60] The only way forward claimed the reviewer was for a Protestant Church Building Society to be formed. Obviously this was a serious suggestion and on 21 November, 1844 a letter from Hugh Stowell of Manchester appeared in the *Record* calling for a National Church Building Society, free from the errors of Tractarianism. On 2 January, 1845 a large advertisement and an editorial were printed in the *Record* calling for support for the 'Church Extension Fund for New Churches' whose chairman was Lord Ashley.[61]

A prominent member of the committee of the Fund was Francis Close of Cheltenham. He made use of Guy Fawkes Day, 1844, to sound an alarm about the dangers to the Church from the Camdenians. Preaching from the story of Jezebel in 2 Kings 18 he declared:

It will be my object . . . to show that as Romanism is taught *Analytically* at Oxford, it is taught *Artistically* at Cambridge – that it is inculcated theoretically in tracts at the one University and it is *sculptured, painted* and *graven* at the other. The Cambridge Camdenians build churches and furnish symbolic vessels, by which the Oxford Tractarians may carry out their principles – in a word, that the *Ecclesiologist* of Cambridge is identical in doctrine with the Oxford *Tracts for the Times*.[62]

Whether he achieved his intention is doubtful but he and many of his hearers were convinced of the relationship. Earlier in the year he had published *Church Architecture scripturally considered from the Earliest Ages to the Present Times*. This was a popular statement but the research which went into the writing of it led the author to conclude that he had made a major mistake earlier in allowing the erection of stone altars in Christ Church, Cheltenham, and at Amberley Parish Church near by.[63]

One writer who firmly believed that there was need both for a Protestant Architectural Society as well as a Building Society suggested a few principles which should govern Protestant Architecture:

1. It is expedient to exclude all imitations of Greek and Roman Temples; and to adhere, universally, to the ecclesiastical style of which the old parish churches of England afford so many beautiful examples.
2. It is not true that Popery forms any essential feature in this style; or that a truly English church will be maimed or injured by the omission of rood-screens, piscinas or sedilias.
3. A simple design of the old English style is as economical as any that can be framed.[64]

Here both the Grecian style, of which a famous example is St Pancras Church, London, and the Gothic style, favoured by A. W. N. Pugin and the Camdenians, are rejected. That which is commended is the Early English style, with very small chancels; this was a style not widely used in the nineteenth century and was probably better adapted to small country parishes than to the demands of the new urban areas.[65]

Whether the Lord's Table is the Christian Altar was a question which was raised by the writings of both the Oxford and Cambridge innovators. In Cambridge James Scholefield, Perpetual Curate of St Michael's and Regius Professor of Greek, had previously attacked Tractarianism in a series of sermons, *Scriptural Grounds of Union*, and now in the University where the Camden Society was beginning to be well known he preached on 23 October, 1842 on *The Christian Altar*. This altar was not the focal point in a church building but, following the argument of the Epistle to the Hebrews, the Cross of Christ at Calvary. The sermon provoked several replies and also helped to cause a division in Scholefield's parish congregation.

The Incumbent of the Round Church, Cambridge, allowed the Camdenians to supervise the restoration of his church and was shocked to find that they included a stone altar and a credence table. So, with the support of the Archdeacon of Ely and the *Record*, he took the matter to the courts. Meanwhile Goode, who had been researching this subject, published *Altars Prohibited by the Church of England* (1844). After a survey of the terminology used in the sixteenth century and afterwards he concluded:

> It is quite clear . . . that according to the rubric and eighty-second canon of our Church, expounded as they ought to be by royal injunctions, archiepiscopal visitations, inquiries, synodal canons and the declarations of our greatest divines, the only thing which properly answers the description of the article of church furniture which is to be used for the administration of the Holy Communion is a *table of joiner's work standing on a frame*, and unattached to any part of the church, the floor of the chancel being paved underneath where it stands, and the wall at the back of it furnished uniformly with the remainder, so as to present no unsightly appearance on its removal. This alone answers the description of what is required by our Church.

Happily for Goode and those who gave money to pay the cost of litigation Sir H. Jenner Fust, Dean of the Arches, decided that stone altars were not permissible in English churches and so gave his judgment in favour of the incumbent. On the same theme S. C. Wilks was able to tell readers of the *Christian Observer* that he had received assurances from various publishers that they would not use again the term 'Altar Services', as they had done in 1842 and 1843, but that they would refer instead to 'Books for the Communion Table'.[66]

Before the question of stone altars had become a major public issue the implementation of the Canons and Rubrics, with reference to the worship in parish churches, was well on the way to becoming a burning issue. The dioceses where feeling appears to have run the highest were Exeter and London. Bishop Blomfield delivered and published his *Charge* in the autumn of 1842. In it he addressed himself to the vexed problem of ritual on which a growing number of clergy, affected negatively or positively by 'Church Principles', had asked his advice or complained about the practice of their neighbours. Insisting that departure from the truth of the Scriptures was more injurious in its consequences than deviation from the prescribed ritual of the Church, he recommended what appeared to many as a moderate position – daily services where possible, preaching in the surplice at the morning service, a weekly or regular offertory of money – especially at Holy Communion to be presented before the Prayer for the Church Militant, and the observance of holy days. But flowers on the the Holy Table, the mixing of water with wine in the chalice, prayers to the saints or for the dead and auricular confession he opposed.[67]

To this *Charge* the *Record* devoted much space. It printed it in full, gave five editorials on it and then allowed many letters in its columns on it; later it often returned to it especially in reporting the confrontation between the clergy of Islington and the Bishop. It was in the early summer of 1843 that Bishop Blomfield went to Islington for a confirmation. Before his arrival, there had been much talk concerning what was understood to be his requirement that there be a weekly offering by the congregation, and the weekly use by the clergy of the words of the prayer for the Church Militant. (His requirement would have meant that when it was not the monthly or quarterly Communion Service the morning service would be Matins, Litany, Ante-Communion, Sermon, Offertory Sentences, Prayer for Church Militant and Blessing – with hymns also.) When he did arrive Daniel Wilson and sixteen other clergy explained that the laity did not want them to take up a weekly offering and that they themselves did not want to do it. Blomfield lifted his ruling but this grant of immunity given in search of peace in Islington, a bastion of Protestantism, was widely reported and became the basis upon which a variety of customs and practices were justified, discontinued or begun in the diocese. Praising the *Quarterly Review* for its condemnation of innovations in ritual the *Record* called upon the laity to preserve their Protestant heritage and to maintain the church services as they had been before 1842. Poor Bishop Blomfield had raised a storm when he intended only to create a gentle breeze and now he could do little to please the *Record*.

Not all Evangelicals were as militant as those of Islington and not all Evangelicals liked the tone of the *Record*. J. W. Cunningham of Harrow felt the need to write to Bishop Blomfield in the following terms:

> I trust your Lordship will allow me to express the deep regret which I feel at the unjust and ungenerous treatment which the *Charge* appears to me to have received in many of the comments of the *Record* newspaper. You would do the greatest injustice to very large numbers who agree with the *Record* in certain leading sentiments, if you should suspect them of not cordially condemning both many of the sentiments of the editor and the spirit in which they are expressed.

Bishop Wilson, father of the militant incumbent of Islington, wrote to Blomfield in such a gracious manner that the latter told Edward Bickersteth:

> I cannot refrain from saying that if the clergy of Islington had acted in the spirit which breathes in the letter of their former excellent Vicar there would have been little disturbance about conformity to the Rubric in any part of the diocese.[68]

But what was done was done and the feelings of the Protestant laity were further inflamed by reports of the arbitrary interpretation of the rubrics given in 1844 by Bishop Phillpotts.

On 1 August, 1842, in reviewing Phillpott's *Charge* of that year, the *Record* had complained of 'the deadness of his perceptions of the things of the kingdom of God', and it continued a vigilant watch over the bishop's actions and publications. Comparing the two bishops on 28 November, 1844 the paper claimed that 'the spirit of the Bishop of Exeter towards the truth of the Gospel we consider far more bitter and his theological code, in action, far more unsound than that of our own diocesan'. Much of the trouble in the West Country centred around Phillpotts' support for the innovations of the Curate of Helston, Walter Blunt.[69] Among other things he refused to bury people in the churchyard if they had not been baptised in the Church of England and he introduced a choir of schoolboys in the chancel. Following a complaint from the churchwardens the bishop ruled in favour of Blunt, following this up on 19 November, 1844 with a *Pastoral Letter* to the diocese in which he required clergy to take up a weekly collection and to wear a surplice in preaching. The Protestant laity in the diocese strongly protested and were supported by the *Plymouth Herald*. From London the *Record* thundered in its denunciations of Phillpotts and the 'hurtful innovations' which he was introducing on behalf of the Tractarians. As a result of these pressures the bishop had to withdraw some of his requirements. One reviewer summed up the situation:

> Seldom a week occurs that we do not hear of some young deacon or priest, fresh from the cloister, in open conflict with the flock he was sent to feed; and that, not upon the interests of eternity, not upon any of those truths which shine conspicuous in the pages of revelation; but it is a surplice, a candlestick, a gesture, a rubrical nicety, which it requires a Prelate versed in acts of Parliament, canons ecclesiastical, and ceremonies of the Church to explain, and when it is explained *ex cathedra* is all wrong in the estimation of the antiquary, and all nonsense in the eyes of the people at large.[70]

In similar vein, Wilks told his readers that, recalling the events of the 1630s, 'Lauds will generate Prynnes' and 'much that is good is in danger of being overwhelmed with what is evil in the tide of popular indignation'.[71] However, the Evangelical press expressed the view that the *Provincial Letter* of Archbishop Howley, sent out in January 1845 and recommending that the content and ceremonial of services be left as they were until further consideration could be given to the problem of ritual, was a helpful statement, which would remove some of the tension. Happily this particular storm appears to have subsided during 1845. The more learned of the Evangelicals had come to the conclusion that a revision of the Canons and Rubrics was necessary and that the body which ought to do this revision was Parliament.[72]

While the Evangelical press kept its readers informed about the question of ritual, it also took space to explain that there was a division within the Tractarian Movement.[73] Perceval, Sewell, Hook and the elder Palmer were seen as the moderates while others, notably Newman, the editors of the *Lives of the British Saints*, and such writers as Ward and Oakeley were seen as committed to 'the development principle'. In Newman's creative mind this principle was to be fashioned into his famous *An Essay on the Development of Christian Doctrine* (1845). One Evangelical who carefully recorded the progress of this principle and who termed it 'the development theory' was C. S. Bird.

Bird's *A Plea for the Reformed Church* (1841) was a reply to remarks in an article by Oakeley in the *British Critic* for July 1841. The subject was Bishop Jewel and his *Apology*; Oakeley, following the example of Froude, had spoken of the Reformation more as a curse than a blessing and in reference to 'Church Principles' he had remarked that 'as we go on we must recede more and more from the principles, if any such there be, of the English Reformation'. Replying Bird wrote:

> It would seem ... that in being required to give up the principles of the Reformation we are asked *to take a leap in the dark*. We are gravely called upon to surrender what we know and what we are perfectly satisfied with for what we know not and think may be worse than the worst we can imagine.

So, at this stage, the development theory only had reference to the actual expansion of 'Church Principles' themselves, now much more elaborate than in 1833.

Bird returned to the exposure with his much longer book, *A Second Plea* (1843). In this defence of the Reformation his use of the expression 'development theory' referred to the extreme Tractarian view that doctrine had rightly and faithfully developed in the Western, Roman Church from its roots in the New Testament. He called the application of this theory, expounded by Ward and Oakeley in the *British Critic*, a 'monstrous proposition'. He wrote:

> Now if this theory were not extended to essential truth – if it were confined to prophetic passages, or to those general rules respecting the order and discipline of the Church which did not receive their full application or their immediate successors whilst the Church was small and persecuted we should not

object to speak of development in such cases . . . But we must altogether refuse to extend this theory to the great practical truths of Holy Scripture. To do this would be to suppose that the early Christians were destitute of some essential knowledge and were yet saved: which is a contradiction in terms. Moreover we can see immediately how liable this theory is to be perverted by enthusiasts or deceivers.

And he saw in this theory a direct route to Rome:

In short, if it was deliberately intended to hand us over, tied and bound into the power of the Romanists this theory appears to me to be the very instrument to effect that purpose, because it lulls us asleep with the idea that in adopting this or that doctrine inconsistent with the first impression of Scripture, we are but following out some hint or notice therein contained to its full conclusion.[74]

At the end of the *Second Plea* Bird provided quotations from Newman's article on Athanasius, also in the *British Critic*, to show the Romeward movement of this group of Tractarians as well as to illustrate further the use of the development theory to justify such doctrines as the Pope's supremacy, the honouring of saints, purgatory and celibacy. The Bishop of Lincoln was so pleased with the *Second Plea* that he offered Bird the important living of Gainsborough, with the attached Prebendal Stall at Lincoln Cathedral.[75]

In March 1843 the *Churchman's Monthly Review* congratulated Bird on his apt designation of 'the development theory' as the 'first attempt to restore among us the dogmas of the Pope's supremacy, saint worship, purgatory and celibacy'. A month later, in a review of Newman's sermon on 'the theory of developments in religious doctrines', the writer commented:

In truth it is difficult to draw any one distinct proposition from it, save perhaps, that Divine truth is not revealed in Scripture; but only *suggested* and the idea given to the Church, to be 'developed' in the lapse of future ages . . . We gather from this new device that the writings of Mr Goode and others have produced a visible and sensible effect, and that the tissue of fallacy requires to be rewoven. A 'theory' accordingly has been constructed. It may be, and probably will, pass for a wondrous work with the juvenile and predisposed.

Criticisms of the theory continued to appear in the *Churchman's Monthly Review* until, with the demise of the *British Critic*, examples of it were not easy to find. The *Christian Observer* came into this exposure later for the theory was first noticed in a review of Oakeley's *A Short and Easy Catechism* (1844).[76] Though detailed responses to the theory had to wait until the appearance of Newman's *Essay*, Bird did point out two problems with it. First, he held that it made 'Faith variable from generation to generation instead of being like its Author and object, immutable', and, secondly, it imparted to the Christian Faith 'the changing character of this sinful, miserable world'.[77]

Not only the Tractarian party was divided by 1845 into a moderate and an extreme wing. In 1843 one observer noted that

The Evangelical party itself, from which better things were to be hoped seemed paralyzed by the boldness of the claims made [by Tractarians], and even to adopt many of them, so as to have split into two portions; some continuing to adhere to the original principles of such men as Cecil and Scott; while a large number were drawn away from these and assumed the very anomalous character of 'High Church Evangelicals'.[78]

Whether this writer truly understood the history of the Evangelical school is open to question, but the context in which it was written suggests that he looked upon the Calvinist position of the *Record*, the *Churchman's Monthly Review* and probably the *Christian Guardian* as being the continuation of genuine Evangelical principles. Therefore the true successors of Cecil and Scott were Francis Close, Hugh Stowell, Hugh McNeile and Edward Bickersteth. An obvious example of a High Church Evangelical would be G. S. Faber, to whom may be added James Garbett and possibly C. P. Golightly.[79] The same observer believed that another effect of the Tractarian controversy had been to 'induce the Evangelical clergy to renounce all intercourse with

Dissenters'. This assertion, though perhaps an exaggeration, did contain an element of truth for when the Evangelical Alliance was formed in 1846 there was a deep division among Evangelical Anglicans as to whether it was right for them to join it. The *Christian Observer* answered in the negative while the *Record* answered in the affirmative.

To attempt accurately to distinguish between all the different types of Evangelicals who were to be found in the United Church of England and Ireland in 1845 is perhaps impossible. What is clear is that in the face of the threat of Tractarianism from within and of Roman Catholicism and Dissent from without there was some polarisation. On the one hand there was a movement towards, and certainly co-operation with, the old school of High Churchmen. As was noted in the last chapter this centre ground was represented in print for several years by two magazines, to which may be added the *Christian's Monthly Magazine* from 1844. On the other side there was a strong movement, with much middle-class lay support, towards an emphasis on 'Protestantism' as a contrary ideology to 'Catholicism'. If it had a centre it was in Exeter Hall, London. The advent of the railway system certainly facilitated this development by making the attendance at London meetings (especially the famous May meetings) relatively easy. The *Record* helped both to create and foster this movement and its adherents were soon termed 'Low Churchmen' because they gave the impression to others that they had a low view of the continuing, historical Church with its succession of bishops. One way to describe the laity would be to call them Evangelical Protestant Constitutionalists because of their great desire to preserve the Protestant nature of British national life and culture.

Between the two extremes were, of course, many clergy and laity. This difficulty in describing the exact churchmanship is well illustrated in some research carried out for the editor of the *Times* in 1844 concerning the principal clergy of London.[80] Out of the ninety-eight listed over half were seen as Evangelicals of one kind or another. There were nine Evangelical Moderates (e.g. Archdeacon Sinclair), eight Evangelicals (e.g. Henry Hughes), three Strong Evangelicals (e.g. Dr A. McCaul), eight Very-Decided Evangelicals (e.g. Thomas Dale), eight Very

Low Churchmen who 'abhor the Tractarian heresy' (e.g. Richard Burgess), six Decidedly Low Churchmen who resisted the *Charge* of the Bishop of London in 1842–3 (e.g. Daniel Wilson), six Extremely Low Churchmen, prepared to take any step against Tractarianism (e.g. W. W. Champneys) and three on the verge of secession into Nonconformity. The last three were John Garwood, Secretary of the London City Mission, Baptist Noel, who seceded in 1848, and H. Montagu Villiers, 'perhaps the most influential clergyman in London' who, strange to relate, eventually became Bishop of Durham.

So the years 1841 to 1845 witnessed changes not only in Tractarianism but also in Evangelicalism. There was polarisation in both parties; in the one towards Rome and in the other towards a cold, tough Protestantism. In both doctrine and ritual Evangelicals were driven on the defensive and thereby laid the foundations for a negative approach even to wholesome renewal, change or innovation. However, for this negativism they cannot be wholly blamed for they were caught up in a situation in which it was difficult to react in any other way. And, furthermore, their reiteration of old Protestant truths was necessary if the Protestant tradition was to be preserved in and for the Church of England.

CHAPTER THREE

FURTHER CONTROVERSIES

1845–1856

From the secession of Newman to that of Robert Wilberforce those whom W. J. Conybeare desribed as 'the exaggerated type of High Churchmen'[1] began to express practically the theological and spiritual emphases implicit in the teaching of the early Tractarians. Although Pusey remained in Oxford the Movement now had no major centre but instead many minor ones throughout the country. First of all there were parish churches or proprietary chapels, usually under aristocratic patronage, in which attempts were made by devoted priests to put into practice what they believed to be the true Catholic teaching – the celebration of the Eucharist on Sundays and holy days, the availability of the sacrament of penance (auricular confession), the use of choirs in surplices, the removal of pews and the instruction of and care for the poor. Examples of such churches are St Saviour's, Leeds; St Barnabas, Pimlico; St Paul's, Knightsbridge; the Margaret Street Chapel, London; St Peter and St Paul, Wantage, and St Peter's, Plymouth. While the introduction of the new ritual caused little trouble in some parishes, in others it was claimed as the cause of dissension and riots.

Secondly, there was the creation of sisterhoods and convents.[2] In 1844 Lord John Manners had founded a community of sisters who ran an orphanage near Regent's Park in West London. Four years later W. J. Butler, Vicar of Wantage, formed a community in his parish to care for prostitutes and unmarried mothers. Also in 1848 Miss P. L. Sellon founded a community, with the blessing of Bishop Phillpotts, in Plymouth to work among the poor who lived near the dockyards. She excelled in her calling and greatly expanded the work. At East Grinstead in 1855 J. M. Neale founded the nunnery of St Margaret. Though much appreciated by the poor, sick and outcasts who benefited from their ministrations, the members of these communities, as well as their founders, were misunderstood and vilified within the Church. The vows of poverty, chastity and celibacy were particularly obnoxious to Victorian Protestants.

Thirdly, while there were no successful male communities in this period, there were significant foundations of schools for boys, who were to be educated in 'Church Principles.' The Woodard Schools at Lancing and elsewhere together with Radley College, founded by William Sewell, are important examples of these.[3]

A further type of centre for the propagation of Tractarian principles was the local Church Union. The English Church Union did not come into being until 1859 but before it there were local Unions of which those in London and Bristol were the largest.[4] Their general purpose was both defence and attack – to promote with all speed the restoration of 'Church Principles' in the Church, to defend the Church from latitudinarianism and to ensure that the parish schools were retained as part of the cure of the parish priest.

Then the persons, activities and influence of prominent Tractarians were centres of attention. Such clergy as E. B. Pusey, R. I. Wilberforce, H. E. Manning, G. A. Denison, John Keble, J. M. Neale and William Butler of Wantage must be mentioned. Less well known but still important were such men as William Gresley, Prebendary of Lichfield, Robert Eden, incumbent of Leigh, Essex, and other parochial clergy. From the laity such names as Beresford Hope, who gave vast sums of money to the Movement, and W. E. Gladstone, who spoke on its behalf in Parliament, need to be mentioned.

Finally, as a means of conveying information and creating unity, there was the press. Between 1845 and 1856 the *Morning Chronicle* appeared daily, the *English Churchman* weekly and the *Christian Remembrancer* monthly (quarterly from 1848).[5] The weekly *Union*, more extreme than any of the others, appeared only from 2 January, 1857 until June 1862 and so it falls outside the period covered by this study. Evangelicals believed that the Union 'was designed for those advanced Tractarians who had outgrown the milk of the *Guardian* [a High Church paper] and the *English Churchman* and longed for strong meat, more highly seasoned with Catholic tradition'.[6]

The Tractarians were not always working and fighting alone. In the famous Gorham case and in the moves to revive Convocation they stood alongside moderate High Churchmen, who like them heartily believed in baptismal regeneration and the rights of the Church to speak authoritatively on matters of faith and practice. Then they also continued to co-operate with and often to influence High Churchmen on the committees of the Church Building Society, the National Society and the Society for the Propagation of the Gospel.

But in this period the Tractarian Movement did have some serious setbacks. The final judgment of the Privy Council in the Gorham affair came as a shock to both High Churchmen and Tractarians. The secession of Henry Manning and Robert Wilberforce weakened the Movement and raised doubts for some of those who remained behind. However, in terms of the influence of the Movement, not only in England and Scotland, but also in the British colonies, and in terms of committed adherents, these years were years of growth.

The issues which the Tractarians raised to which other Churchmen responded were basically centred on the Church, her nature, authority, ministry and sacraments; questions concerning the rule of faith and justification remained in the background.

I. ISOLATED CONTROVERSIES, 1845–8

At the close of 1845 it appeared to S. C. Wilks that the progress of Tractarianism had not yet been checked:

> Tractarianism, in its essence, we fear is scarcely checked among us. It is inflicting its ravages in our parishes and in invidious forms; it is working its way in schools, colleges and training establishments; it is poisoning the very fountains from which should flow the streams of life in missionary labours; and it has made gigantic efforts by means of the press to extend its baneful influence.[7]

However, at the end of 1847, in a final editorial note in the

Churchman's Monthly Review, which was ceasing publication, the editors wrote of 'the apparent declension of that formidable party in the Church, against which at the outset, our efforts were most especially directed'. They went on:

A great change has taken place during the eight years of our existence. The leaders of the Tractarian party have taken that step which we ever declared they *must* one day take; namely, a departure from our Protestant Church. And their literature, formerly so flourishing, has departed with them. We say not that Tractariansim is *dead*; but at least its apparent and active vigour and energy is gone.

This was to misunderstand the situation. The vigour which had earlier gone into literary productions was now diverted into a greater variety of means of disseminating 'Church Principles'.

Between 1845 and 1848 most Evangelical observers appear to have agreed with Wilks that the poison of Puseyism was being digested within the great Church societies – the Society for the Propagation of the Gospel and the National Society for Education. And they added that it was making an impact in parishes and in old and new educational establishments. In the pages of the *Record* fears had been expressed from as early as 5 December, 1842 concerning the acceptance by the Society for the Propagation of the Gospel of candidates holding Tractarian views.[8] On 1 June, 1846 the same paper carried discussions of the adoption of Tractarian teaching and practices by tutors in Codrington College, Barbados, Bishop's College, Calcutta, and Cobourg College, Canada, while the Bishop of Toronto was frequently criticised for his espousal of Puseyism. Likewise the foundation of the new college named after St Augustine of Canterbury was criticised because of the 'strong Tractarian leaven' which distinguished 'many of the men (e.g. A. J. B. Hope Esq.) who had exerted themselves in this affair'. The teacher-training institutions at Westminster, Battersea and Chelsea were also frequently assailed from 1845. It was declared that the purpose of the National Society, which ran the colleges, was 'to send into our villages and hamlets, as well as into our mining and manufacturing districts, schoolmasters initiated into all the ecclesiastical millinery and ceremonies of Puseyism'.

Not surprisingly the foundation of the new Training School in the parish of Cheltenham was greeted with rejoicing. 'We have long held', declared the *Record* on 8 April, 1847, 'that the foundation of new Training Schools on an enlarged scale was of paramount importance as it regards the permanent orthodoxy, security and spiritual prosperity of our beloved and venerated Church.' But also a careful watch was kept on other establishments, the result being that Malborough College was declared to be leavened with Tractarianism and Robert Eden of Leigh was strongly rebuked for his attempts to crush the schools munded by Lady Olivia Sparrow in the parish in order that he foight found new ones on Tractarian principles. These and other examples led to a call for an Evangelical Protestant Education Society, but that had to wait until 1853.

It has been noted that the amount of controversial literature decreased in this period. Even so, one author, William Gresley, seemed determined to incite the Evangelicals to wrath. In the decade after 1846 he was in controversy with at least four Evangelicals, one of whom was Close, sometimes called 'the Pope of Cheltenham'.[9] His battle with the latter began with his brief but pungent *The Real Danger of the Church of England* (1846). In this he celebrated the new school of churchmen who had asserted 'Church Principles' and declared that the Evangelical clergy posed a threat to the maintenance of these principles in the Church. His booklet went through six editions within a year and was noticed in all the Evangelical press. According to one critic Gresley's aim was 'to divert the attention of the public, and more especially the Church's rulers from the secessions to Romanism which have lately occurred and are still occurring; and to get up an alarm in a totally different direction'.[10] One of Gresley's major assertions was that 'the denial of baptismal regeneration is the leading doctrine not only of Dissenters from the Church, but of the Evangelical or Puritan party within it; and in this they have entirely departed from the doctrine of the reformers'. There was a mixture of truth and error in this claim. Gresley also accused the 'Puritan clergy' of resisting the restoration of the genuine services of the Church, making particular reference to the opposition of the *Record* and the Islington clergy in 1843 to the requests made by the Bishop of London in terms of the reading of the Liturgy. Furthermore, he accused Evangelicals of neglecting 'Church societies' such as SPCK and SPG and preferring to work through their own societies, the CP-AS and the CMS, thereby bringing danger to the unity of the Church. The *Record*, which had complained about the religious fiction of both Gresley and F. E. Paget in 1842, took Gresley's accusations seriously and declared:

> Such little manufacturers of little stories and books as Mr Gresley may continue their little operations in the Church in the time to come, or follow the objects of their admiration into Rome as circumstances may direct, and few would be able to say whether they were better placed here or there; but the men whom he has libelled and abused in this discreditable pamphlet are men of higher and nobler nature and their work, while a sure work for eternity is also a safe foundation amidst the mutations and perturbations of time.[11]

Close, a frequent correspondent in the columns of the *Record*, also wrote against Gresley in a hasty composition *An Apology for the Evangelical Party, being a Reply to the Pamphlet of . . . W. Gresley* (1846). Not very convincing, it ended on the pessimistic note that 'the moderate and considerate of the Evangelical clergy may gather from these pages of how little use it is to attempt to propitiate such a body as these ultra High-Church Anglicans.' For Close, not only co-operation but also dialogue with Tractarians was now useless and in asserting this he spoke for many 'Recordite' Evangelicals.[12]

2. CONTROVERSY IN OXFORD, 1845–8

Though the dispersion of Tractarians meant that Oxford University was no longer the major focal point of the Movement the eyes of the country were, nevertheless, turned towards it on several occasions. The first of these was connected with the sermon preached by Pusey on 1 February, 1846 in Christ Church, some two years after his suspension. Always on the lookout for incipient Romanism, Golightly was at the centre of the efforts to ensure that Pusey affirmed a true Protestant faith before he actually preached the sermon. Earlier he had sent letters to the

Morning Herald and *Standard* newspapers in which he pointed out Romanising tendencies in the *Oxford and Cambridge Review* and claimed that 'Stonyhurst Jesuits' were being intruded into Oxford.[13] From Gainsborough Vicarage Bird wrote to tell Golightly, 'I think you are entitled to the gratitude of the Church of England for protecting her children, especially her choice ones at the Universities, from the plague likely to be communicated by the *Oxford and Cambridge Review*.' Later in the letter, after discussing the welcome appointment of Samuel Wilberforce as Bishop of Oxford, he expressed the view that one of his first episcopal duties should be the suspension of Pusey from preaching, just as Bishop Blomfield had suspended W. G. Ward earlier.[14] Another correspondent, Archdeacon Browne, who had been involved in the stone altar case at the Round Church in Cambridge, referred to Pusey's propagation of erroneous doctrine in various publications as nothing less than 'flagrant and atrocious dishonesty'.[15] As the date for the delivery of Pusey's sermon approached, Golightly examined recent writings in the Tractarian press, articles and letters reputed to be by Pusey; he brought to the attention of Oxford colleagues and far flung correspondents four letters, which had appeared anonymously in the *English Churchman* on and after 2 October, 1845 and which appeared to defend the doctrines of purgatory and invocation of the saints.[16] He also wrote and had printed for general circulation a letter to the Vice-Chancellor, Dr Symons, in which he requested that before Pusey preached his University sermon he should be required to affirm his belief in the teaching of the Thirty-Nine Articles, especially Article XXII (Of Purgatory).[17] In encouragement Goode wrote from London to state that 'Dr Pusey's present position at the University of Oxford seems to me a standing scandal and therefore that the only question to my mind is *how* this case can best be taken up.' He proceeded to express the view that to bring charges in the Vice-Chancellor's court would be difficult since the articles in the *English Churchman* were anonymous.[19] The Vice-Chancellor was likewise cautious and in a letter of 14 January, 1846, a copy of which was sent to Pusey, Golightly was politely told that nothing could be done before the preaching of the sermon, but if the sermon was judged to be heretical then the statutes of the

University provided a remedy.[19] So the sermon, based on John 20.21–3, was duly preached in Christ Church to an attentive congregation and when printed was entitled *The Entire Absolution of the Penitent*. Since the preacher was careful to keep to the teaching concerning absolution given in the Ordinal and in the Service for the Visitation of the Sick, it was impossible to delate him a second time. Even so, his critics were still persuaded that he taught erroneous doctrine.[20]

The second occasion when the national press showed great interest in the Tractarian question at Oxford was connected with the elections for Parliament in 1847. At the height of the contest a writer in the *Guardian* commented on 26 May, 1847: 'It is the election of elections. The Member will be the elect of the elected.' It was taken for granted that Sir Robert Inglis would be re-elected as one MP and so the contest was between those who stood hoping to gain the second seat. At first it appeared that the battle was between W. E. Gladstone and Edward Cardwell, nephew of the Principal of St Alban Hall. At this stage Evangelical Protestants were not happy for they saw little to choose between the two men, since, in the words of John Hill, both men had given 'support for popery' in their previous voting in Parliament.[21] So when C. J. Round of Balliol, the Recorder of Colchester and late MP for North Essex, was proposed as a candidate the *Record* saw him as the champion of the Protestant cause and immediately called upon Oxford men to support him. On 17 May Hill attended a meeting at the lodgings of Dr C. A. Ogilvie, the first Regius Professor of Pastoral Theology; here it was resolved that Mr Round be proposed in Convocation as a candidate. Later Hill served on the committee which sought to gain support for Round. However, despite the hard work of Round's Oxford and London committees he was not elected; Gladstone received 997 votes and Round 824. In this particular battle the Evangelicals lost but in that Inglis continued as MP, they could claim in him a sympathetic defender of their cause.

On the day before the meeting at Dr Ogilvie's lodgings Hill had taken tea with Dr Shirley, now the Bishop of Sodor and Man, who had commenced his Bampton Lectures two days earlier. His topic was the supremacy of Scripture in matters of faith and conduct because he understood the unanimous choice of him by the Heads of Houses as 'a decided act of the University against Tractarianism'.[22] Regrettably due to illness and subsequent death he was never able to finish the series. The Bampton Lectures for 1848 were given by another Evangelical, Edward G. Marsh, a former Fellow of Oriel, and now incumbent of Aylesford, Kent. Working from the traditional doctrine of justification he expounded the way in which God's children grow in holiness. These lectures were published as *The Christian Doctrine of Sanctification* (1848). It must be admitted that neither of these series made much impact either in Oxford or elsewhere. In fact the lecturers would probably have served the Church and Evangelical cause better had they addressed themselves to the doctrine of the Church.

3. THE GORHAM CASE AND ITS AFTERMATH, 1847–52

The Gorham controversy has often been described and its outlines are well known.[23] Gorham was a decided Evangelical having studied at Trinity College, Cambridge, in the days of Simeon, and having been a curate at Clapham. Had he looked for an incumbency in any other English diocese than Exeter in 1847 he would probably have experienced no trouble at all, his name then going down into history as one of the six thousand Evangelical clergy in the Church of England. With Bishop Phillpotts, however, he came face to face with a decided High Churchman, who not only knew what he himself believed but who also claimed to know exactly what the Church should teach. The theological topic which brought the Bishop and his presbyter into open conflict and which then threatened to divide the Church of England was the doctrine of regeneration in infant baptism. This subject, intimately connected as it was with the words of the Service of Holy Baptism for Infants in the Prayer Book, had already been a cause of controversy between Evangelicals and High Churchmen in previous decades of the century. And after the publication of Pusey's *Tracts on Baptism* in 1835 the topic had been constantly raised in pamphlets, tracts, sermons and magazines. The consistent Tractarian doctrine that spiritual regeneration always accompanies baptism led the

Record to declare on 24 January, 1848 that 'the prevailing error of the day in our Church is that of the spiritual regeneration of every infant in baptism'. Earlier, on 12 October, 1840, in an account of the Tractarian system of theology the same paper had claimed that the root of the system was baptismal regeneration.

Unlike the doctrines of Reserve or Sacramental Confession, the teaching that the implantation of divine life in the soul takes place whenever the sacrament is correctly administered was a doctrine in which the majority of High Churchmen agreed with the Tractarians. Among Evangelicals it was generally agreed that, while God could, and sometimes did, actually implant divine life in the soul of the baptised child, it was impossible to affirm, on the grounds of either Scripture or experience, that spiritual regeneration always takes place in baptism. If it did, personal conversion to God in later life would not be necessary and the openly sinful life of so many baptised as infants would be incapable of explanation.

As the two viewpoints collided first in the fight of the two gladiators in the West Country, and then throughout the kingdom, much dust was raised and in this dust were other controversial areas of doctrine and practice. Since the ritual troubles of 1844 Phillpotts had been seen by Evangelicals as a semi-Tractarian and his controversy with Gorham and the support he received from Pusey and the Tractarian press only served to confirm this.

Immediately after the lengthy examination of Gorham by the Bishop himself, which stretched from December 1847 to March 1848, Phillpotts sent a letter to his Archdeacon, which was printed in the *English Churchman* on 6 April, 1848. The letter was not explicitly related to the Gorham examination but contained the Bishop's reaction to the clause concerning the Thirty-Nine Articles proposed for insertion in the Clergy Offences Bill, which was before Parliament. Phillpotts objected to the elevation of the Articles above the Book of Common Prayer as the supreme doctrinal standard of the Church. He would have been content with equal status for both. Drawing upon his detailed knowledge of English Church History Goode responded in *A Defence of the Thirty-Nine Articles as the Legal and Canonical Test of Doctrine* (1848). He denied that the proposed clause would 'rob the Church of its most sacred and dearest principles'. Both men knew that the Articles did not explicitly teach baptismal regeneration. Phillpotts was not a man easily to be silenced and in his *Charge* of that summer he returned to the subject seeking to meet the arguments of Goode, who himself replied in *A Vindication of 'A Defence . . .'*. Because the supremacy of the Articles over both Prayer Book and Ordinal was so fundamental to Evangelical thinking, Goode, now editor of the *Christian Observer*, commissioned eight articles on 'Clerical Subscription to the Articles' which appeared between May and December 1849. It seemed clear to some Evangelicals (but not all) that since the Articles did not explicitly teach the regeneration of infants in baptism neither could the Prayer Book, even if the natural sense of the words of the Service appeared so to teach. In calling for support for Gorham the *Record* declared on 4 May, 1848 it was now time for action against the Bishop because for 'too long has Dr Phillpotts been permitted to import the passions of a political pamphleteer and the domineering spirit of an intolerant Tractarian into the management of the see of Exeter'.

Meanwhile the Evangelical clergy of the Exeter diocese, led by John Hatchard, Vicar of St Andrew's, Plymouth, and son of John Hatchard the publisher, openly challenged the Bishop over the orthodoxy of his domestic chaplain, William Maskell, who had been closely involved in examining Gorham.[24] In a Visitation Sermon at Totnes in October 1848 Maskell had expressed his belief in the doctrines of auricular confession and priestly absolution, subjects on which he was later to challenge Pusey as he moved into the Church of Rome.[25] Twenty-one clergy, led by Hatchard, protested about the sermon; letters from the clergy to the Bishop and the Bishop to the clergy appeared in the *Plymouth Herald* and were reprinted in the *Christian Observer* (published by Hatchards), being dated between 13 October and 20 November. Though they did not examine the baptismal issue they did help to charge the theological atmosphere in Exeter and in the Evangelical constituency and thus they added to the importance of the Gorham case. Phillpotts was now seen as the tool or the mouthpiece of the Tractarians.

Among the many publications which now began to appear on

the doctrine of infant baptism, two may be noted. First, the published sermon of Professor James Scholefield, preached before Cambridge University on 25 November, 1849, and printed as *Baptismal Regeneration as maintained by the Church of England* (1849). Writing to Scholefield, who at this time was doing work as an editor for the Parker Society, Bishop Daniel Wilson stated that he thought 'it far the most Scriptural view of our Church's tenets on Infant Baptism which has yet appeared'.[26] At this time Wilson had probably not seen the major treatise of William Goode, *The Doctrine of the Church of England as to the Effects of Baptism in the case of Infants* (1849).[27] Both authors attempted to prove that the doctrine of the Church does not require clergy to believe that each and every infant who is baptised is necessarily regenerated by the Holy Spirit. Both Archbishops were in general agreement with this position and in the very month that the Dean of Arches gave his judgment that infants are always regenerated in baptism, the Archbishop of York issued a *Charge* proclaiming that the effects of infant baptism were open to a variety of interpretations, and the Archbishop of Canterbury, now J. B. Sumner, presented William Goode, the major opponent of Phillpotts, to the Rectory of All Hallows the Great in London.

Even with the support of Archbishops, Evangelicals rightly felt that the judgment of the Dean of Arches brought them into a crisis. The *Christian Observer* declared that 'we believe no such crisis has occurred in our Church for at least two centuries' after Goode had subjected the Judgment of Sir H. J. Fust to a lengthy scrutiny. With others Goode believed that 'new tenets of orthodoxy' were being used by the Court and instead of plain statements of the Articles of Religion being quoted 'inferential reasoning from certain non-dogmatical Formularies of the Church' was being substituted.[28] From the *Record* came full support for Gorham and praise for Goode's writings which were often quoted. It called upon Evangelicals to support the 'Bramford-Speke Fund' so that Gorham would not personally be burdened with all the legal expenses. Its columns were now filled with letters from leading Evangelicals bitterly criticising the Judgment and from the pen of Edward Bickersteth came five long letters in December 1849 on the subject of the Prayer

Book Services of Baptism. With the support of thousands of clergy and laity Gorham took his case to the highest court and to the relief of Evangelicals and Broad Churchmen the Judicial Committee of the Privy Council declared that Gorham's doctrine was not contrary to the Church of England's teaching. Naturally this was seen by the *Record* as an answer to fervent prayer. A massive exodus of Evangelicals from the ministerial ranks of the Church was avoided.

While the Evangelicals blessed God for the Gorham Judgment the High Churchmen and Tractarians were shocked and humiliated and thus made gigantic efforts to have the decision reversed. In St Martin's Hall, Long Acre, a massive protest meeting was held on 23 July and so many were in attendance that an overflow meeting was needed at the Freemasons' Tavern. Richard Bagot, now Bishop of Bath and Wells and the only representative of the episcopate present, put to the meeting a protest which asserted the doctrine of baptismal regeneration, repudiated the findings of the Judicial Committee and petitioned the Queen and Bishops for the restoration of synodical government within the Church. Reporting the meeting the *Record* recalled the experience of ancient Israel and declared: 'What was considered a propitious day for the great sacrifice to the Baal of Tractarianism having at length been found it was offered in a music hall in Long Acre.'[29] Immediately after 'The Day', as Tractarians called 23 July, 1850, Manning drafted a *Declaration touching the Royal Supremacy in Matters Ecclesiastical*, which, with a *Letter*, signed by Manning, Wilberforce and Professor Mill, was distributed among the clergy for their signatures.[30] The three Tractarians declared that 'we do not and in conscience cannot acknowledge in the Crown the power recently exercised to hear and judge in appeal the internal state or merits of spiritual questions touching doctrine or discipline, the custody of which is committed to the Church alone by the law of Christ'. The *Declaration* attracted only 1,800 signatures and several printed criticisms from Evangelicals.

Hugh McNeile of Liverpool, who attempted to teach Bishop Phillpotts what was true Anglican doctrine concerning baptism,[31] now corresponded with Wilberforce on the question of the meaning of the Royal Supremacy. He declared:

I look upon the Sovereign as the chief member of the Church, under Christ the Head; and I look upon any other member of the Church, lay or clerical, who denies or disputes the supreme authority of the Sovereign as refractory or rebellious. The Divine Head of the Church has given us His own Supreme Law to which our Sovereign, as well as ourselves, is bound to yield implicit obedience. This is our security and the only security the nature of the case admits of . . . The loud opponents of Erastianism are after all Erastians. *Their* sovereign is a *majority* liable to all the fluctuation of popular election. Ours is an individual ascending an hereditary throne and surrounded by the hallowed precedents of a Royal ancestry.[32]

A further correspondence between Manning and Goode revolved around the question whether the Articles and Canons of the Church taught the same doctrine of the Royal Supremacy as did the Statute Law. Manning answered in the negative claiming his conscience was bound only by Church Law and Goode answered in the affirmative claiming that historically it could be shown that the two sources of law gave a unanimous decision.[33] Editorials in the *Record* represented the viewpoint of the Protestant laity who wanted Parliament to continue the plenary exercise of the old Royal Supremacy as the only way of preserving for the Church the truths and principles of the *Reformation*.[34] In the pages of the *Christian Guardian* Henry Walter, an editor for the Parker Society and a frequent contributor to the *Record*'s columns, proceeded to criticise the Address to the Queen from some forty-five tutors at Oxford. In this Her Majesty was petitioned not to interfere through the Privy Council in ecclesiastical doctrine. Guided by Pusey these tutors had also sent protests to the parents of their scholars. Walter, who had written a history of England and was editing the works of William Tyndale, argued on historical grounds for the exercise of the Royal Supremacy in 1850 through Parliament, to which the monarch had yielded it.[35]

While Evangelicals rejoiced in the fact that secession had not been necessary there was nevertheless a widespread concern in their ranks about the maintenance of Protestantism in the national Church. Daniel Wilson the younger, spokesman for many London clergy and laity, published *Our Protestant Faith in Danger* (1850) which was an appeal to the Evangelical members of the Church in the times of crisis immediately following 'The Day' which Wilson had viewed with horror.[36] This appeal was longer and more influential than a similar one from J. C. Miller of Birmingham entitled, *'Subjection; No; not for an hour'. A Warning to Protestant Christians in behalf of the 'Truth of the Gospel' as now imperilled by the Romish doctrines ... of the Tractarian heresy* (1850). Wilson described the crisis facing religious liberty in the following terms:

> The question at issue is, whether the Church of our fore-fathers shall henceforth be the faithful depository of that pure Scriptural truth which is comprised in her recognised formularies, or whether she shall gradually be permitted to relapse into vain superstitions and unmeaning ceremonies, holding the name without the power and life of Christianity, sub-mitting her conscience to the dogmatic teaching of assumed dictators of her faith, and thus preparing at no distant period to drop her distinctive appellation as a Reformed Church and to resume her ancient position as a vassal of the See of Rome.

Tractarianism, the cause of the crisis, he then examined in its historical development. It had gained ground because the Evangelical clergy, though numerous, had been involved in large parishes and active service for various societies, leaving little time for polemical theology. Since the bishops had failed to do their duty 'the heresies which now threaten us might apparently have been nipped in the bud'. Commenting on the Gorham case he wrote :

> I regard the baptismal controversy merely as one of the phenomena of the present critical position of our Church. It was the spark thrown among the combustibles which created a sudden explosion. It has not altered materially for better or worse the state of the Church. It has given a temporary check to the movement party, which has led them more distinctly to avow their ultimate designs. The cry of oppression and

spiritual bondage which they now raise is simply the expression of disappointment and chagrin that a legal obex has for the present been placed against their further advance.

He called for unity and vigilance in the Evangelical ranks for he feared that a Convocation would in the future attempt to interpret the Articles and the Prayer Book in a Roman way. Thus 'the Evangelical body must either arise to the emergency or they will be eventually excluded from the Church'. But the problem was how the Evangelicals should arise and on this not all the reviewers agreed with Wilson's suggestions.[37]

The section of Calvinistic Evangelicalism whose spokesmen controlled the *Christian Guardian* believed that the only way to prevent the débâcle of another Gorham case was to reform the Liturgy so that it could not be interpreted in anything but a Protestant sense. In an article entitled 'The Duty of the Evangelical Party', printed in October 1850 as protests for baptismal regeneration were still being heard, faithful Protestants were called upon as a body to follow Wilson and Miller and to protest and remove Tractarian abuses and blemishes from the Church. An urgent need, it was strongly argued, was to press also for the reform of the Liturgy and enlist Lord Ashley in the crusade: 'The policy of attempting such a revision of our Book of Common Prayer as shall at once preserve its services from the profanation incident to their present necessarily indiscriminate administration, and the avoidance of cavil or offence to tender consciences from the use of ambiguous terms or declarations not positively supported by the plain statements of Holy Writ.' Then began a series of articles, printed over the next two years, by John Jordan of Enstone, Oxfordshire, C. H. Davies of Nailsworth, Gloucestershire and one, who declared only his initials of 'C.A.',[38] on liturgical and ritual reform, with occasional reference to administrative reform. Articles appeared providing new services for Baptism, Holy Communion, the Visitation of the Sick and the Burial of the Dead, and improvements for virtually all parts of the Prayer book and Ordinal were suggested. The magazine also reported with enthusiasm the foundation of 'the Wycliffe Church Reform Association' at a meeting on 28 May, 1851 at Freemasons' Hall, London.

This group of churchmen, who were in sympathy with the Evangelical Alliance and believed Anglicans should be involved in it, were of course quite convinced that the Liturgy of 1662 did not speak with the clarity of the Thirty-Nine Articles on doctrinal points and thus there was a need, as they saw it, to complete the work of the Reformers of the sixteenth century. While they admired the efforts of the editor of the *Christian Observer* (J. W. Cunningham) and the former editor, William Goode, to make the whole Liturgy speak the language of the Articles, they believed that such men as Phillpotts had more than a grain of truth on their side in pleading that immediate baptismal regeneration is the obvious meaning of the Service of Holy Baptism for infants. This point of view is reflected in a review of a long tract by a rising star of the Evangelicals, J. C. Ryle, Vicar of Stradbroke, Suffolk, on *Regeneration*.[39] Ryle followed Goode in arguing for 'the hypothetical principle of the presence of faith and its promised result' – 'the charitable supposition' as it was called. Ryle's position was criticised on the grounds that in a national Establishment it is impossible to secure the discipline to make sure that only converted Christians bring their children to baptism; and even if it were, it is impossible on biblical grounds to defend the thanksgiving prayer in the rite when God is thanked for regeneration which is now a reality. The reviewer, C. H. Davies, attempting to be positive, actually provided a prayer which he thought could replace the prayer in the rite.

On 'The Day' a call had been made for the restoration of synodical government to theChurch in terms of the revival of the Convocations of York and Canterbury and this pressure was continued. It was also made by men who were not High Churchmen, Archdeacon Hare for example. In their ancient structure the Convocations were weighted in favour of the senior clergy with the lower clergy having little representation and the laity having no representation. While W. E. Gladstone looked hopefully for the eventual inclusion of a lay element, Pusey and Robert Wilberforce wanted only a clerical synod. The latter were convinced that the Catholicity of the Church could best be preserved if only clergy were admitted. Samuel Wilberforce disappointed Evangelicals by becoming the main protagonist in the House of Lords for the revival of Convocation.

Evangelicals opposed the revival of Convocation even as they had opposed the diocesan synod called by Phillpotts. The moderate Archdeacon of Middlesex, John Sinclair, published his Charge on the topic as *Synodal Action in the Church unreasonable and perilous* (1851). He examined and then rejected the various reasons given by High Churchmen for Convocation and argued that the Church already had many blessings and these could well be lost if a national clerical synod ruled over all. In similar fashion the Archdeacon of Chichester, James Garbett, argued in *Diocesan Synods and Convocation* (1852) that it was better to do without any synods and thereby preserve the Church from internal strife and disruption. Furthermore he believed that it was now impossible for the Church to move in this way without the consent and co-operation of the laity. A similar message came from C. S. Bird in his *The Danger attending an immediate revival of Convocation* (1852). J. W. Cunningham commented that 'the great mass of the laity are decidedly opposed to the doings of a Convocation and will not tolerate the re-imposition of its yoke (as at present constituted) upon the neck of the Church'.[40]

After many sorties against those who would revive Convocation the *Record* of 8 November, 1852 summed up its arguments against the move as follows:

First, that a power of synodal or corporate action is inherent in every branch of the Church of Christ and that in certain cases of urgent necessity, or high practical utility, it might be incumbent on all faithful members of the English Church to resume it by some means or other. Secondly, that any synodal action at the present juncture, with our large openings for useful activity, and the state of parties within the Church, would lead to endless strife, with no counteracting benefit, and ought to be opposed by every lover of the Gospel and every friend of peace and practical Christianity. Thirdly, that if synodal action were desirable, the Convocation is quite disqualified for the work and this for four or five reasons. The laity have no voice at all which is a fatal defect and intrudes a Popish element into its composition the moment it assumes the representation of the whole Church. The Irish Church has also no voice in it. The parochial clergy, instead of three-fourths, their natural share, are little more than a fourth of the whole, and the two provinces have a distinct Convocation each framed in a different way. Fourthly, the Convocation is just as ill-qualified to be a constituent and legislative body. Our parishes and our dioceses are living features of the Church. The Convocation is both a dead and mis-shapen body . . . And, lastly, even if the most unwise steps were taken of reviving Convocation, to revive it now at the last moment would have been an insult to common sense, and a direct fraud upon the great body of the Church, in favour of a faction of zealots who are either secret or open traitors to the cause of the Reformation and to the truth of the Gospel.

This was written before the Convocation of Canterbury had its brief sessions in November 1852, sessions which inaugurated the revival of the southern synod. The northern one did not resume until 1861.

The revival of Convocation shocked many of the Protestant laity and, led by Lord Shaftesbury (he had ceased to be Lord Ashley eighteen months earlier), the Protestant Defence Committee called a meeting at Freemasons' Hall on 15 November. 'We are here', the noble Lord told the great crowd, 'to say that we will not submit to any clerical Parliament that will make the laity of the Church and of these realms mere "hewers of wood and drawers of water" [Joshua 9.21] to a select knot of sacerdotal dignitaries.'[41] A protest was also made against the growing practice of auricular confession. There followed further large meetings in English cities but they were not able to stop the process which had begun. Happily, their worst fears were never realised for there soon appeared the Church Congress and then the Church Assembly in which the laity had a voice. The protest over auricular confession continued in the following years reaching a peak in 1858 when there were many protest meetings throughout the country; but, again, the Protestant laity were not able to stop the growth of this practice in the English Church.

4. FROM THE PAPAL AGGRESSION TO 1856

As the initial effects of the Gorham Judgment were being assimilated by the Church the controversy between Evangelical and Tractarian was given a new twist by what has become known as the Papal Aggression, the establishment of thirteen Roman Catholic bishoprics in England and Wales, with an Archbishopric at Westminster. The Pope's decision became widely known in mid-October 1850 and a series of protests and riots began as the endemic Protestant feeling of the country was stirred. On 5 December Shaftesbury was at the Freemasons' Hall at the head of a large and influential gathering of the laity of the Church in order to protest and to send a petition to the Queen.[42] According to the *Record* 'the two chief features of the Meeting were the speech of the Noble Chairman and the deep, strong and unmistakable determination of the assembled multitude'.[43] Earlier the same paper had printed the full text of the letter sent by the Prime Minister to the Bishop of Durham, fully agreeing with Lord Russell that Tractarianism had helped to pave the way for this act of papal arrogance.

As did other clergy, Goode addressed his parishioners on the subject in the gravest of terms and then with them sent an Address to the Queen expressing their disgust over the action of the Pope and noting the connection of the Aggression with Tractarianism:

We regret to be compelled to add our conviction that what has tended more than anything else to produce this act of Papal aggression has been the late rise of a Romanising party in the Church of England. Of those who have already seceded to the communion of the Church of Rome, we say nothing; but as it respects those who, while they remain in the ministry of the Church of England, are countenancing, directly or indirectly, doctrines and practices essentially Popish, and denying that supremacy of the Crown in spiritual matters which they have solemnly pledged themselves to uphold – or, what is worse, casting contempt on the exercise of it – we would humbly but earnestly represent to your

Majesty the dangers that must ensue from such a state of things, not merely to the interests of the Church itself, but to the peace and welfare of the community; and respectfully entreat your Majesty to take such measures as may tend to preserve unimpaired the Protestant character of the Church of England and secure the faithfulness of its ministers to their engagements.[44]

If this is how the leading theologian of the Evangelicals was thinking it is easy to understand how others could be led to violence and riotous behaviour. Though not a storm in a tea-cup, the protests did eventually cease and the Roman Catholic hierarchy gradually became a part of the English religious scene. But in the meantime Evangelicals found it difficult to forgive the Tractarians for assisting, as they thought, the progress of the religion of 'the Man of Sin' in Protestant Britain. In January 1851 those who met in Islington Vicarage for the annual Clerical Meeting discussed the topic, 'How may we most effectually promote a revival of spiritual religion in our own Church?'[45] and soon afterwards their president, Daniel Wilson, published his *A Revival of Spiritual Religion the only effectual remedy for the dangers which now threaten the Church of England* (1851). He looked for a movement of the Holy Spirit such as that which had occurred through the preaching of George Whitefield, William Romaine and John Newton.[46]

In the parish of Islington was the Islington Protestant Institute, founded in 1846 as an interdenominational centre for the conversion of Irish immigrants and for the propagation of the Protestant Faith.[47] Wilson, its first president, did not doubt that Presbyterian, Lutheran and Congregational ordinations made true ministers of Christ. Thus he and other Evangelicals had no theological problems to face concerning opening their pulpits to foreign pastors if this seemed the appropriate thing to do. In April 1851 the Protestant-Aid Society, whose chairman was the Marquis of Cholmondeley, had been in correspondence with Bishop Blomfield about the availability of churches for services in foreign languages and the latter had been very sympathetic to this need.[48] The Great Exhibition, which opened in April 1851, brought many foreigners to Britain among whom was a group of pastors, including Dr Merle D'Aubigné. His inaugural lecture in the Protestant Academy in Geneva had dealt with Tractarianism and was made available in an English translation by the efforts of Edward Bickersteth under the title *Geneva and Oxford* (1843). So while no Evangelical would doubt the validity of D'Aubigné's ordination, or that of his colleagues, every Tractarian who knew of him had to doubt it and view him merely as a layman.[49] On 8 June, 1851 he preached at a public service in Woburn Chapel, London, after Richard Burgess, incumbent of Upper Chelsea, had read prayers. A critical report of this incident was printed in the *Morning Chronicle* of 11 June where it was pointed out that under the Act of Uniformity of 1662 D'Aubigné was liable to be prosecuted and put in jail for three months. The Swiss Professor immediately composed a reply to this report defending himself on what he believed were scriptural grounds in *A Letter to the Archbishop of Canterbury*, whom he counted as a personal friend.[50] Commenting, the *Record* declared on 12 June that 'the principle at issue in the whole affair is this: the Reformed Churches and the Church of England with them place Evangelical truth *first* and Church order in the second place. But Rome, and the Romanizers, make Episcopacy and the Apostolic Succession the test, the sole test of a true Church.'

Unfortunately more bitterness was to come. On the following Sunday D'Aubigné and a colleague preached again in Woburn and Portman Chapels. Hearing of this W. Upton Richards, priest in charge at the Margaret Street Chapel (whose services the *Record* had severely criticised), sent a letter of protest to the Bishop of London, pointing out that their preaching had been a violation of the law. Blomfield took the point and informed the ministers of the Chapels, Thomas Dale and Thomas Reeves, that they should explain to their foreign guests what was the law of England. Whether these men did do as the bishop requested is not clear but what is clear is that a certain W. R. F. Gawthorne, a friend of Upton Richards, wrote to Archbishop Sumner on 18 June and thereby caused much trouble. Instead of using his surname he wrote as Mr W. Francis, utilising his Christian names. Pretending to be an Evangelical, he claimed that he was offended by the actions of Upton Richards and

Blomfield, and thereby played on the known respect which the Archbishop had for D'Aubigné. The Archbishop took the letter seriously and in all innocence replied. After explaining and defending the action of the bishop he went on to make what was to be regarded as a momentous assertion: 'I hardly imagine that there are two Bishops on the Bench or one Clergyman in fifty throughout our Church, who would deny the validity of the orders of these pastors, solely on account of their wanting the the imposition of Episcopal hands.' This was as a red rag to a bull and Gawthorne immediately made the contents of the letter known to his Tractarian friends. Pamphlets appeared containing the correspondence; the matter was taken up by newspapers and magazines and the poor Archbishop was maligned in letters printed in the *Morning Chronicle* written by Beresford Hope. Happily the Evangelicals stood by the Archbishop, in strong but calm language in the *Christian Observer* and in powerful but less dignified language in the *Record*.[51]

The 'Exeter Synod' took place soon after the incidents involving the foreign pastors and it was not unexpected that those clergy in the diocese who supported Phillpotts should also be in sympathy with members of the London Church Union who had made complaints to Blomfield and Sumner. From these clergy came an Address to the Archbishop maintaining that the only valid ordinations are those by bishops in the apostolic succession. And from Archdeacon Edward Churton of Yorkshire came a letter published in the *Guardian* of 19 November, 1851 criticising the new Bishop of Manchester, James Prince Lee, for his declaration that the clergy of the Church of Scotland, though ordained by presbyters, are still true ministers of the Church of God and are so recognised by the canon law of England. (To understand the difference of opinion here it is necessary to recall that the order of bishops was removed from the Church in Scotland only in 1638 and that the canons of the Church of England dated from 1604.) Into the arena once more stepped William Goode to engage in a correspondence with Churton in the columns of the *Guardian*. He argued that the fifty-fifth canon of 1604 in requiring prayer for the Holy Catholic Church and especially 'for the Churches in England, Scotland and Ireland' did refer to the 'Presbyterian' Church of

Scotland and not the Episcopalian Church in Scotland. The Church of Scotland of 1852 was the obvious historical continuance of the Church before 1638. Another person with whom Goode did battle at this juncture was Archdeacon Harington. The latter had provided what he believed to be a convincing 'catena' from Anglican divines on the question of the invalidity of non-episcopal orders but Goode's response was that the 'catena' actually proved the opposite; 'His *nominal* thesis of the Apostolical institution of Episcopacy they will no doubt support; but his *real* one of the indispensable necessity of Episcopacy to a valid ministry and a real Church they distinctly oppose.'[52]

Next Goode turned his eyes towards Exeter and addressed a pamphlet to Bishop Phillpotts. A year or so earlier he had defended his archbishop from what he termed the 'groundless, unjustifiable and offensive' accusations made against him by Phillpotts following the Gorham Judgment.[53] Now in *A Reply to the Bishop of Exeter's Second Arraignment of his Metropolitan in his 'Letter to the Archdeacon of Totnes'* (1852) he sought to prove on historical grounds that the Church of England in the sixteenth and seventeenth centuries did not doubt the validity of the orders of foreign Protestant Churches. He had to make this point because Phillpotts had supported his clergy who had sent the Address to the archbishop mentioned above. He proceeded to make the further point that to believe that only episcopal orders are valid is one thing; to prove that the Church of England makes this belief its official teaching is another. It seemed to be the case that both Phillpotts and the Tractarians confused their beliefs with the facts of the case.

The question of orders also lay behind some of the controversy surrounding the Jerusalem Bishopric. In 1846 the ordination and consecration of Samuel Gobat as the second Bishop of Jerusalem had not gone unchallenged by the vigilant Phillpotts and the Tractarian leaders, and had not gone without strong support from the *Record*.[54] Throughout his episcopate Gobat's activities were carefully watched or reported by his critics. As a result he was accused in High Church circles of seeking to proselytize from the Eastern Church, a serious offence for those who had a branch theory of the Church, but a good activity to those

who, like a writer in the *Record*, spoke of the 'apostate and idola-
trous Greek Church'. Matters came to a head in 1853 when
John Mason Neale, an admirer and student of the Eastern
Churches, organized with the help of other Tractarians, a protest about Gobat's alleged misdemeanours. This protest, bearing about one thousand signatures, was sent to the Archbishop
of Canterbury, with copies being sent to the Eastern Patriarchs.
Evangelicals of all shades of opinion rose to the defence of
Gobat;[55] and theirs was not an isolated voice for the four British archbishops (two English and two Irish) took the unusual
step of issuing a joint letter to state that the Memorial to the
Eastern Patriarchs did not emanate from the United Church of
England and Ireland but from private individuals.[56]

Following these disagreements over the validity of orders and
the true state of the Eastern Churches came controversy between 1853 and 1857 over the doctrine of the Eucharist. First of
all there was the trial of Archdeacon Denison for alleged heretical views. Evangelicals, who were not impressed by his attempts to dominate the educational policy of the National
Society, both initiated and pressed charges against him concerning the contents of sermons he had preached in the cathedral at Wells on the Eucharist. Secondly, from the pens of R. I.
Wilberforce, E. B. Pusey and John Keble there came weighty
publications expounding the developed Tractarian doctrine of
the Holy Communion and, predictably, this exposition produced both a popular and a learned Evangelical response.

As the trial of Denison has been described by others there is
no need here to repeat the details.[57] Found guilty by the Diocesan Court of Bath and Wells of teaching doctrine contrary to
the doctrine of the Church of England on the subject of the presence of Christ in the sacrament, he would have been deprived
had not the Judicial Committee of the Privy Council in February 1858 declared that the sentence was invalid because of a
technical point. It is generally assumed that the Evangelical
Alliance set the trial in motion but there is no evidence for this
apart from the assertions of Denison and Liddon.[58]

In February 1856 one writer made the point that 'Archdeacon Denison enjoys the unenviable distinction of having
given more trouble with less benefit to a larger number of men,

than perhaps any man in the kingdom'.[59] Why Evangelicals, and Goode in particular, felt so strongly about him is revealed in the following quotation from Goode's book on the Eucharist.

> In direct contradiction . . . to the statement of our XXVIIIth Article that 'the mean whereby the Body of Christ is received and eaten in the Supper is faith', the Archdeacon maintains that it is received and eaten by the *mouth*; and in direct contradiction to the statement of the XXIXth Article that the wicked 'eat not the Body of Christ' . . . he maintains that the wicked receive the Body and Blood of Christ in the Lord's Supper as well as the faithful . . . Now these two points formed the leading points of disagreement between our early Reformers and the Romanists in their disputes previous to the martyrdom of the former. These were *two of the more important of those points of doctrine connected with the Eucharist, to oppose which Archbishop Cranmer and Bishop Ridley laid down their lives.*[60]

The Protestant Alliance, founded in 1851 and led by Shaftesbury, and the *Record* also demanded that Denison's 'Roman' doctrine be declared heretical. It is probably true, however, to state that the prosecution failed because the Evangelicals were not of one mind and did not always act together against Denison. Certainly all agreed that his doctrine was unsatisfactory, yet while Goode, Shaftesbury and Haldane were convinced that he was a heretic and that the courts should declare him to be so, Archbishop Sumner, sitting in the 'hot seat', and some moderate Evangelicals such as Professor Heurtley, became convinced that a long legal battle was inappropriate and so they tried to stop the legal proceedings. In the end the moral victory won by the prosecution was hailed by the *Record* as a sufficient indication of the error of Denison's doctrine. From the High Church and Tractarian side there was relief that Denison had escaped punishment for his position and certainly his personality had not commanded universal approval in their ranks.[61]

Before Denison's trial began Archdeacon Wilberforce published *The Doctrine of the Holy Eucharist* (1853), and Pusey published *The Presence of Christ in the Holy Eucharist* (1853); during the trial Pusey defended the teaching of the earlier book with *The Doctrine of the Real Presence as set forth in the Works of divines and others of the English Church since the Reformatiom* (1855); and after the trial Keble published *On Eucharistical Adoration* (1857). Of these books the one by Wilberforce, following as it did his major study of the Incarnation, caused the greatest comment. The *Christian Observer* had carried a long review of *The Doctrine of the Incarnation* in 1850. The writer, C. S. Bird, accepted that since no major English divine had hitherto devoted a whole volume to this doctrine Wilberforce was to be credited with some praise for his learned effort. Yet Bird felt that the volume was ruined by the adoption of Newman's doctrine of Justification, by conceding the principle of doctrinal development, by adopting an exclusive doctrine of apostolic succession, by putting the Visible Church in the place of Christ and by cutting off from union with Christ pious non-Episcopalians. Three years later Bird reviewed the volume on the Eucharist and criticised it for teaching that the union of the Christian with Christ is effected primarily and continuously through the body, that is, by the eating of the bread and wine of the Holy Sacrament. He claimed that 'to prevent rationalism he would extinguish reason. To escape from pride he would fly to formalism. To exalt the Church he would abase Christ.' Furthermore he believed that in Wilberforce's teaching the work of the Holy Spirit was superseded by that of the earthly priest so that 'faith loses its proper object. The Church is thrust before Christ. The Heavenly Intercessor is less thought of than the earthly mediator. The priest's performance is more regarded than God's promises. Instead of resting on Divine Testimony faith is called to take the testimony of antiquity for its foundation.'[62] For a balanced doctrine of the Eucharist Bird commended Bishop Edward Reynolds *Meditations on the Holy Sacrament of the Lord's Supper* (1679, reprinted 1826).

To satisfy public demand Bird's articles were printed in an expanded form as *The Sacramental and Priestly System Examined* (1854).[63] In the preface to this book Bird argued that the theological system of Wilberforce, 'the Coryphaeus of the Tractarians', was 'nothing less than the Philosophy of the Schoolmen which bewildered and subdued the intellect, and the

Sacramental and Priestly System of the Medieval Ages which almost extinguished subjective and personal religion and reduced Christianity to a round of vicarious performances, equally deadening to the people and the performers'. With less sophistication an editorial in the *Record* on 22 September, 1852 declared that Wilberforce wished to introduce a daily Eucharist, understood as a propitiatory sacrifice, with the laity communicating in only one kind and at the great festivals. After the appearance of these books there was little or no surprise when it was announced that the Archdeacon had seceded from the Church of England in order to enter the Church of Rome.[64]

In order to do justice to the Victorian Evangelicals it is necessary to mention three other matters before concluding this chapter. These are the continuing Evangelical response to the High Church/Tractarian domination of the National Society and other educational bodies, to the growth of female religious communities and to the ritualism of certain parish churches.

First, the problem of ritualism. It was noted above that when the practice of auricular confession began in a parish the organised Protestant opinion soon spoke out against it. A good example is the activism of the Protestant Committee in Brighton, which, after protesting about the ritualism of Sackville College, where J. M. Neale was Warden, turned its attention to the alleged practice of auricular confession encouraged by Gresley, who had recently come to the town, and by A. D. Wagner of St Paul's Church, where Gresley assisted.[65] Supported both by the *Record* and the *Brighton Gazette* as well as by visits from Shaftesbury, M'Ghee and other itinerant lecturers of the Protestant Association, the Protestants of Brighton managed to publicise widely their case. Yet having done this they appear to have done little in practical terms to halt the practice of confession in Brighton and Sussex.

But auricular confession was only one part of the general phenomenon of ritualism which was now gradually becoming less unfamiliar in parish churches in England. Protestant spies, alarmed by this growth, visited such London churches as St

Paul's, Knightsbridge, and St Barnabas, Pimlico, and then reported in the press what they had seen. In an editorial on the activities of Robert Liddell, the priest at St Paul's, Knightsbridge, the *Record* said on 28 April, 1851:

> It is for the laity to stand up in defence of their Protestant faith and Protestant usages, and not to allow these to be thus tampered with under the pretext that they are of little moment. It was a matter of little moment in one sense whether the Red flag or the tri-coloured should be hoisted in France, but every statesman felt that this trivial difference involved the cause of good order and good government. So it is in regard to popery. Stone altars and crosses, shrouded chancels and sedilia and piscinae, and all the main millinery of Tractarian vestments are in themselves of no more importance than the pagan idol, which the apostle declares to be in itself *nothing* (1 Cor. 8). But all these mummeries, as well as all forms of idolatry, do in fact involve principles and doctrines of the highest importance to the welfare of the Church and the salvation of the people.

Later when Liddell was prosecuted by his churchwarden, Charles Westerton, the *Record* appealed for funds to assist him with the expenses. This was the first of the ritualist prosecutions and though the verdict went to the Protestants the sympathies of many Englishmen began, perhaps slowly at first, to move towards the 'hardworking priests' with the result that, though prosecutions were to increase, ritualism also was to increase as it assumed the mantle of the martyr's cause.

For the Protestants there was a natural connection between ritualism in parishes and ritualism in religious communities. As early as 25 April, 1850 the *Record*, having in mind the support by Phillpotts and certain noble Lords, remarked that 'monasticism in the Church of England is basking in its growth not only under the fervid heat of diocesan sunshine but also on the hot-bed of aristocratical and high sounding names'. The same paper gave a lot of editorial space, as well as inches in the letters columns, to reviews of the pamphlets which appeared attacking or defending Miss Sellon and her community in Plymouth. Underlying all criticisms was the basic theme that such religious communities were essentially papist institutions in principle and therefore condemned by the Word of God. In 1857 Evangelical Protestants claimed to be shocked by the serious charges brought against J. M. Neale and the Community of Sisters he founded at East Grinstead. The charges were brought by John Scobell, Evangelical incumbent of Southover and Prebendary of Chichester, whose daughter Emily Ann Elizabeth had joined the community without his permission. She was, however, in her late twenties when she made this decisive move and it was apparently based on rational thought. Part of her work involved nursing patients with scarlet fever and she caught the disease and died. This tragedy was widely reported and feelings were intensified so that there was a near riot at her funeral.[66]

Turning to the question of education it can perhaps be claimed that Protestant sentiments here were on a more rational basis than some of those surrounding the criticism of nunneries. For years Evangelicals had protested about the Tractarian principles evident in the teacher training institutions of the National Society and the efforts of 'the pugnacious Archdeacon' Denison from 1850 to 1852 to dominate the Committee of the Society did not help matters. A crisis came in June 1852 when the Committee arbitrarily rejected a petition asking for changes in policy and signed by about three thousand Evangelicals. Francis Close led others in resigning from the Society. On 26 May, 1853 the *Record* announced the formation of the Church of England Education Society:

> We bless God that at length we see instituted a society which will prevent the education of the youth of this country from being committed into the hands of the National Education Society, with its Romanizing training schools at St Mark's, Chelsea, and its continued efforts to reduce our country parishes under the influence of Tractarianism.

To found a new Education Society and a new teacher training college at Cheltenham was not enough: error in other institutions had still to be exposed. Thus the *Record* denounced the Tractarianism in the Woodard Schools at Shoreham and Hurstpierpoint in Sussex.[67] And, though he had never been to the school but had only read a volume of Sewell's sermons preached there, Close published *High-Church Education Delusive and Dangerous: being an exposition of the system adopted by . . . W. Sewell, Warden of St Peter's College, Radley* (1855).

Evangelicals were also concerned that the training of the clergy should not get into Tractarian hands. In practical terms this meant making every effort to maintain the Protestant character of Oxford and Cambridge, as well as the new Colleges in London and Durham. Therefore when St Edmund Hall was lost to Evangelicalism with the forced resignation of E. A. Litton, the Vice-Principal, plans were set in motion to create a new Evangelical Hall, which was allowed by a new Oxford University Statute of 19 May, 1855. It was called Litton Hall and had the double aim of preserving Christian learning from both neologian and Tractarian principles.[68] It existed only from 1856 to 1861 and never had more than eight students in any one year. Thus it made little impact on the very problems it was created to confront. Evangelicals were also active in opposition to the formation of diocesan theological colleges but here again their arguments were dependent on the universities, maintaining their Protestant heritage. Editorials in the *Record* expressed the same viewpoint as did the editor of the *Christian Observer* when he wrote:

Against another scheme held in high esteem by the same class of divines as are eager for 'Convocation' we must more distinctly raise our voice – we mean the establishment of Theological Colleges in our various dioceses. One grand objection to them is the, to us, immeasurable evil of substituting an exclusively clerical education for that of a more general and promiscuous character – a monkish for an University education. The insufficiency of the theological instruction hitherto supplied by the Universities is indisputable. But this *may* and now *will* be one of the first results of the new bills for University Reform. But the effects of Diocesan education would be to divide the clergy still more completely from the laity, to raise a barrier between the two bodies, and so, in the end, both to deteriorate the clergy and to estrange the laity and thus hasten the downfall of the Church of England.[69]

Here were excellent principles, but the practical situation was

such that eventually Evangelicals felt the need to found colleges, connected wherever possible with the universities.[70]

The appearance of Goode's *The Nature of Christ's Presence in
the Eucharist* was one of the last serious Evangelical, theological
responses to Tractarianism. Though it was followed by significant books from John Harrison and Nathaniel Dimock, the
controversy between Tractarians and Evangelicals for the next
four decades was primarily concerned with ritualism.[71] Evangelicals looked confidently to litigation to stop it and it seemed
at first that they were succeeding, but they made martyrs out
of popular priests and the policy eventually failed. In other areas
of church life they now had not only their own foreign and home
missionary societies but also their own Church Extension
Fund, Education Society and teacher training colleges. So
they were able to go their own way in evangelism, missions and
education without being over concerned about the work of
other societies such as the Society for the Propagation of the
Gospel.

PART TWO

THEOLOGICAL

CHAPTER FOUR

THE RULE OF FAITH

In August 1844 Christopher Wordsworth, Canon of Westminster, visited the famous editor and publisher, Jacques Paul Migne, in his Imprimerie in Paris. When Migne spoke of the great help that his *Patrologia Latina* would be to the Church of Rome, Wordsworth 'ventured to assure him that no one would welcome his publications with greater satisfaction than the Bishops and Clergy of England', who were 'as conversant with the works of the Fathers as their brethren in France'. Two weeks later he visited the publishers, Messrs Gaume, and was told that the principal market for their recent editions of Augustine, Chrysostom and Basil had been in England.[1] An interest in the early Fathers runs throughout the history of the Church of England but at no period was the interest more intense than in the 1830s and 1840s. On the one side Tractarians claimed patristic support for the teaching they sent forth in sermons, tracts and books, and, on the other, patristic support was claimed by some who opposed Tractarian teaching. The task in this chapter is not to survey any aspects of the teaching of the Fathers but rather to examine how the use of their writings by Tractarians was challenged by Evangelicals in controversy over the place of Tradition in the Rule of Faith. By Tradition is intended the contents of the writings of the Fathers along with the Creeds and Canons of Councils and the ancient Liturgies.

I. INTRODUCTION

It was noted in Chapter One that the Tractarian publications which especially caused the Evangelicals to believe that Tradition was being elevated to a position co-equal with Scripture were Keble's *Primitive Tradition* (1836), Newman's *The Prophetical Office of the Church* (1837) and Manning's *The Rule of*

Faith (1838). In a long appendix to the latter a short summary of the general position was provided:

1. All points of faith necessary to salvation must be proved by Holy Scripture.
2. All interpretations of Holy Scripture in matters of religious belief must be made in accordance with the faith of those on whose evidence we receive the writtten Word of God itself.
3. The faith of the primitive Church, on whose testimony we receive the Canon of Holy Scripture, is presented to us in the Creeds and universal consent of Christians. This consent is the basis of the Doctrinal Articles of the Church of England.
4. All primitive interpretations, prevalent though not universal, claim their several measures of deference from us, and we may not lightly contradict them.
5. Where we have no external evidence of primitive interpretation, we have no other rule than our own judgment, aided by the laws of criticism and unauthoritative exposition.

The principle behind these assertions was 'that universal agreement with the Church of the apostolic ages is the surest test of agreement with the doctrine of the Apostles of Christ'. The 'apostolic ages' were the first five or six centuries of the Christian era.

Newman's exposition of Tradition in his *Prophetical Office*, which followed his debate with the Abbé Jager, was more sophisticated than that of Manning, whose gifts were in clarity of exposition rather than creative development of ideas. Newman had come to distinguish between 'Episcopal tradition' and 'Prophetical tradition'. He maintained this distinction while agreeing with Manning that 'Scripture is interpreted by Tradition, Tradition is verified by Scripture' and 'Tradition teaches and Scripture proves'. He understood 'Episcopal tradition' as the transmission from bishop to bishop in each ancient see of the essentials of the Faith, the fundamental doctrines necessary for salvation. He explained 'Prophetical tradition' in terms of the general teaching of the Church passed on within the churches from one generation to the next: this teaching included the writings of theologians, liturgical practice and form, decrees of councils and ecclesiastical customs. It appears that Evangelicals did not seek to challenge this way of expounding Tradition although at least one author, as will be noted, did question Newman's confidence in our knowledge of the contents of the 'Episcopal tradition'.

There is a further dimension to the Tractarian doctrine of Tradition which needs to be noted and that is the admiration of the *Disciplina Arcani* (the Discipline of the Secret). Though Newman had expounded this practice in his book on the Arians it came most obviously before the public in Isaac Williams' *Tracts 80 and 87*, which were entitled *On Reserve in Communicating Religious Knowledge* and were addressed specifically to the clergy. It was admitted by Tractarians primarily because they believed it to have been central to the way in which the teaching of Christian truths to pagans, catechumens and the baptised was conducted by the Early Church. Whether in fact it was as widespread and important as they supposed, or whether it represented a borrowing by the Church from the pagan mysteries, were not questions which the Tractarians publicly faced. The Discipline of the Secret with its stress on reverence and the mystical interpretation of Scripture was well suited to their understanding of piety and the authority of the Church and priesthood.

The major issues as seen by the Evangelicals may be put in the form of three questions: Where is Divine Revelation to be found? What is the value of Tradition? What are the limits and duties of private judgment? These will form the headings for three sections of this chapter. No account will be taken of the views on the development of dogma since this particular problem was raised in an acute form by Newman in his *Essay on the Development of Christian Doctrine* (1845), which belongs to his Roman Catholic period. Further, note was taken in Chapter Two of initial Evangelical reaction to Tractarian comments in this area.[2]

2. EVANGELICAL LITERATURE

The oldest writer to be used is G. S. Faber, the author of three books whose titles all began with the words 'the primitive doctrine of' – *Election* (1836), *Justification* (1837) and *Regeneration* (1840). This form of title reflected his belief that our understanding of the teaching of the New Testament is to be checked and confirmed by the testimony of the Fathers of the early centuries. He was described as 'one, who, so far from being inclined to slight the force of alleged Catholic Tradition, verges rather to the extreme of paying too great deference to it'.[3] His viewpoint was often misunderstood and opposed in the Evangelical press.

Using information and material supplied by Josiah Pratt, Daniel Wilson, Bishop of Calcutta and Metropolitan of India, had opposed the views of Keble as early as 1838 in his *Charge*; but he set out his views in greater detail in a printed sermon with appended notes entitled, *The Sufficiency of Holy Scripture as the Rule of Faith* (1841). He attacked the tendency (as he saw it) of the Tractarians to make Tradition a joint Rule of Faith: 'By placing herself first, and pre-occupying the mind as the channel through which divine truth must flow Tradition in fact invalidates the inspiration of Holy Scripture and casts everything into her own mould.'

W. A. Shirley, Bishop of Sodor and Man, accepted the appointment of Bampton Lecturer since the invitation was the unanimous act of the Heads of Houses. Because of his busy life he came to the conclusion that 'My Bible must be my subject – the supremacy of Scripture: and that same Bible, unlocked by prayer, must be in a great measure my Library'. Regrettably illness and subsequent death prevented his delivering the whole series but four of the lectures were printed as *The Supremacy of Holy Scripture* (1847).

The youngest author to be used is William Fitzgerald of Trinity College, Dublin, who became an editor for the Parker Society and later Bishop of Killaloe. He published *Episcopacy, Tradition and the Sacraments, considered with reference to the Oxford Tracts* (1839) and *Holy Scripture the Ultimate Rule of Faith to a*

Christian Man (1842). The latter does not specifically mention the Tractarians but it is written in such a way as to defend the traditional Evangelical Protestant position of the sole authority of Scripture against both Tractarianism and Roman Catholicism. As the title indicates it was also a defence of the right of the individual Christian to read the Scriptures which were, argued Fitzgerald, perspicacious with reference to the essential message of salvation.

Without any doubt the most learned and elaborate reply to the Tractarian doctrine of Tradition came from the pen of William Goode. Taking over 1,200 pages *The Divine Rule of Faith and Practice* (1842, reprinted 1853) defended the position that Holy Scripture has been and is the sole, divine Rule of Faith and practice to the Church. Edward Hawkins, Provost of Oriel, from whom Newman had learned to look carefully at Tradition, especially at the doctrine of baptismal regeneration, appreciated Goode's work calling it 'a learned discussion'; and the Bishop of Chichester, Dr Gilbert, presented copies of it to the deacons whom he ordained.[4] Evangelicals thought it struck a death-blow at Tractarianism. According to Goode the major question was 'whether there is sufficient evidence of the divine origin of anything but Scripture to entitle it to authority over the conscience as a divine revelation?' Put another way the question was 'whether in the testimony of the Fathers there is to be found anything which either in form or in substance we are bound to receive as the Word of God delivered to the Church by the apostles and consequently forming part of our *Divinely-revealed Rule of faith and duty*'. He made the attempt to provide an accurate summary of the view of Newman, Keble and Pusey on the relation of Scripture and Tradition. They believed,

1. That consentient patristical tradition, or 'catholic consent' is an unwritten word of God, a divine informant in religion, and consequently entitled, as to its *substance*, to equal respect with the Holy Scriptures.
2. That such tradition is consequently a part of the divinely revealed rule of faith and practice.
3. That it is a necessary part of the divine rule of faith and

E

practice, on account of the defectiveness of Scripture, for that, –

(1) Though it does not reveal to us any fundamental articles of faith and practice not noticed in Scripture, Holy Scripture containing, that is, giving hints or notices of, all the fundamental articles of faith and practice, it is yet a necessary part of the divine rule of faith and practice as the interpreter of Scripture, and as giving the full development of many points, some of which are fundamental, which are but imperfectly developed in Scripture; and

(2) It is an important part of that rule, as conveying to us various important divinely revealed doctrines and rules not contained in Scripture.

4. That it is a necessary part of the divine rule of faith and practice, because of the *obscurity* of Scripture even in some of the fundamental articles, which makes Scripture insufficient to *teach* us even the fundamentals of faith and practice.

5. That it is only by the testimony of patristical tradition that we are assured of the *inspiration* of Scripture, what books are *canonical* and the *genuineness* of what we receive as such.[5]

This position, Goode maintained, was virtually identical with that of the Roman Catholic Church. He then moved on to argue 'that there are no writings extant entitled to the name of Apostolic Traditions but the Canonical Scriptures' and 'that patristical tradition is not a "practically infallible" witness of the oral teaching of the Apostles, nor receivable as a divine informant'. The general argument in the second volume was to establish the grounds on which Protestants assert that Scripture is the sole Word of God, and supremely authoritative in controversies of religion, in the 'credenda' of religion and over the individual conscience. Finally, the third volume contained a series of 'catenae' from the early Fathers and Anglican divines to show that they viewed Scripture as the sole and complete rule of faith and judge of controversies. This final volume was intended to beat the Tractarians at their own game by showing that the authors whom they quoted, often in brief snippets, did not in fact support the viewpoint for which they were being quoted.

If Goode's was the most learned reply to the Tractarians, then Isaac Taylor's treatise was the most daring and original. It appeared in instalments until the first volume (four parts) was completed in 1839 and the second (four parts) in 1842. A Supplement, whose purpose was to modify and extend the argument in the light of criticisms of the work, appeared in 1843.[6] Both volumes were dedicated to Thomas Bewley Monsell, Archdeacon of Derry and father of the hymn writer, J. S. B. Monsell. Informed readers quickly realised that the general thesis of the work, if true, was a devastating argument against not only Tractarianism but also parts of the traditional Anglican appeal to the Fathers.[7] In view of this, proportionately more space will be given here to a description of the contents of *Ancient Christianity* than has been given to any of the previous books.[8]

Convinced that the available 'church histories scarcely lift a corner of the veil that hides from us the recesses of the ancient church', Taylor decided that his task must be that of laying 'open the real condition, moral, spiritual, and ecclesiastical, of the ancient church' of the first six centuries.[9] As a layman with access to the necessary literature, he had no secular interests at stake in ecclesiastical questions and so he thought himself better placed than clergymen, be they High Churchmen, 'Political Churchmen' or Evangelical Churchmen, to pursue this task.

Recognising that he had to confine himself to a specific yet central subject which 'must be well adapted to the general purpose of bringing into view, vividly and distinctly, the general, and the specific merits and faults of the time in question', he chose the practices of celibacy and virginity. He attempted to prove that they were found from early times in the Eastern, African and Western Churches and so came within the general application of the rule of Vincent of Lérins. It was his argument,

That the notions and practices connected with the doctrine of the superlative merit of religious celibacy, were at once the causes and the effects of errors in theology, of perverted moral sentiments, of superstitious usages, of hierarchical usurpations; and that they furnish us with a criterion for estimating the GENERAL VALUE OF ANCIENT CHRISTIANITY; and, in a word, afford reason enough for regarding, if not with jealousy, at least with extreme caution, any attempt to induce the modern church to imitate the ancient church.

He was convinced that the medieval practices of celibacy and virginity were no worse than, and could even have been an improvement on, the system of the age of the Council of Nicea. Furthermore, he showed that the teaching on celibacy within the ancient church was a perversion of the teaching on celibacy in the teaching of Jesus (Matt. 19.12).

Taylor held that for careful students of the New Testament the rapid corruption of the visible Church and the later rise of the Roman Papacy provided no surprise for they were implied in the teaching of Jesus and his apostles. To explain this Taylor expounded and illustrated certain parables of Jesus (the seed in the field, for example, in Matthew 13) and certain sayings of Jesus (in John 17 and Matthew 24) with historical material. And, of course, he pointed out that the nature of the 'Church' and the 'Gospel' which the Tractarians were wanting to revive was that which the Lord had already condemned in his predictions concerning the visible Church.

We turn now to the second volume which, as Taylor told Monsell in the dedication, would also face the fact that 'the question concerning antiquity is a question between the GOSPEL and the Superstition which so early supplanted it'. The first task which the author undertook was that of clarification, as his purpose had been misunderstood by some reviewers. He wrote:

> The question IS NOT what ought to be said of Basil; or of Pope Gregory, or of Pope Hildebrand; but whether the SYSTEM which they severally promoted . . . was such that we should do well in taking it as our model.
>
> The question IS NOT whether a certain amount of delinquency, or corruption of manners – less or more, attached

to this or that ancient community: – But, whether the church SYSTEM of the early ages embraced elements which contravened the spirit of the Christian institute – which were at variance with explicit apostolic injunctions, and which were of a tendency that, by the experience of many centuries, and in all climates, is proved to be unfavourable to morals, nay, productive of greatest evils.[10]

Then, following long quotations from the social history, *De Gubernatione Dei*, written by Salvian in the middle of the fifth century, he gave his own conclusion concerning the state of the Nicene Church.

That, while there were then to be found, here and there, MANY INDIVIDUALS, eminent for piety (according to the dark notions of the age) and who, for the most part, had fled into the wilderness, or had shut themselves up in monasteries, the mass of the christianised community – the accredited recipients of the sacraments, exhibited scarcely any indications of genuine spirituality; while the morals of those who crowded the churches ranged far below a mean level; and, in a word, that a degree of grossness, and of violence – a sensuality, a frivolity and a fierceness marked the social body (of all ranks) to which a parallel could *now* be found nowhere in protestant countries; and only in catholic countries where no protestant or biblical influence has ever been admitted.[11]

Having affirmed this he could not miss the opportunity to bring in Vincent of Lérins, a town where Salvian had also lived: 'The ingenuous modern reader of the "Commonitorium" if uninformed of *history* imagines nothing else but that he is listening to a voice, echoing the blameless confession of a holy church. Yet around the very islet to which Vincent had retired, this catholic church was wallowing in pollutions at the sight of which heretical barbarians blushed.'

Having dealt with celibacy in the first volume he now turned to the examination of what he called 'demonolatry', by which he meant the adoption by the Church of forms of worship formerly used in paganism. He showed that this was so widespread as to qualify as *semper, ubique et ab omnibus*. Also he examined various miracles (e.g. the bleeding relics of St Euphemia) which were claimed for the fourth and fifth century Church in support of its system of faith and worship; he concluded that they were not authentic miracles and he provided ten reasons to support his conclusion. Then he summarised his findings:

1. That the veneration of relics, the invocation of the dead saints, the adorations and festival-worship carried on at celebrated shrines, and the custom of making pilgrimages to such shrines, were as prevalent in the Fourth, as in the following centuries; and that they constituted the prominent feature of the popular religion of the times.

2. That this system of worship was not merely winked at by the leading men of the church, but was zealously promoted by them, and received their warmest commendations; and was held in credit by a species of support on particular occasions which touches too nearly, their reputation for common honesty and piety.

3. That this worship was constantly and intimately connected with a system of professed miracles, which, if real, should compel our approval of the same worship; or at least must preclude our condemnation of it; or *if spurious*, must be held to mark broadly the church system of the fourth century with the deepest stains of fraud, idolatry and blasphemy.[12]

Thus the Church which the Tractarians admired was seriously infected with corruptions and errors.

All that was now left for Taylor to do in the final part of the second volume and in the supplement was to apply his findings to the Church of England. In short he was convinced that the English Reformers of the sixteenth century truly desired to reform the Church by the Word of God and that this central principle lies at the heart of the Articles, Homilies, Prayer Book and Ordinal. However, he did point out that in the sixteenth century there was a mistaken belief that the Church of the age of Cyprian of Carthage was pure; also, there was a readiness to use in the Homilies quotations from a 'miscellaneous commonplace book' of extracts from the Fathers, and thus certain Fathers were being quoted in support of doctrines which they did not teach or which they regarded as erroneous.[13] So he suggested that when next the Formularies of the Church were revised the reliance on the Fathers should be removed from them. At least one Evangelical magazine took up this point and agreed with him.[14]

A modern scholar would probably argue that Taylor's was a drastic apologetic and that he was too selective and overstated his case, even on his selected points. He read back into the language of the Fathers developments of belief to which their language afterwards lent itself but which it did not necessarily originally imply. Invocation of saints, for example, was not prevalent in the fourth century even though the first moves in that direction were being taken then. Concerning the Reformers and their use of the Fathers, Taylor again overstated his case. Cranmer and Jewel, who composed many of the Homilies, used the Fathers mainly to show that the teaching of Rome was late, not to establish their own teaching.

3. WHERE IS DIVINE REVELATION TO BE FOUND?

Both Tractarians and Evangelicals were agreed that the Holy Scriptures contained the inspired Word of God. They were at one in affirming that Divine Revelation is recorded in the Bible. The area of their disagreement lay outside Scripture in the area of a possible oral tradition from the Lord and His Apostles, which because of its inspired origin, should also be regarded as Divine Revelation. Evangelicals denied that there was such an available tradition and Tractarians affirmed its existence. Our concern now is to explicate the Evangelical response to this Tractarian affirmation.

(i) *The Apostles' Creed cannot be regarded as Divine Revelation*
Newman had called the Apostles' Creed 'the formal symbol which the apostles adopted and bequeathed to the Church' and 'a collection of definite articles set apart from the first'; he claimed that 'it is delineated and recognised in Scripture itself, where it is called the *Hypotyposis*, or "outline of sound words" '.[15]

Goode was convinced that Newman was wrong and reminded

him that 'an overwhelming majority of the learned divines of the last three centuries' were against him. Quoting at length summaries of doctrine from Irenaeus and Tertullian, Goode showed that there was no set form of words left by the Apostles as the Christian Creed.[16] He went on to prove that what is called 'the Apostles' Creed is merely the ancient Creed of the Church of Rome, and no more entitled to the name ["Apostles"] than any other of the ancient Creeds', and 'that two at least of the articles it now contains were not inserted in it before the fourth century'.[17] Finally he argued that the Creeds of the primitive Church were derived from Scripture. To do this he examined the internal evidence of the Creeds found in the writings of Irenaeus, Tertullian, Origen, Lucian the Martyr, Cyril of Jerusalem and Augustine. He was prepared to admit that 'Irenaeus, Tertullian and Origen appeal to the consentient teaching of the Churches founded by the Apostles agreeing with the Creeds they delivered, as an argument in favour of their truth', and, he went on, 'at that early period such testimony formed *distinct* and *independent* evidence of their truth of considerable weight'; however, 'this fact does not militate against the assertion that those statements of the faith were drawn from Scripture'. In a further admission, he agreed that the ancient Creeds, being summaries of the chief articles of the faith, 'were justly called by the Fathers the *rule of faith*'. Again, this fact did not affect the priority of the Scripture as the source of Creeds. With a claim of Manning particularly in mind, W. A. Shirley stated that,

It is ... important ... to protest against the logical fallacy which is contained in a phrase which has formed the staple of many arguments on this subject; namely, that 'the substance of the Creed is older than Scripture'. The correct statement of this proposition would be that the substance of the Creed is older than the substance of Scripture, which every one may perceive is only true in the sense in which it becomes identical. The facts and doctrines contained in the Creed were doubtless taught before any part of the New Testament was written, because what is contained in the New Testament ... was first orally communicated; but there

is no evidence that the Creed acquired a fixed or written
form until long after the volume of inspiration was completed, written and published.[18]

In this general position the Evangelicals were in agreement.[19]

*(ii) The supposed consentient testimony of the patristic literature does
not contain Divine Revelation*

To the proof of this point Goode devoted nearly three hundred
pages, including quotations and references to both patristic
literature and the writings of leading Anglican divines of the
sixteenth, seventeenth and eighteenth centuries. He fully recognised that the argument of his opponents was that 'catholic
consent in the whole primitive Church for several centuries in
favour of any doctrine or interpretation of Scripture or other
matter is a sure proof that it was derived from the apostles'.
In other words, 'consentient patristical statements must have
had a common origin in the teaching of the first preachers of
Christianity'. His method of argument was to discredit this
basic assumption and to show that the Rule of St Vincent (*quod
semper, ubique et ab omnibus*) could not be used as the Tractarians
were using it. First of all he attempted to show that it was impossible to know exactly what the whole Church (comprising
all pastors and all the faithful) of the first three centuries had
always and everywhere believed; there was just no way of find-
ing out. Also it was quite impossible to ascertain what the
pastors actually believed; the only summaries of the Faith that
are extant for the first three centuries are the creeds of Irenaeus,
Origen and Tertullian.

Goode developed this line of argument by emphasising that
the extant records of the Church of the first three centuries
are totally inadequate to supply the information which the
application of Vincent's rule requires. In fact we do not possess
the writings of more than about twenty authors for this period
and they were produced, wrote Goode, 'in reply, either to the
heathen opponents of Christianity, or to heresies' which in the
nineteenth century 'would be equally despised by all parties'
involved in the conflict in the Church of England. These few
writings provide a very partial view of the Church and exist

because the ruling party in the Church allowed them to be preserved. So Goode concluded on this particular point that:

> It is impossible, then, to consider the remains we have of the ancient ecclesiastical authors, as beyond doubt exhibiting to us all the variations of doctrine that were to be found in the primitive Church; and therefore we could not regard even the consent of these writings, as representing the catholic consent of the whole Church. It is no aid to the cause of orthodoxy to put forth such a claim.[20]

Making use of Thomas James's *A Treatise of the Corruption of the Scripture and Fathers* (1611) he proceeded to demonstrate that our view of antiquity is seriously affected by the 'way in which the works of the Fathers have been mutilated and corrupted and works forged in their name'.

In the next long section Goode attempted to prove that 'the witness of Patristical Tradition, even in the writings that have been preserved, is of a discordant kind, and that even in fundamental points'. He looked at such topics as the divinity of the Holy Spirit, the divinity and generation of the Son, the procession of the Holy Spirit from the Father and the Son, the Nestorian, Eutychian and Pelagian errors, the millennium, the date of Easter, the re-baptism of heretics and the interpretation of Proverbs 8.22 in order to make good his contention. His conclusion was that 'it is evident, then, that the notion that there is a consentient testimony to the doctrines of revelation, even among the authors that remain to us, is a mere dream of the imagination, and *that*, even as it respects the very highest points of faith'.[21] Thus, while the theory of the Tractarians was that 'catholic consent' only can be relied upon, that which they '*practically* rely upon to prove this consent is often the dictum of half a dozen Fathers'.

Not content with having taken his argument so far, Goode continued to hammer nails into the coffin by insisting that 'consent, even in the writings that remain to us, is not to be expected' for the simple reason that consent must assume that the apostles left not only the Scriptures but also interpretations of them, with statements of doctrine as well, which would immediately negate all heresies that would arise in the Church at all times. The hypothesis of consent is an extremely improbable hypothesis, for all sound reason and historical testimony militate against it. Continuing, he argued that even if a small and partial consent can be ascertained, there is no proof that it came from the apostles. For, 'it needs no proof', he wrote, 'that any corruptions of the faith suited to the natural feelings and prejudices of the human mind would be likely, at the very earliest period of the Church, to obtain extensive circulation, especially if they were supported by a few able and unfluential men'. A further point which Goode made (and in this Isaac Taylor fully agreed with him) was that the New Testament itself makes it clear that 'from the very beginning there were many heresies, errors and false doctrines prevalent among the professed followers of Christ' and that 'such errors were maintained and propagated among those who formed what was called the Catholic Church'. He held that Jesus Christ had prophesied this in his parable of the wheat and tares growing together until the harvest. There was never a time when there was only 'wheat', and so again to find consent *semper, ubique et ab omnibus* was impossible.

Bishop Wilson argued at a more practical level. Since Protestants allowed the use of all means (creeds, catechisms, commentaries, etc.) in the understanding of the Scriptures, there was no need to exalt Tradition to a joint rule of faith. He admitted that it might appear to some who had not marked the bearings of the controversy 'that there can be no great difference between all these [creeds, writings of Fathers etc.] being admitted as means of arriving at the sense of Scripture, and their being made a joint rule of faith'. But, for Wilson, the difference was immense:

The supreme authority of Holy Scripture is, next to Jesus Christ, the foundation-stone of the Gospel. To exalt Tradition to a share in it, is to make the witness to Holy Writ, the judge. It is to convert the keeper into the interpreter of the Bible. It is to substitute a gloss upon our heavenly Father's will, for the original. It is to distil the doctrine of inspiration through the alembic of the Fathers. It is to put the word of man for the word of God.[22]

Further, he asserted that 'Tradition, when exalted into a joint rule of faith, increases the difficulties in the sacred volume which it pretends to remove' and brings in another Gospel.[23]

(iii) Divine Revelation is now only found in the Scriptures which are therefore the sole Rule of faith and practice for the Church and individuals

This assertion was, of course, the fundamental theme of all the authors whom we are considering. For them the Rule of Faith was simply the Holy Scriptures.

> By 'the Rule of faith' we understand a testimony which shows us *infallibly* those doctrines which we are *bound by our duty to God* to receive; and one which has such evidences of its divine origin, as making it binding upon the consciences of all men; and of that Rule, therefore, nothing can form a part, which has no reasonable evidence of its being the word of God.
>
> And if Holy Scripture is thus the sole infallible and authoritative Rule of faith, it follows, of course, that it is to its decision alone that we must appeal, as of absolute authority and infallible, in *controversies concerning the faith*; and hence it is justly called the sole infallible *Judge of controversies of faith*, as being that which alone gives an infallible testimony on the subject. That it cannot *end* controversies, forms no valid objection to this appellation, for no testimony on the subject, however clear and definitive, could do that; nothing in fact but a living Judge who has power to *silence* every dissentient from his sentence.[24]

Before writing this Goode had argued for the divine origin of the books of the New Testament on lines familiar within Protestantism – the inner testimony of the Holy Spirit within the believer's heart to their inspired character, the witness of the early Church to the Canon of the New Testament and the moral evidence of the books themselves.[25] And the Hebrew Scriptures, forming the Christian Old Testament, were accepted on the authority of Jesus Christ and the apostles. Against Tractarian claims that the Scriptures need Tradition by way of complement or explanation, Goode claimed that 'there is no such inadequacy in the Holy Scriptures, as it respects what are considered by our Church the fundamental articles of the faith'. Further he sought to show that

> all the doctrines received by us as revelations from God, and therefore articles of faith, and all the rites held by us to be of divine institution, are delivered to us in the Holy Scriptures; so that there is no article of faith maintained by us, of which, or any part of which, our belief rests upon the testimony of Tradition, our belief in all such points resting wholly upon Scripture; and no rite received by us as of divine institution on any other than Scripture testimony.[26]

In expounding this latter contention, Goode dealt with a variety of rites and doctrines to show that some (e.g. infant baptism) were accepted by the Church of England because they were grounded in Scripture and confirmed by tradition, while others (e.g. purgatory) were rejected since they were grounded only in tradition.

Reverting to the essentials of Christianity, Goode proceeded to argue that 'all the fundamental and essential points of faith and practice are clearly and plainly delivered in the Scriptures; and consequently that the Scriptures are well adapted and amply sufficient to *teach* men all such points'. The burden of his proof for this argument was the internal testimony of Scripture and the claims that it makes for itself as being 'profitable for doctrine, for reproof, for correction, for instruction in righteousness that the man of God may be perfect' (2 Tim. 3.15–17). He moved on to argue that 'however obscure . . . any of the less fundamental doctrines or statements of Scripture may be considered to be, there is no plainer report of them than what we find there, that can come to us with any authority to bind the conscience to belief. They are *as* plainly delivered in the Scriptures as, *to our knowledge*, they are revealed.' Finally he repeated the basic Protestant hermeneutical rule:

> The best and only infallible expositor of Scripture is Scripture; or, in other words, that the best mode of judging of the sense of any passage is by a comparison of it with the testimony of Scripture in other parts; first, by comparing it with

the *context*, with passages *similarly* worded, with such *plain* places of Scripture as can illustrate its meaning, and with all that is stated in Scripture respecting the *subject* treated of; and secondly, by considering it in connexion with the whole scheme of doctrine clearly revealed in Scripture.[27]

His second volume ended with a long quotation from the High Churchman, Bishop S. Horsley of St Asaph, to show that what he had been arguing was fully in accord with the teaching of the 'standard divines' of the Church of England.[28]

(iv) Many of the Fathers of the first five centuries expressly declared that divine Revelation is to be found only in the Scriptures

Since the Fathers did not face the particular questions concerning the source of revelation, which the Tractarians raised, but necessarily faced problems of their own times, to use them to disprove the claims of the Tractarians was not a simple matter. Goode was very conscious of this, but yet felt it necessary to provide 'catenae' from patristic literature in the five basic areas to which he had devoted his first two volumes: that is, whether catholic consent is a source of revelation, whether Scripture is the sole and complete Rule of faith, whether Scripture is the sole Rule of practice, whether Scripture is sufficiently clear to teach the faith and whether patristical tradition is the ground upon which belief in the inspiration of Scripture is to rest. His conclusions were stated briefly and undogmatically, for he believed that the long quotations from the Fathers needed little comment. He wrote:

> The passages adduced from them [the Fathers] by our opponents and the Romanists fall far short of the statements required for the support of their views; for, however strongly the Fathers may appeal to the teaching of what they considered 'the Church' and her earlier divines, they never put such teaching as binding on the consciences of men.[29]

The teaching of the Fathers, Goode believed, was that only the revelation contained in Scripture could bind the consciences of men.

4. WHAT IS THE VALUE OF TRADITION?

Since the Evangelicals were involved in the exercise of denying
the excessive claims on behalf of Tradition made by the Tractarians, it is possible, in a cursory reading of their writings, to
gain the impression that they saw no value in the patristic
literature – other than of merely an antiquarian interest. Such
an impression would be a false one, for, intertwined with the
criticism, we find positive assertions about the value of the
writings of the Fathers, and of the Creeds. The general position
adopted may be summarised in the statement that Tradition is
a witness to facts, not an independent authority for faith and
practice.

For example, Garbett argued that accepting the Canon of
Scripture on the testimony of the early Church was right and
not the same as accepting every doctrine or rite taught by any
early Father:

> Nor is there any contradiction in principle that we receive
> the Scriptures upon the testimony of the ancient Church, and
> yet reject, in other points, its authority over our faith ...
> For that general consent by which we are assured of the
> authenticity of the Scriptures, is, *in itself and of itself*, credible.
> All that it binds upon us is this – to accept whatever else shall
> be similarly attested to us, as the acts and sayings of the
> Apostles – to that it does unquestionably bind us, but no
> more.[30]

Isaac Taylor likewise affirmed that 'we cannot but refer to, and
avail ourselves of, the judgment and decision of the early church,
concerning the canonicity of each portion of the New Testament'.[31]

Goode asserted that 'the testimony of the early Fathers respecting facts and practices *of which their senses were cognizant,*
is sufficient to assure us, that such facts and practices took place
in their time in the Primitive Church'. And he continued by
maintaining that 'the usage of the Primitive Orthodox Church
from the Apostolical times (as far as it can be ascertained) may
justly be taken as a guide to show us, how rites and practices
enjoined in Scripture are to be carried into effect; and also, to

a certain extent, in its general rites and practices, that is, so far as to recommend them to our attention, and perhaps to justify modern Churches in following them, inasmuch as it is not probable, that, *from the very first*, the Orthodox Church should have adopted a superstitious or improper usage'. Developing this he argued that in such matters as the keeping of the Lord's Day, the practice of infant baptism, the regular Eucharist and the threefold order of the ministry the value of tradition was to confirm what a careful study of Scripture reveals.[32] In other areas where there is no specific Scriptural warrant – such as the sign of the cross in baptism– each National Church having the authority to decree what rites and ceremonies are to be in use may follow primitive practice as long as any such practice is not required as necessary to salvation.

Faber developed a point concerning the use of the Fathers which is found minimally in Garbett and Goode but, as we have noted, was rejected by Taylor.[33] Faber was aware that as the eleventh Article of Religion refers to the Homily of Salvation for a fuller statement of the doctrine of Justification, so the Homily itself appeals to the early Fathers for the confirmation of the same doctrine. Thus he claimed that

> In this procedure, the wise writers of the Homily in question exemplify the sound Principle of the Church of England; the principle to wit: that Scripture is the sole Rule of Faith; but that, since no Rule can be practically used as a Rule until it be first interpreted and understood, we must, for the interpretation of this our Sole Rule, Scripture, resort, not to the wantonness of our own arbitrary dogmatism, but to the ascertained Concurrence of the Primitive Church from the beginning.[34]

He also made use of the Canon of 1571 which read: 'Preachers shall especially take heed, that, in the course of their sermons, they never teach any thing to be religiously held and believed by the people, save what is agreeable to the Doctrine of the Old or New Testament, and save what the Catholic Fathers and Ancient Bishops have collected out of that very Doctrine'.[35] So he was convinced that the method used in his works on the primitive doctrines of election, justification and regeneration, as also on the apostolicity of trinitarianism, he was following the principle of the Anglican Church, which was, in his own words,

In the settlement of Articles of Faith on the authority of Scripture the only Rule, the PRINCIPLE of the Anglican Church is that of AN APPEAL TO THE RECORDED CONSENT OF PRIMITIVE ANTIQUITY FROM THE VERY BEGINNING.

He believed that this consent could be found 'either in the early Creeds, or in the early Apologies, or in the early Liturgies *so far as they accord with the early Creeds* or in the concurring statements and unanimous exposition of the early Fathers'.[36] While the consent as he understood it led him to see 'Protestant' doctrine in the early Fathers, the same consent as the Tractarians understood it, led to a different conclusion, a fact not unnoticed by the Evangelicals.[37] Though Goode never mentioned Faber's writings in his three volumes it is clear that much of the argument used by Goode against the Tractarian reliance on the Vincentian Canon applies to the claims of Faber. If Isaac Taylor went too far in a negative direction then G. S. Faber went too far in a positive direction; they represent the two poles of the Evangelical position. Goode represented its central and balanced position.

Though Taylor and Faber held different views of the usefulness of patristic teaching they did agree in condemning the teaching on Reserve. In this condemnation they were joined by others, C. S. Bird, Hugh Stowell and George Townsend, for example. The doctrine of the *Disciplina Arcani* was not new to Faber who in 1828 was involved in a controversy with the Roman Catholic Bishop of Strasbourg, J. F. M. Trevern, who among other claims argued that the doctrine of transubstantiation was part of the Secret kept from pagans and others in the Early Church.[38] Further, in his *Apostolicity of Trinitarianism* (1832), he devoted a whole chapter to the way in which the doctrine of the Holy Trinity was kept in reserve in times of persecution by the churches.[39] Thus in 1838 Faber was well prepared to examine *Tract 80*. While admitting that in times of persecution the Early Church kept back from pagans and possible catechumens certain central Christian doctrines, he insisted that there were no secrets of doctrine as far as the baptised membership was concerned. For the latter the whole counsel of God was there to be learned.[40] Bird relied upon Newman's account of Reserve in the *Arians* and, following J. Daillé and Bishop Warburton, claimed that the Early Church had in this particular adopted the method of the pagan Mystery religions. He lamented the fact that the Fathers had not 'a deeper and nobler faith' and pointed out that if they had lived to see the fatal effects of their system in the hierarchy of the priesthood in Popery they would never have devised or adopted it.[41]

Taylor likewise believed that those Fathers who taught the doctrine of Reserve had learned it from pagan sources. But the strong point which he made was that in adopting this principle the Tractarians were doing what Jesus had condemned the Jewish doctors of the Law for doing – taking away the key of knowledge from the people (Luke 11.52). Thus he was happy to quote against Williams words of Pope Gregory from his Commentary on Job in which he urged the common people to know the contents of Holy Scripture which was as 'an epistle of Almighty God to his creature'.[42]

Evangelicals did not disagree with all aspects of Tractarian teaching. Stowell wanted it to be known that 'in so far as they insist upon a godly reverence in handling the things of God we entirely go along with them. Nothing is more unbecoming, irrational or repulsive than to trifle with what is sacred.' Also that 'their authors are right in demanding that the truth of God should not be denuded of the heavenly garments with which her Father hath robed her, and clad instead with the coarse texture wrought in the looms of earth.' Yet, he went on, 'where they argue in favour of keeping the distinguished truths of the Gospel in the shade and of not allowing the atonement of Christ to hold a very prominent place in . . . preaching' they are wrong. This insistence by Stowell (and the other Evangelicals made the same point) that the saving work of Christ on the Cross for the salvation of sinners had to be proclaimed loud and clear was necessary, they believed, because of the contention of Williams in *Tract 80* that the doctrine of the Cross was to be taught gradually (and more profoundly than did

Evangelicals) as the baptised lived more obediently to the will of God. 'In their system', he continued, 'as that of Rome, it is clear that the reservation of the free grace of God through his Son is essential to the maintenance of that moral thraldom on the part of the people, and that sacerdotal power on the part of the clergy, which are too plainly the drift of the whole scheme.'[43] Though these results might well have been seen had the doctrine of Reserve been introduced into the English Church, the motivation of Williams, Newman and Pusey was hardly to put people into a false subjection to the clergy.

Where the Evangelicals were on strong ground was in their insistence that whatever was appropriate in times of persecution in ancient times was not necessarily appropriate in modern times in a Christian country and in a Church whose public Liturgy openly declared the central truths of the Faith. Townsend made the point that if the doctrine of Reserve was adopted 'our services must be re-constructed and our congregations classed, like large schools, according to their knowledge, talents, powers of expression and general proficiency. Pride of intellect would succeed to holiness of heart.'[44]

5. WHAT IS THE ROLE OF PRIVATE JUDGMENT?

It was probably the horror of what Faber often called 'insulated, uninformed and independent' private judgment which was a factor in leading him to seek for greater certainty in interpreting the Scriptures from the testimony of the early Church. Certainly the danger is always present that once the Scriptures are freely available in the vernacular people will interpret according to their 'whims and fancies' and without reference to any proper hermeneutical principles. The Tractarians were very conscious of this danger and claimed to see its results in popular Protestantism. Therefore Newman argued that an individual Christian has the right to interpret the Scripture only in areas where the Church has not already given an authoritative interpretation.[45] He wrote: 'In matters of inferior moment both the Church and the individual have room to exercise their own powers.' So by the right of private judgment he meant not that 'all *must*, but that all *may* search Scripture and determine or

prove their creed from it: that is, provided they are duly qualified', and provided they subject their reason to the Tradition
of the Church.[46]

Goode traced the origins of the doctrine of private judgment
to the Reformation of the English Church in the sixteenth
century.

> With the doctrine of the Supremacy of Holy Scripture to
> the consciences of individuals, and the right of private judg-
> ment in contradistinction to 'the authority of the Church'
> she stands or falls. For, her Reformation was effected by com-
> paratively a few individuals acting against the authority of
> the Church both of the East and West, and going back . . .
> to the word of God, to draw from it the pure doctrine of the
> Gospel of Christ . . . And that which alone enabled her to
> effect her Reformation was, the gracious providence of God
> inclining the Civil Power to aid a minority of the clergy and
> laity in re-establishing a Scriptural faith in the place of the
> corrupt system of Rome. The very ground, therefore, upon
> which our Church stands, is that of the right of private
> judgment.[47]

This was a rather large claim and would hardly be made by
historians today. In fact the doctrine of private judgment was
formulated as Protestants defended their view of Scripture
against Roman Catholic critics, and thus the classic English
statements of this doctrine appear in the controversial literature
of the seventeenth century.[48]

Following the general position adopted in this controversial
literature both Goode and Fitzgerald asserted both the right
and duty of individuals to enquire into the truth of God by
searching the Scriptures. 'Upon the very same grounds upon
which our opponents admit the right and duty of private judgment in determining between the various forms of religion existing in the world', wrote Goode, 'do we contend for the right
and duty of private judgment in determining between the
various meanings affixed by nominal Christians to the word of
God contained in the Holy Scriptures.'[49] Fitzgerald admitted
that there was inherent in the Protestant position many pitfalls;
yet, he claimed that

If it be allowed that the Scripture is sufficient when studied with care, humility and candor, to inform all, even the most simple, in all things absolutely necessary to be known, and to inform those of higher abilities and attainments, still (as before) supposing proper care, humility and candor in such other useful truths as God has seen fit to reveal – then all is granted that we contend for. Nor is it at all contrary to the supposition that Scripture is sufficient for this end, but rather perfectly consistent with that supposition that when men of meaner abilities endeavour to judge of things which they are not competent to judge of, or when men of greater abilities but of perverted minds, apply their abilities to the distortion of Scripture, or fail in diligence or moral qualifications, such persons should frame wrong interpretations of the writings of the apostles and evangelists, since, under the same circumstances, they would be sure to frame wrong interpretations of any other writings.[50]

So, narrowing the range of the perspicuity of Scripture, he held that 'it was not God's purpose to secure unity, either of opinion or practice, absolutely in his Church, but only conditionally; that is, to provide such means as, when properly used, should be sufficient to teach men all things necessary to salvation, and instruct them to differ in other matters without breach of charity, but not to prevent them from neglecting or misusing those means.'[51] Apart from the basic obligations of diligent reading, humility and prayerfulness, the use of means – creeds, catechisms, commentaries, teachers and preachers in the churches – was encouraged. But in the last analysis the right and the duty of the individual to make up his own mind was acknowledged.

CONCLUSION

Within the first nineteen centuries of the Christian Church four different views of the relation of Scripture and Tradition emerged.[52] According to the 'coincidence view' the teaching of Scripture and Tradition coincide, that is they are in essence identical; the best example of this would be the Church of the first century when the Apostles were alive and when their writings were beginning to be circulated. Later in the history of the Church a need was felt to supplement Scripture by teaching from Tradition and this is the 'supplementary view'. Gnostics adopted this position in the second century and it was the commonly held view in Roman Catholicism from the sixteenth to the nineteenth century. The viewpoint adopted by the leading reformers of the sixteenth century may be termed the 'ancillary view'. They regarded Tradition not as a normative interpretation of Scripture nor as a necessary addition to Scripture; rather it was a tool to assist the Church to understand Scripture. Finally there is the 'unfolding view' which was adopted by Newman as he left the Church of England and as he explained it in his *Essay on the Development of Christian Doctrine* (1845). In general this viewpoint works on the assumption that what is implicit in the New Testament or early Tradition is expanded and made explicit in the life and work of the Church over the centuries. If we are to put the Tractarians and Evangelicals into compartments then we have to say that the Tractarians adopted the 'coincidence view' and the Evangelicals the 'ancillary view'. In asserting this it is of course recognised that within each view there was a certain breadth of interpretation, and it is realised that Evangelicals believed the Tractarians adopted the 'supplementary view'.

It is now obvious that in terms of the extensive claims they made, Newman, Keble, Pusey and their colleagues were not sufficiently familiar either with the general position of Anglican divines or with patristic literature in general. Goode regarded the various 'catenae' from English divines which appeared in the *Tracts for the Times* and other publications as 'one of the most extraordinary and painful features in the whole case'. Further,

> the fact is, that almost the only witnesses to whom they could properly refer as at all supporting their *system*, are a few individuals, such as Brett, Hickes, Johnson and others, forming a small and extreme section of a small and extreme party in our Church, namely, the Non-jurors; and even among these it would be difficult to find one who agreed with their system as now developed.

The extracts from the works of Anglican divines were, for the most part, 'general and loose and indefinite passages, whose meaning depends altogether upon the context, and which are *applied* by the Tractators in a sense which the views of the writers, gathered from their works as a whole, altogether repudiate'.[53]

Similarly Goode was convinced that their references to the early Fathers were 'almost equally incorrect and fallacious'. On several occasions he referred to the 'blunder' which Newman made in the interpretation of the phrase, 'evangelical tradition', in a passage from Athanasius.[54] This mistake showed 'a want of acquaintance with the phraseology of the Fathers'; but Newman's error was of minimal importance compared with the errors which appeared in the periodical publications of the Tractarians. These latter authors needed 'to go to school on the subject on which they would fain be the teachers of others'.[55] But why, it may be asked, had the *Tracts* and their 'catenae' seemed so convincing to many clergy. The answer, claimed Goode, was at least partly to be found in 'the low state of ecclesiastical learning' among the clergy in the early nineteenth century. They had no immediate means of checking the accuracy of the claims from the Tractarians.

The general accuracy of Goode's understanding of the teaching of Anglican divines from the sixteenth to the nineteenth centuries has been shown by the studies of recent writers.[56] Also that he was much nearer to the truth in his assessment of patristic literature than were the Tractarians has been demonstrated in recent studies.[57] Further, the second generation of 'Tractarians' led by Bishop Gore narrowed considerably the range of their appeal to Tradition.[58] Their commitment only to the Creeds, the threefold ministry and an efficacious sacramentalism was not only an attempt to come to terms with 'modern knowledge' but was also an admission that Newman, Keble and Pusey had claimed too much on the basis of Tradition. To claim all this for Goode is not necessarily to state that his position is viable today in a situation where the relation of Scripture and Tradition is very much in debate and being re-assessed; it is merely to say that he had the better of his opponents in the situation of the 1840s and 1850s.

We have remarked that the Tractarian position was modified in the late nineteenth century. It is also true to say that as a result of this controversy two tendencies already present in Evangelicalism were further developed. First, the prestige of the early Fathers as theological guides significantly dropped. At the academic level a few men, of whom C. P. Heurtley, the Lady Margaret Professor, is a notable example, produced important works on the Fathers, but at the parish level the Fathers were found not to be helpful, although, of course, the Creeds were recited and accepted.[59] Secondly, the doctrine of private judgment was emphasised as being one of the three great principles of the Reformation; this historical mistake would not have been of great importance had both the *right* and the *duties* involved in reading and interpreting the Scriptures been given equal emphasis. As it was much was made of the right but little of the duties, that is the use of the means available to ascertain the true meaning of any passage (e.g. commentaries and lexicons).[60]

CHAPTER FIVE

JUSTIFICATION

To Luther is attributed the statement that Justification by Faith is *articulus stantis vel cadentis ecclesiae* (the article of faith that decides whether the Church is standing or falling).[1] In 1843 a writer in the *British Critic* asserted that Evangelicals clave 'to the soul-destroying heresy of Luther on the subject of Justification'.[2] Since Justification by Faith was regarded in orthodox Protestantism as the *material* principle of theology, determining its substance, it is not surprising to learn that in this area of controversy the Evangelicals believed they were fighting for nothing less than the preservation within the Church of England and Ireland of the Gospel of Christ.

I. INTRODUCTION

During 1837 two letters from John Henry Newman, defending views expressed in the *Tracts on Baptism* by Pusey, appeared with lavish editorial comment in the *Christian Observer*. The second letter ended with a promise from Newman that he would write on justification; commenting on this the editor claimed that his readers eagerly awaited this production which related to 'far the most important of the questions at issue' between the doctrine of the *Tracts* and of the *Articles of Religion*. Indeed, Wilks was convinced that the tendency of Tractarian teaching was towards the revival within the Church of the Romanist doctrine of justification by infused righteousness. An opportunity to assert this conviction was provided by the publication of G. S. Faber's *The Primitive Doctrine of Justification Investigated* (1837), which attempted to prove, against Alexander Knox, the Irish lay theologian, and against Joseph Milner, the Evangelical historian, that the Protestant doctrine of justification by Faith was actually taught by the early Fathers, before its corruption in the medieval period.[3]

A long review of Faber's book appeared in the first three

issues of the *Christian Observer* for 1838. The writer of it declared that 'we see no substantial difference between the doctrine of Trent and the doctrines of Mr Knox and the Oxford Tracts'. In all three cases 'by qualifications and blending Scriptural truths with false inferences error is often made to appear so plausible that it is not easy to attack'. So a controversy over the doctrine of justification and related truths was anticipated: 'If the battles of the Reformation are to be fought over again, not with avowed Romanists but with professed Anglicans, who account popery their "dear sister" and consider Protestantism as a rational neologian schism, the friends of the pure Gospel of Christ, unsophisticated by human devices, have only to take up the spiritual arms of their godly forefathers, and with the Bible in their hands to contend for the faith once delivered to the saints.' And this is what happened, the battle being fought by Evangelicals according to traditional Protestant strategy learned in the lengthy Protestant–Catholic controversy, a controversy which had been given a new lease of life in Britain because of the religious and political problems of Ireland.[4]

Newman never sent a third letter to the *Christian Observer* on the subject of justification. However, he did deliver a series of lectures in the Adam de Brome Chapel of the Church of St Mary the Virgin, Oxford, on this topic, which he later published in a revised form as *Lectures on Justification* (1838). The thirteen lectures contained an attempt to restate the doctrine of justification in such a way that the primary biblical aspects of both the traditional Protestant and Roman Catholic viewpoints were preserved and fused into one new doctrine. So the idea of the external righteousness of Christ being reckoned (imputed) to the believing Christian and the righteousness of Christ being infused into the soul by the Holy Spirit at regeneration were brought together. Indeed, as Thomas L. Sheridan SJ has argued, it was Newman's high view of regeneration as the impartation of the full presence of Christ into the soul, a position to which he came in the late 1820s, which was the basis for his new view of justification, as being inseparably linked to regeneration.[5]

It is now generally agreed that the root of Newman's emphasis on the inseparable relation of justification and regeneration was the teaching he found in the Greek Fathers, especially Athanasius, on the divinisation or deification of the Christian, through baptism and the Holy Spirit.[6] However, his critics believed he had learned his doctrine from Western Medieval or Roman Catholic sources, a belief which is easy to understand when it is recalled that 1838 was the year when Froude's *Remains*, praising medieval Christianity and edited by Newman, were being widely read. And in the preface to the *Lectures* Newman admitted that one of his major aims was to show that the views of salvation expressed in the *Tracts* did not entail the inclusion of human merit as earning salvation. While Döllinger believed the *Lectures* to be one of the best theological works of the nineteenth century, G. S. Faber found them to be confused and confusing.[7]

Following his correspondence and personal interview with Newman, Faber introduced into the second edition of his book on justification two appendices which related to Newman and his doctrines.[8] Although he claimed to have devoted more time to the study of the *Lectures* than to any other book in his life, he found it impossible to create a harmonious view of the subject out of Newman's seeming contrary principles. At one and the same time, he believed, Newman taught that:

1. We are justified by Faith: we are justified by Obedience: we are justified by Baptism: we are justified conjointly by the two Sacraments of Baptism and the Lord's Supper.
2. Our Justification precedes our Faith: and our Faith precedes our Justification.
3. Justification is a judicial process, by which a sinner is accounted and declared righteous in the court of Heaven: but still our moral renewal is fitly called our *Justification* . . .
4. The word *Justification* cannot bear two meanings, yet it clearly does bear two meanings, to wit, the accounting righteous and the making righteous.
5. There is but *one* act of justification: nevertheless, there are *ten thousand* justifications.
6. When the English Church declares, that Faith is the *sole* mean or instrument of Justification, without making any exceptions or distinctions: we must not, by such a

declaration understand that she wishes to deny the existence of sundry other instruments in sundry other senses of the term ... Thus, for instance, the instrumental power of faith cannot interfere with the instrumental power of Baptism.

7. ... when the Homilies speak of Faith being *the sole instrument*, though they *seem* to predicate of it both *soleness and instrumentality*, they *really* teach, that Faith is not at all an *instrument*, but that it is purely a symbol.

So, though he loved Newman as a brother, he was obliged to to state that the *Lectures* exhibited 'a strange and mischievous attempt, to mix up together, wholesome food and rank poison, the sound doctrine of the Church of England and the pernicious dogmas of the Church of Rome; Scriptural Orthodoxy and Popish Heterodoxy'.[9] In the private correspondence Newman tried to justify his position to Faber, but the latter remained convinced that Newman's position contained irreconcilable elements.

Immediate support for Newman came from Pusey in his *Letter to the Right Reverend Father in God, Richard, Lord Bishop of Oxford* (1839) who declared in his explanation of Article xi 'Of the Justification of Man':

The Anglican doctrine, or that which we conceive to have been the teaching of the majority of our Church differs ... from the Roman, in that it excludes sanctification from having any place in our justification: from the Lutheran in that it conceives justification to be not imputation merely, but the act of GOD imparting His Divine Presence to the soul, through Baptism, and so making us temples of the Holy Ghost ...

Or, in words taken from Newman: 'Justification comes *through* the sacraments, is received *by* faith, *consists* in God's inward presence, and *lives* in obedience.' From a former Evangelical in Cambridge came support for this viewpoint. Francis Whaley Harper, a Fellow of St John's, argued in his *A Few Observations on the Teaching of Dr. Pusey and Mr. Newman concerning Justification* that Evangelicals had nothing to fear and much to accept in the teaching of Newman. But his was a lonely voice.

As was noted in Chapter One, defences of the traditional

Anglican doctrine of Justification by Faith came from men of varied churchmanship, from the gentle High Churchman Philip Shuttleworth, the supposed liberal, R. D. Hampden, and from various Bishops.[10] However, since our task here is to understand the Evangelical Anglican response we shall use primarily the books of G. S. Faber, Bishop J. B. Sumner, Bishop C. P. M'Ilvaine, Professor James Garbett and C. A. Heurtley, which together provide a wide spectrum of Evangelical thinking. Since the theological sections of this chapter will consist of quotations from and summaries of these books, we shall first provide a brief description of the publications in question. Following this descriptive section we shall study the Evangelical response as it answered three basic questions: What is justification? How does a sinner receive justification? and, What is the relation after baptism between justification and forgiveness?

We shall find that in all this Evangelical literature it is pre-supposed that the traditional terminology of Reformational and Post-Reformational debates is valid for nineteenth-century controversy within the Church of England and is therefore the correct way to discuss the doctrine of justification. The key expressions were, the *formal cause*, the *meritorious cause* and the *instrumental cause*. Happily Roman Catholic and Protestant controversialists had long been agreed that the *meritorious cause* of justification was the Work of Christ in his death and resurrection. By his sacrifice for sin he had purchased for men the salvation of God. On the *formal cause* of justification, that by which God actually pronounces and accepts a sinner as righteous, there had never been agreement. The traditional Roman Catholic position was that at baptism God infuses into the soul his divine grace and that this grace purifies the soul. On seeing this infused righteousness in a human being God accepts him or justifies him. This new grace of the soul is thus the *formal cause* of justification and is at the same time the means of sanctification. With this view Protestant scholars had no sympathy. They argued that once God's grace enters the soul it becomes a human righteousness and no human righteousness is sufficient in quality to be the basis for justification and full acceptance with the eternal God. So they pointed to the external righteousness of Christ the Mediator and argued that his righteousness was imputed or reckoned to the Christian as the *formal cause* of acceptance and justification. Within both the camps, the Roman and the Protestant, there was a limited variety of teaching within the fixed limits of either the infused, inherent righteousness or the external righteousness of Christ, as the *formal cause*. The *instrumental cause* was the means by which, or the channel through which, God actually achieved the justification of the sinner. Here again the two sides emphasised two different instruments. Roman Catholic divines spoke of baptism as the instrument through which grace was infused into the soul to achieve justification, while Protestant divines spoke of saving faith in the heart of the repentant sinner as the instrument through which union with Christ, through the Holy Spirit, was achieved for the purpose of justification. Catholics did not deny the importance of faith but made baptism primary, and Protestants did not deny the importance of baptism but made faith primary.

Of course within the theological tradition of the Church of England there had been attempts to find a doctrine of justification which mediated between the two extreme positions, and for attempts in this direction one turns to the writings of such theologians as Jeremy Taylor and George Bull.[11] However, while it is correct to see Newman's doctrine as an attempt at mediation it is wrong to see it as the nineteenth-century exposition of an earlier Anglican position. Newman's study of the Greek Fathers had given him new insights and had led him to expound a position which, though bearing certain similarities to earlier Anglican teaching and to classic Roman Catholic teaching, was a new synthesis. The idea of an implanted 'presence of God' attached to, or affiliated to, the soul (and thus commonly called 'an adherent righteousness') and set in the large biblical context in which Newman placed it, was novel and few seemingly understood him.

2. EVANGELICAL LITERATURE

Though G. S. Faber wrote his *Primitive Doctrine of Justification* (1837) against the teaching of Alexander Knox, not surprisingly it was regarded by many people as also an answer to the teaching of the Tractarians. The general aim of Faber, as appears in his dedication to the Bishop of Chester, was to show that there were basically only two possible methods of justification:

> The one system grounds our justification upon our own Intrinsic Righteousness, infused into us by God, through our faith in the Lord Jesus Christ. The other System grounds our Justification upon the Extrinsic Righteousness of Christ appropriated and forensically made our own by faith as by an appointed instrument.

In the pages of the book he sought to demonstrate that the systems of Knox, of the Council of Trent and even of Bishop Bull were, at root, the same, and were different from the system contained in the formularies of the Church of England. Also he argued that the teaching of the New Testament was uniform (Paul and James being complementary rather than contradictory) and was captured in the official doctrine of the Reformed Church of England. Further, he attempted to prove that the earliest of the Fathers did in fact teach in essence the same doctrine as that of the English Reformers. So confident was he that the early Fathers taught the doctrine of 'Justification upon the Extrinsic Righteousness of Christ appropriated . . . by faith', and so were faithful to the New Testament, that he used the word 'primitive' in his title. As we have noted the second edition contained appendices relating to the views of Newman. By 1842 Faber had come to believe that the system of theology behind the *Tracts for the Times* was an 'unscriptural delusion based ultimately upon a gross perversion of the vital doctrine of Justification on account of the sole external Merits of Christ'.[12]

Since John Bird Sumner had recommended his clergy regularly to read Richard Hooker's *A Learned Discourse of Justification* it was no surprise that he was opposed to the Tractarian position. His views on justification were clearly stated in his *A Charge delivered to the Clergy of the Diocese of Chester* (1841), his *A Practical Exposition of the Epistle of Paul to the Romans and the First Epistle to the Corinthians* (1843) and his brief

Tract on Justification (SPCK, 1843).[13] To the clergy of the diocese he declared that

> Those have now risen up who affirm that the doctrine of the Gospel, the propitiation made for sin, is a doctrine too dangerous to be openly disclosed, too mysterious to be generally exhibited, and would thus deprive the sinner at once of his motive to repent and his comfort in repenting. It has been another part of the same system to involve the article of our justification in obscurity; what has been done for us and what is to be wrought in us, are confused together; and practically, man is induced to look to himself and not to the Redeemer for acceptance with God.[14]

Therefore he felt the need to reassert what he understood to be the doctrine of the English Reformers. Into his *Practical Exposition* he introduced some long introductory 'Prefatory Remarks on the Doctrine of Justification as propounded in the Epistle to the Romans' against Tractarian innovations, and these 'Remarks' were the basis of the Tract.[15]

Across the Atlantic, where the *Tracts for the Times* and related literature were also being published, Bishop C. P. M'Ilvaine of Ohio, whose family roots were in Scotland and whose doctrinal sympathies were with the British Evangelicals, followed these publications with care and concern.[16] Eventually he decided that, as a teacher of the Church, he must reassert the Evangelical Protestant character of her theology at its pivotal point and expose what he judged to be the errors of the views set forth in the Tractarian literature. So he published a volume of over five hundred pages entitled *Oxford Divinity compared with that of the Romish and Anglican Churches with a special view of the doctrine of Justification by Faith* (1841).[17] This book appeared both in New York and London, with the Evangelical House of Seeley and Burnside handling the British edition.

The bishop's method was to link Tractarian teaching with that of Alexander Knox and then to compare this 'Oxford-Divinity' with that of the Schoolmen, the Council of Trent and the Roman Catholic Church to show their likeness. In particular he noted that both the Tractarians and the Roman

Catholics taught the doctrine of justification in and through the sacrament of baptism. Having shown the similarity of the Oxford teaching to that of Rome, his next task was to show that it differed from that of the Articles, Homilies and standard divines of the Church of England. His conclusion was that 'the whole ground-work, on which they teach the sinner to rely for justification and acceptance before God, is the very reverse of that which we have learned from the Scriptures and which our Fathers have declared unto us'. After the publication of the book, which his friend Bishop Daniel Wilson in Calcutta called 'a masterly treatise', he remained very concerned about the spread of Tractarian doctrines.[18] For example, addressing his clergy in 1843 he declared that this controversy over justification was 'about the very life of Christianity'.[19]

James Garbett, the Oxford Professor of Poetry, did not write a treatise on justification but in the printed version of his Bampton Lectures, *Christ as Prophet, Priest and King* (2 vols, 1842), two important chapters are devoted to this subject. In the preface to the book he claimed that he had nothing new to say since he was in agreement with Faber and M'Ilvaine. The chapters on justification followed two on 'Christ as High Priest and Sacrifice' wherein the Protestant doctrine of the substitutionary atonement of Christ was asserted. With this background he argued that justification by faith was fundamental to the Gospel and this he illustrated from both Old and New Testament Scriptures. He emphasised that while Protestants and Roman Catholics agreed in the meritorious cause of justification (the Work of Christ), they were at variance on what was usually called the *causa formalis*. For Protestants the formal cause was not infused, inherent righteousness but the extrinsic righteousness of Christ. The latter was imputed to the sinner by God, being appropriated by faith, the instrument of justification. Far from being opposed to the production of holiness, this doctrine of justification by faith, he argued, was, when rightly understood, the only true basis for holy living. In a final section he provided arguments against the notion of an adherent righteousness (that is, the presence of God attached to the soul) as the formal cause of justification. While Garbett's discussion is very much in the context of the controversy

F

during the Reformation it is prosecuted with the views of Newman very much in mind, but without detailed reference to the Greek Fathers.

In 1845 Charles A. Heurtley, Rector of Fenny Compton, gave the Bampton Lectures and published them as *Justification* (1846). He viewed this volume as a sequel to his previous book entitled *The Union of Christ and His People* (1842) which had its origin as sermons before the University. It was his view, as he declared in the preface, that

> Whatever blessings we either have or hope for, pertaining to life and godliness, are given us *in Christ*, and become ours, *through our union with Him*. Justification is one of these: and to be viewed rightly it must be viewed in connection both with the root from which it springs and also with the kindred blessings, which spring with it from the same root.

While the lectures of 1845 do not particularly refer to Tractarian publications and doctrines, they do nevertheless take up and provide replies to the major questions raised by the Tractarian theology. And, as we shall see, they represent an Evangelicalism which is seeking to be faithful not only to Articles and Homilies but also to the Baptismal Services in the Book of Common Prayer. The subjects covered were: Man fallen in Adam, Man restored in Christ, Imputed Righteousness, Inherent Righteousness, Faith, the connection between Faith and Justification, the connection between Baptism and Justification, and Justification in Continuance (Sanctification).

3. WHAT IS JUSTIFICATION?

(i) *The Tractarian doctrine*

In his *Lectures on Justification*, which are basically an exercise in biblical theology, Newman developed a comprehensive definition of justification. He argued in the third lecture that the Word of the Lord is creative and powerful and brings into being what it declares:

> Justification is an announcement or fiat of Almighty God breaking upon the gloom of our natural state as the Creative Word upon chaos; that it *declares* the soul righteous, and in

that declaration, on the one hand conveys *pardon* for its past sins, and on the other *makes* it actually *righteous*. That it is a declaration, has been made evident from its including, as all allow, an amnesty for the past; for past sins are removable only by an imputation of righteousness. And that it involves an actual creation in righteousness has been argued from the analogy of Almighty God's doings in Scripture, in which we find His words were represented as effective.

[margin note: NOT TRUE. only by DEATH.]

He claimed that this position was set forth in the Articles of Religion XI and XIII. From this basis he stated in the fourth lecture that justification and sanctification are not separate acts of God:

> Justification, then, which in its full meaning is the whole great appointment of God, from beginning to end, may be viewed on its two sides, – active and passive, in its beginning and its completion, in what God does, and what man receives; and while in its passive sense, man is made righteous, in its active, God calls or declares. That is, it will stand either for imputation or for sanctification. Thus divines, who in the main agree in what the great mercy of God is *as a whole*, may differ as to what should be called justification; for according as they view it as God's giving or man's receiving, they will consider it God's accounting righteous or man's becoming righteous.

'In some sufficient sense Christ, as our righteousness', he held, 'fulfils the Law *in us* as well as for us; that He justifies us, not only in word, but in power bringing the ark with its mercy seat into the temple of our hearts; manifesting, setting up there His new kingdom, and the power and glory of His Cross.'

As was noted above, the classic question concerning the *causa formalis* could not be avoided in the 1830s and Newman did not shrink from it. Rejecting Luther's answer, and the traditional Roman Catholic answer, he argued in the fourth lecture that the formal cause must be 'at once the special fruit of Christ's sacrifice and also an inward gift possessed and residing within us'. And this was 'the *habitation* in us of God the Father and Word Incarnate through the Holy Ghost'. So to be justified was 'to receive the Divine Presence within us and be made a Temple of the Holy Ghost'. He held that his own doctrine of the righteousness of Christ 'both imputed and imparted by His real indwelling' was superior to the Roman Catholic view in that it involved not an 'inherent righteousness' but an 'adherent righteousness', which depended 'wholly and absolutely upon the Divine Indwelling'. So the formal cause of justification was internal, adherent righteousness, that is, the presence of Christ by the Holy Spirit in the soul.[20]

(ii) *Evangelical Response.* (a) *Tractarian doctrine is in essence the same doctrine as that of Alexander Knox and the Council of Trent*
In the preface to his *Lectures*, Newman, referring to the criticism of Knox's views by Faber, asserted that his own work had been written without reference to either of them, and so he declared he would leave it to the reader to decide to what extent he agreed with Knox and to what extent with Faber. M'Ilvaine did not doubt that Newman agreed with Knox and sought to prove the point both by quotations from Knox and from the *British Critic*. In the latter magazine it had been written of Knox that 'he is an instance in rudiment of those great restorations which he foresaw in development. He shares with the eminent writers of the day in the work of advancing what he anticipated.'[21] One of these restorations was the doctrine of justification, defined as follows by Knox: 'In St Paul's sense, to be justified is not simply to be accounted righteous; but also and in the first instance to be made righteous by the implantation of a radical principle of righteousness.'[22] So, claimed M'Ilvaine, Knox and the Tractarians were agreed in defining justification primarily in terms of inherent righteousness, infused by God. Faber, of course, had already equated the teaching of Knox with the teaching of the Schoolmen and Tridentine Fathers; they agreed, he had argued, in making 'the procuring cause of Justification, or the ground of our acceptance with God, to be our own infused and therefore inherent or intrinsic righteousness'.[23]

If the doctrine of Knox and the Tractarians was the same, and if the doctrine of Knox and the Roman Catholics was the same, then obviously the doctrine of the Tractarians and the Roman Catholics was the same. And this latter claim is exactly what

M'Ilvaine sought to demonstrate in a carefully argued section of Chapter Four of his book. He set out three propositions and then defended them.[24] The first was 'that the Schoolmen described the righteousness of Justification precisely as do our Oxford Divines'. In support of this he quoted both Newman and Aquinas. The former admitted that 'Lombard and Thomas Aquinas declare that the Holy Spirit indwelling is the formal cause of Justification' and the latter stated that 'Justifying Grace is something real and positive in the soul, a supernatural quality.' The second proposition was that

> they felt the same necessity . . . of finding out a distinction between an indwelling righteousness that justifies and an indwelling righteousness that sanctifies, and that they fell upon precisely the same subtle and shadowy expedient.

Having noted that both Newman and Pusey were at pains to state that sanctification can have no place in the justification of a sinner, the bishop went on to show that Aquinas himself had also carefully distinguished the two. Therefore, while Newman's charge that Romanists identify justification with renewal might be true of post-Reformation Catholics it was not true of certain medieval divines. Aquinas himself distinguished between the *gratia justificans* (the justifying righteousness) and the 'habit' of love, the latter belonging to the will and the former to the essence of the soul.[25]

The third proposition was 'that this very distinction of the ancient Schoolmen which equally characterises the divinity of our Oxford Schoolmen, is used by our ancient writers as one distinctive characteristic of Popery'. It was sufficient here to quote from John Keble's edition of the *Works* of Richard Hooker:

> The Schoolmen, which follow Thomas, do not only comprise in the name of grace, the favour of God, his Spirit, and effects of His Spirit; but, over and besides these three, *a fourth kind of formal habit or inherent quality*, which maketh the person of man acceptable, perfecteth the substance of his mind, and causeth the virtuous actions thereof to be meritorious. This grace they will have to be the principal effect of sacraments; a grace which neither Christ nor any apostle of Christ did

ever mention. The fathers have it not in their writings, although they often speak of sacraments and of the grace we receive by them. Yea, they which have found it out, are as doubtful as any other, *what name or nature* they should give unto it.

Thus the confusion of the Medieval Scholastics is shared by the Oxford Tractarians, for both, thought M'Ilvaine, preferred 'heathen dialectics to Holy Scripture, the words of Aristotle to the writings of the Christian Fathers'. Here, perhaps, the Bishop of Ohio was overstating his case.

James Garbett emphasised that the point at issue was that which had been long known as the *causa formalis*. To him, as to Faber, the Tractarian doctrine was self-contradictory:

> . . . supposing that such a substance – itself a term of Aquinas – could be considered as *ad*herent rather than *in*herent, it must still be forensic, therefore our justification being placed *in it*, depends on a *forensic* formal cause. Wherefore then, not on Christ, rather than on this ideal substance? If it be replied, that it is *in* us, though not of us, then it is *righteousness inherent*, the *direct* confession of which the whole scheme is intended to elude.

Further, Newman's idea of God's indwelling the soul (adherent righteousness) was philosophically unacceptable to him. Admitting that there is a sense in which it is true to say that God indwells his creation, and fully recognising that there is the hypostatic union of the divine essence with the humanity in the Person of Christ, he went on to state that

> There remains but one more sense in which God can be united to the soul, and that is morally – that is an acting *upon us*, and *in us*, as we are intelligent and spiritual beings, by His purifying energies – and so, by strengthening our faculties, and the exercise of them, through heavenly communications, He renews them into the image which they have lost and brings us into a harmony with the heavenly will, and a perception and enjoyment of His adorable perfections. But there is no affixture of a divine substance, different from our own essence: it is only the activity of the divine Spirit

within us, the motion of that which, wherever it is, morally or physically, is *actus purissimus*.

So Newman's view of adherent righteousness was only possible if 'we give grace a quasi-solid form and consider it as Aquinas says, *positivum et reale* – enfolding in itself all goodness and glory'.[26]

(iii) *Evangelical Response*. (b) *The Tractarian doctrine is similar to the condemned teaching of Osiander*

Andreas Osiander (1498–1552) became a Professor at Könisberg, where he published in 1550 his treatise, *De Justificatione*.[27] In this he taught that the *formal* cause of justification is the presence of the divine gift of righteousness in the soul. This teaching, which seemed to contemporaries to be the doctrine of the Schoolmen in Protestant dress, led to a major controversy within Lutheranism and to the condemnation of the new teaching both by Melanchthon and by Calvin.[28] Newman knew of Osiander's doctrine and attempted to deny that his teaching was similar. He claimed that Osiander's doctrine bore the same relation to his own 'as the Manichaean blasphemies concerning the union of the substance of God with the natural world, to the Scripture truth that in Him "we move and live and have our being" '.[29]

The Archbishop of Cashel, Richard Laurence, was not convinced by Newman's disclaimer and in a special section to a new edition of his *The Visitation of the Saxon Reformed Church* which appeared posthumously in 1839 he quoted a summary of Osiander's doctrine of justification and then remarked that perhaps the principal point in controversy was 'little more than a logomachy', for Newman affixed 'a peculiar sense to the word Justification which with the exception of Osiander no Protestant ever affixed before him'.[30] This charge of reviving Osiander's errors was taken up by both Garbett and M'Ilvaine. The latter believed that Osiander like Newman spoke of justification sometimes as 'the communication to us of the essential righteousness of the divine nature' and sometimes as 'our own personal holiness', and Garbett connected Osiander's and Newman's doctrines with that of the Schoolmen.[31]

(iv) *Evangelical Response.* (c) *The Tractarian doctrine is not that of the formularies and 'standard divines' of the Church of England*

Lying behind this assertion there was of course the belief that the formularies gave a correct presentation of the biblical teaching on justification. The Articles of Religion which deal with justification are XI, XII and XIII, and the Homily referred to is Homily 3 'Of the Salvation of all mankind'.

Heurtley, whose presentation is basically biblical, endeavoured to show 'that our Justification consists not ... in our being *made* righteous ... but, as our own church teaches (Article XI) in our being *accounted* righteous; God dealing with us, in Christ, as though we had perfectly fulfilled the whole law, not because we have done so or can do so, but because our guilt in transgressing the law has been laid upon Christ, whose members we are.' Or, in greater detail:

> In the fulness of time, the eternal son took man's nature upon Him, in the womb of the blessed Virgin, that He might become a second Adam, the federal Head of a second race, the Fountain and Source of life to all, who, by a second birth, should be born of Him. These great truths, the incarnation of the eternal Son, and the union between Christ and His Church, of which the incarnation is the basis, lie at the foundation of what the Scriptures teach us respecting our salvation ... Whatsoever we either have or hope for, in reference to eternal life, is given us *in Christ* and by virtue of our union with Him. And it is therefore available to us, because He, in Whom it is given, and with Whom we are united, is one also with the Father and the Holy Ghost.
>
> Justification is one of the precious gifts thus bestowed upon us, and it consists, not in an *imperfect* righteousness of our own *inherent* in us, but in Christ's *perfect* righteousness *imputed* to us, – ours because we are one with Christ, and Christ with us.[32]

Then he went on to quote from Hooker's *Discourse on Justification*, to show that this understanding of justification was that commonly held in the Church of England.

So the issue was that according to the Evangelical understanding of the Scriptures and Formularies the doctrine of justification was the declaring of a sinner righteous by God through the imputing or reckoning to him of the forensic righteousness of Christ, while for the Tractarians justification was a declaring righteous because of the possession by the sinner of the gift of righteousness in his soul, the presence of divine life within him. Faber, quoted with approval by M'Ilvaine (who equated the doctrine of Knox and the Tractarians), summarised the matter as follows:

> Mr. Knox and the Tridentine Fathers and the Schoolmen, with whatever subtle distinctions and explanations, make the *Procuring Cause of Justification,* or *the Ground of our acceptance with God,* to be OUR OWN INFUSED AND THEREFORE INHERENT OR INTRINSIC RIGHTEOUSNESS.
>
> The Church of England, on the contrary, and along with her all the other Reformed Churches, make the *Procuring Cause of Justification,* or *the Ground of our acceptance with God,* to be THE EXTRINSIC RIGHTEOUSNESS OF CHRIST APPRE-HENDED AND APPROPRIATED BY THE INSTRUMENTAL HAND OF FAITH.[33]

Thus, as Garbett emphasised, the point at issue was the old problem of the formal cause of justification: was it the imputed righteousness of the Mediator or was it the infused gift of righteousness in the soul?[34] Without hesitation the Evangelicals, following the Articles and Homilies, declared that it was the imputed extrinsic righteousness of Christ whereby a sinner was justified and accepted by God.

4. HOW DOES A SINNER RECEIVE JUSTIFICATION?

(i) *The Tractarian doctrine*

Recognising that Article xi declares that 'we are justified by faith only', and wanting to do full justice to what he believed to be the intimate relation between baptism and justification, Newman proposed to call faith 'the internal instrument' and baptism 'the external instrument'. He wrote:

> The instrumental power of Faith cannot interfere with the instrumental power of Baptism; because Faith is the *sole* justifier, not in contrast to all means and agencies whatever

(for it is not surely in contrast to our Lord's merits, or God's mercy,) but to all other *graces*. When, then, Faith is called the sole instrument, this means the sole *internal* instrument, not the sole instrument of any kind.

There is nothing inconsistent, then, in Faith being the sole instrument of justification, and yet Baptism also the sole instrument, and that at the same time, because in distinct senses; an inward instrument in no way interfering with the outward instrument. Baptism might be the hand of the giver and Faith the hand of the receiver.

Thus 'Faith does not precede justification; but justification precedes faith and makes it justifying'. And 'Baptism is the primary instrument, and creates faith to be what it is and otherwise is not, giving it power and rank, and constituting it as its own successor'. So he rejected the 'Lutheran' idea of faith as trust in the atonement of Christ and saw it instead as a complex virtue in which is included 'love and fear, and heavenly-mindedness, and obedience, and firmness, and zeal and humility'.[35]

Thus for Newman and his colleagues justification was received at baptism and was sustained by faith and the Eucharist.

(ii) *Evangelical Response.* (a) *The Tractarian doctrine is in essence the Roman Catholic doctrine of Baptismal Justification*

Taking up Newman's claim that 'the Act of Justifying is expressly ascribed to Baptism', Faber wrote: 'I recalled not that the dogma, *We are justified by Baptism*, occurs EXPRESSLY anywhere in Holy Scripture. At all events our familiar clerical oracle, Cruden, announces not the existence of any text of this description. If there be such a text, let it be produced: and the matter will be settled at once.'[36] The doctrine came either from Newman's private judgment or from Rome. M'Ilvaine believed it came from the latter and devoted a chapter of his book to a comparison under six headings of the Tractarian and Roman Catholic teaching. These were:

1. That faith before baptism is not and cannot be a living faith, that 'which worketh by love'.

2. That faith before baptism is said to justify or to be an instrument of justification, only as a *sine-qua-non*, only as a necessary preparation for, and that which leads to, baptism, which itself is the only real instrument of justification.

3. This faith, so dead, is nevertheless a *divine, supernatural* gift based on the testimony of God, through the creeds and traditionary doctrines of the Church, independently of a direct application to the Scriptures, as the primary and only authoritative Rule of Faith.

4. That this faith, before baptism, instead of being in any sense justifying, until after the sinner becomes justified *in baptism*, must itself be first justified, or made a *living* faith by baptism.

5. That faith when regenerate and justified in baptism, is not such a *trust* in the divine mercy as *apprehends* and *accepts* remission of sins through the mediation of Christ, and justifies the soul through his righteousness accounted to the believer.

6. That after it has become a *regenerate and lively faith*, by the love of God shed abroad in the heart by baptism, so that it is now joined with hope and love, it then only *continues* or *sustains* that justification already completed, in baptism, before it was alive; and even this not in any proper sense, as an instrument applying the righteousness of Christ, but only as united to, and acting in common with, all other virtues and works.

In order to prove the similarity of Tractarian and Tridentine teaching the bishop had to give himself to some tortuous reasoning and perhaps some quotations out of context. His conclusion was that there was no essential difference for both took an *opus operatum* view of the efficacy of baptism and he added, for good measure, that 'this *opus operatum* has ever been considered, among Protestants, a dark and deadly plague-spot of Popery'.[37] The *opus operatum* is simply the efficacy of the sacrament without respect to the state or condition of the recipient, except that he does not shut up his soul against the grace infused. Opposing this, Protestant theology had always insisted on the need for faith and repentance (in the one to be baptised or in the sponsors) as a preliminary of the administration of the sacrament.

(iii) *Evangelical Response.* (b) '*By faith alone*' *is the teaching of the Scriptures and the Church of England*
No one asserted this more strongly than did John Bird Sumner, Bishop of Chester. In his *Charge* (1841) he declared:

> The Scriptural truth is as clear as it is simple. 'When all were dead [in sin], Christ died for all'; so that 'he that hath the Son hath life and he that hath not the Son hath not life'. By one way alone can man possess the Son; that is, by believing in him. And therefore, faith alone can justify; faith alone can appropriate to us that remedy, which God has appointed for the healing of our plague: faith alone can give us an interest in that sacrifice which God has accepted as satisfaction for sin. Thus 'being justified by faith we have peace with God through Jesus Christ'.

And in the 'Preface on Justification' to his *Practical Exposition of Romans* (1843) he wrote:

> When our Church says that we are accounted righteous before God for the merits of Jesus Christ by faith; this must not be understood as if faith were a work of obedience or an act of duty, which God accepts instead of other duties or other obedience, and that therefore the man who has faith is justified, whilst the man who has not faith is condemned for for wanting it. The meaning is that Christ has 'redeemed from the wrath to come' 'as many as receive him and believe in his name': but that he must be trusted by those whom he redeems: that his death must be relied on, in order that it may be efficacious for salvation: faith being, as it were, the graft by which a believer is united to the 'true vine' and separated from the natural corrupt stock to the root of which the axe is laid.

Of this justifying faith Garbett wrote: 'By its very nature it is *self-renunciatory* – it rests upon the merit of another – and in this forensic relation it has its very being and exhibits its vigor'.[38]

Heurtley devoted a chapter to the topic of 'the connection of faith and justification' and had the following to say about faith:

> We are justified by faith, because faith, instead of holding out something of our own to rest upon, whether pointing to works done, or calling our attention to itself as the root and foundation of all works, remits us simply and at once to Christ, who is 'the Lord our righteousness', that we may receive in Him and from Him, what we have not, and cannot have, of ourselves, both that perfect righteousness of Justification which we may boldly plead before God, and also that inherent, though as yet imperfect, righteousness of Sanctification, which shall qualify us for admission into His presence.[39]

The last sentence introduces the relation of Justification and Sanctification and to this we shall return below.

(iv) *Evangelical Response.* (c) *The true relation of Baptism and Justification*

In the Articles of Religion there is no specific mention of baptism in relation to justification. However, in the services of Holy Baptism in the Book of Common Prayer, baptism is clearly connected with the forgiveness (washing away) of sins, which is a part of justification, and in the creed the words 'I believe in one baptism for the remission of sins' occur. M'Ilvaine and Heurtley each devoted a whole chapter to the stating of the relation of baptism and justification and their slightly differing emphases indicate that within Evangelicalism there were several viewpoints. We shall first set forth Heurtley's position concerning each point covered and then indicate or describe M'Ilvaine's attitude.

Heurtley explained, with reference to adult baptism, that 'the office of baptism is the solemn ratification of the great Christian covenant, between God and the faithful recipient'.

> In adults . . . faith is instrumental to our incorporation into Christ in that . . . it leads us, on the one hand, to accept salvation . . . as God's free and unmerited gift, bestowed upon us in Christ; on the other, to consecrate ourselves and

all we have unreservedly to His service. Faith produces the cordial and unfeigned assent to this covenant in our hearts.

So before baptism 'the covenant is already made in intention; only it is not made formally. The soul is betrothed to Christ, but the marriage ceremony has not taken place.'

> Baptism completes what is yet lacking. It is the solemn signing and sealing of the covenant by both the contracting parties. And consequently, it actually conveys and makes over to both of them the benefits to which they respectively become entitled. Thus, on the one hand, God does, in and by baptism, incorporate the baptized person, as a living member, into Christ's mystical body, and invest him with the full privileges and immunities, so far as he is yet capable of them, of that blessed fellowship . . . On the other hand, the baptized person renounces for ever all other lords; he accepts Christ, and God, in Christ, as his only Master; and he solemnly engages himself to the performance of whatsoever duties . . . are involved in this new relationship.[40]

Justification is, of course, along with Adoption into God's family, one of 'the privileges and immunities'.

For M'Ilvaine this covenant emphasis, which Heurtley seems to take partly from Vossius (1577–1649), is not so prominent. He wrote that

> Baptism is a *sign* of separation from the world, and consecration to God; a _seal_ of the Promises of God to those who truly repent and believe; an *effectual* sign and seal, whereby the grace of repentance and faith is confirmed and increased.[41]

This type of definition reflects the Anglican Calvinistic tradition of William Romaine and Thomas Scott.

Both writers were conscious that the early Fathers and even the Reformers had used language of the sacraments which could be interpreted as teaching an *opus operatum* doctrine. Heurtley admitted that 'the fathers . . . in speaking of baptism often use language, which might seem to put its efficacy upon another ground, besides this of its being the ratification of the Christian covenant'. He concluded that 'such language is obviously to be understood mystically'.

We are truly said to be in baptism washed in Christ's blood, yet not because the element of water is substantially changed into blood, but because the blood of Christ is really, though mystically, applied to us in the sacrament.[42]

M'Ilvaine was content to follow Jewell and Augustine and state that sacraments 'receive the names of the self-same things they signify'. So baptism is called 'baptism for the remission of sins' because it signifies remission of sins and it is called 'the washing of regeneration' because it signifies that washing. So,

> when we speak *sacramentally*, it is right to say of those in general who are baptised, that in Baptism they are *born of God*, because then the profession of newness of life is made; then, the seal of the Church is set upon that profession; then the promises of God to those who embrace them are visibly pledged and assured; then the man is received into visible fellowship of the household of faith, and communion with the people of God. Then, therefore, his Christian life, as one of the children of God, visibly and professedly begins.

Therefore in stating that remission of sins comes at baptism the Church is saying that baptism is like the delivery of a deed: 'A man is said to have received the conveyance of an estate, which he has been long enjoying, and of which, before God, he had long been the rightful owner.'[43]

Heurtley put the last point in somewhat stronger relief; and in so doing took a position that was not common in nineteenth-century Evangelical theology:

> But the question may be asked, What is the condition of those, to whom God has already given the grace of faith, but who are not yet baptised? I answer, Their condition is an imperfect condition: their union with Christ is, as it were, in an incipient state, but it is not formally effected; they have life in some sort, but not life fully developed; the life of the womb, not the life which is given at birth.

He did admit that 'indispensable as baptism is to salvation under ordinary circumstances, we may not doubt, but that where men are prevented from receiving it by unavoidable necessity, the faith, which desired the sacrament, is accepted instead of the sacrament'.[44]

The discussion thus far has referred to adults. Concerning infants Heurtley proposed that

> Infants need the grace which adults receive in baptism as truly as adults. They need to be admitted into God's covenant; they need to be incorporated into Christ's body; they need remission of sins. And they are certainly capable of these benefits.[45]

The sin remitted in infant baptism is the guilt of Adam and so, normally justification may be said to occur at baptism, but is a reality which has personally to be appropriated and recognised later by the child. M'Ilvaine wrote that in infants

> Original Sin is thus remitted on account of the imputed righteousness of the 'Second Adam' without their personal faith, just as they have been brought, without any act of theirs, under the curse of the sin of the first Adam. When baptized infants come to be capable of what is called *actual sin*, that is, *sin after baptism*, then they must personally 'repent and believe on the Lord Jesus Christ' or else they cannot be saved; but their baptism, as to all participation in God's mercy, will be then as if they had not been baptized; just as the circumcision of the Jews was made, by unbelief, 'uncircumcision'.[46]

So the state of justification could be lost by a child who refused to obey the Gospel.

To summarise this long section we may say that the Evangelicals, while seeking to preserve a very intimate relation between justification and baptism, differed from the Tractarians in that they insisted that justifying faith in adults is always preliminary to the sacrament and though increased and enriched by the sacrament is not the fruit of it, as Tractarians taught.

5. WHAT IS THE RELATION AFTER BAPTISM BETWEEN JUSTIFICATION AND FORGIVENESS?

(i) *Differences in terminology*

Within Evangelical Protestant theology it was usual to distinguish carefully between justification and sanctification, justification and regeneration, regeneration and sanctification. Justification was seen as the act of God declaring the believing sinner to be righteous in Christ; sanctification was seen as the work of the Holy Spirit in the believing sinner gradually making him righteous; regeneration was seen as the implantation of divine life (or a new nature) in the soul of the believing sinner at the same time as justification and thus being the beginnings of sanctification. Thus while justification was seen as an act of God within his heavenly court, regeneration was seen as an act of God within the soul of the believing sinner. Sanctification then began immediately and its purpose was to make righteous that person whom God had already declared to be righteous in Christ. Naturally Protestants emphasised that the true outcome of justification by faith was the life of increasing holiness and good works (a point which our authors strongly asserted) in which could be enjoyed the assurance of sins forgiven and peace with heaven.[47]

As we have seen the Tractarians used the words justification and sanctification in a different way from traditional Protestantism and this made the Evangelicals claim that they used the terminology of the Schoolmen and the Council of Trent, to propound doctrines similar to those of Roman Catholicism. And it was because the Tractarians had such strong doctrines of baptismal regeneration and baptismal justification that the problem, of how sins committed after this unique washing of regeneration were to be forgiven, arose.

(ii) *The Tractarian doctrine of the forgiveness of sins after baptism*

In his *Scriptural Views of Holy Baptism*, Pusey had surprised and shocked many churchmen by his apparent teaching that there was no sure possibility of full assurance of the forgiveness for sins committed after baptism. This sacrament was, for him, the

God-ordained means of both the implantation of divine life into the soul and the remission of sins. Baptism was the washing of regeneration. Yet, since baptism was by its very nature administered only once, the problem of the forgiveness of post-baptismal sins was a vital one. On this point Pusey shared the view of certain teachers of the Early Church that the faithful could never know with full assurance that sins committed after their baptism were cleansed until after death.[48] He maintained his original position in his *Letter to the Bishop of Oxford* (1841) where in his explanation of Tractarian teaching on Article xvi 'Of Sin after Baptism' he wrote:

> She [our Church] has no second Baptism to give and so she cannot pronounce him altogether free from his past sins. There are but two periods of *absolute* cleansing, Baptism and the day of Judgment. She therefore teaches him continually to repent, that so his sins *may be* blotted out, though she has no commission to tell him absolutely that they are.[49]

The question of repentance by Christians was taken up by Charles Wordsworth, second Master of Winchester School, in a printed sermon entitled *Evangelical Repentance* (1841). Wordsworth, who later became Bishop of St Andrews, advocated the restoration in the Church of public penance, arguing that forgiveness of sins after baptism can be received only through much self-abasement. Of the Prodigal Son he wrote: 'It was the very extremity of pain and misery which humbled the Prodigal's pride; it is by definite *acts* of self-punishment and self-abasement that we shall best humble ours' and thus be in the position to be forgiven. W. G. Ward was very impressed by Wordsworth's reasoning and stated that 'it is impossible to add anything to the masterly treatment it has received at Mr. Wordsworth's hands, and we would anxiously refer any one who at present takes on trust the popular views [Evangelical] on that awful question, to examine carefully the arguments there adduced'.[50] It is interesting to note that when Newman came to write his *Essay on the Development of Christian Doctrine* in 1845 he expressly stated that the whole system of penance which developed in the Early Church was inherent in the idea of baptism as the 'Washing of Regeneration'. Pusey himself realised that his position as set forth in the *Tracts* of 1835 was severe and so later he preached several sermons setting forth the comforts afforded by the Gospel to penitents. The first of these was the famous *The Holy Eucharist a Comfort to the Penitent* (1843).

(iii) *Evangelical Response. A full assurance of the forgiveness of sins is promised under the Gospel*

Evangelicals, without exception, held that the Scriptures, Article xvi 'Of Sin after Baptism', and the service of Holy Communion promised to Christian people full forgiveness after baptism upon the condition of repentance for the sin and faith in Christ the Saviour. Bishop O'Brien, author of the classic exposition of justification published in 1833, took up this matter in his lengthy *Charge* of 1842 and insisted that as there was a welcome and forgiveness for the Prodigal Son, so there was a welcome and forgiveness from God to all the unbaptised or baptised who repented of their sins and turned in faith to Christ. God did not require a perfect repentance. The reason why Evangelicals asserted that the full forgiveness of sins was the continuing privilege of the baptised Christian, who remained repentant for sins and trusting in Christ, the Saviour, was not only because of the 'comfortable words' of Holy Scripture (which are quoted in the service of Holy Communion) but also because of their doctrine of justification and the Baptismal Covenant of Grace. God's declaration of forgiveness, imputation of the righteousness of Christ and adoption into his family, ratified in baptism were constant realities from God's side and human sin merely destroyed the experience of them; but the breach caused by sin was lovingly healed, and the barrier of sin readily removed by God when he found repentance for sin and trust in his Son by the sinner. The offer of the Gospel, Evangelicals affirmed, included not only the forgiveness of past sins but the promise of the forgiveness of future sins, on condition of faith and repentance.

M'Ilvaine was severe in his criticism of Pusey's teaching and likened it to Roman Catholic doctrine; Heurtley stressed the positive side of the matter. 'We may not doubt', he wrote, 'but that God's arms of mercy are still open to receive those who

truly and earnestly turn to Him, even though they have for-
saken the guide of their youth, and forgotten the covenant of
their God.' Like O'Brien he referred to the Prodigal Son and
insisted that the human side of the covenant of grace is faith
and repentance and when these truly occur then God welcomes
and fully forgives the person in question.[51]

6. CONCLUSION

It is difficult to avoid the conclusion that the Evangelicals
never really answered the doctrine of justification proposed by
Newman. They were so wedded to looking at the subject in
terms of the possible formal causes, either internal or external,
that they looked for a scholastic basis for Newman's doctrine of
an internal adherent righteousness and believed they found it in
the teaching of Aquinas. So their response to the Tractarian
teaching was governed by their knowledge of the controversy
between Protestants and Roman Catholics in the sixteenth and
seventeenth centuries. And, it must be said, they faithfully
expounded the position of the Protestant Reformers as far as the
doctrine of Justification by Faith was concerned. But they did
no fresh biblical exegesis and only in the case of Heurtley is
there the glimmer of an attempt to look once more at the
teaching of the apostles. If the Evangelicals had responded by
examining the roots of Newman's views (that is the teaching
of the Greek Fathers) and challenged these roots by the teaching
of the Apostle Paul and James, then the whole controversy
(and perhaps the development of Evangelical theology) would
have taken on a different character. Though Pusey certainly
felt the need to explain the Tractarian doctrine of justification
to the Christian public, it appears that Newman never felt that
his *Lectures* had been seriously challenged. The same, however,
cannot be said of Pusey's teaching concerning the forgiveness
of sin after baptism. He expounded an extreme position as
early as 1835 and it did not necessarily follow from Newman's
doctrine of justification, which achieved full flower only in
1837–8.

Justification by Faith, as expounded by Luther and his
contemporaries was a liberating doctrine. It was a doctrine

which described a joyful experience of the pardon of sins and of peace with heaven. In polemical theology it became an integral part of a system of doctrine, the *material* principle of the Reformation, as it was called. It is possible to hold to a doctrine both in its experiental and its polemical aspects and it appears that many of the first, second and later generations of Protestants managed to do this. The great danger which Evangelicals faced in the Victorian period was that of reducing this great Protestant doctrine to a party slogan as they fought what they saw as erroneous systems around them, the teaching of salvation by works or salvation by sacraments. It is easy to claim that such a corruption of Justification by Faith occurred in the 1830s and 1840s and was the religious, ideological platform of members of the various Protestant societies and Orange orders. Yet, even in this context, where it was so easy to reduce the experiental aspects of justification to a minimum, one finds a man such as Lord Shaftesbury, whose 'Diary' clearly reveals that he knew a similar experience as the Reformers described, and the stalwart Protestant, Alexander Haldane, also appears to have had a deep experiental sense of the forgiveness of God.[52] So all that can be safely said is that the tendency of this battle with the Tractarians was in the direction of reducing the prominence of the experiental aspects of the doctrine, which had been primary in the work of the Evangelical leaders of the eighteenth and early nineteenth centuries, and enlarging its polemical and ideological aspects.

It is interesting to observe that in each of the three National Churches of the United Kingdom during the third, fourth and fifth decades of the nineteenth century there were sensitive thinkers challenging the traditional doctrine of forensic justification within Protestantism, based as it was on the analogy of the law court. In Ireland there was the layman, Alexander Knox; in Scotland there was Thomas Erskine, another layman, and John McLeod Campbell, minister of Row, near Cardross on the Gareloch; and in England there was John Henry Newman and Frederick Denison Maurice.[53] The systems which these men produced were different but perhaps a common thread which united them was the search for an internal and an ethical approach to, and account of, justification.[54] In defending the forensic account of justification the Evangelicals in the Church of Ireland, the Church of Scotland and the Church of England fought a common fight with common weapons, and because they were on the defensive they brought no new light from Scripture to shine upon this important area of Christian doctrine and experience. Perhaps their failure can be overlooked in that even today biblical scholars cannot seemingly agree as to what exactly is the New Testament or the Pauline, doctrine of justification.[55]

CHAPTER SIX

CHURCH, MINISTRY AND SACRAMENTS

At the time when the Oxford Movement began, Anglican Evangelicals were engaged in a sometimes bitter controversy with some of their Nonconformist brethren concerning the biblical, theological and political justification for an Established Church. Apparently they convinced few Dissenters but they did strengthen their own conviction that they were in an institution which was within God's will for his universal Church and for Britain. They welcomed the famous *Lectures on Church Establishments* by Dr Chalmers and gave support to the position outlined by two of their number – Hugh McNeile, the eloquent Irishman, in his *Lectures on the Church of England* (1840) and R. B. Seeley, the publisher, in his *Essays on the Church* (1833).

Controversy with Tractarians over the doctrine of the Church and related issues was a different matter. Ironically, in this case, Anglican Evangelicals who were staunch defenders of the national Church were accused of being open or disguised Dissenters or Puritans within the episcopalian structures. Thus while Evangelicals zealously argued from biblical teaching (often from the Old Testament) and political theory to defend Church Establishments against Nonconformists, they argued with a similar zeal against Tractarians from what they heartily believed to be New Testament principles and the teaching of the Anglican Reformers.

I. INTRODUCTION

The nature of the Church, ministry and sacraments constituted an area of doctrine to which Tractarians gave increasing attention as the years from 1833 passed by. In the earliest *Tracts* clergy were reminded of the apostolic ministry which was theirs and the efficacious sacraments of grace which they administered in Christ's name. In later treatises a *via media* course for the

Church of England was plotted between popular Protestantism and Romanism, a full-blooded doctrine of baptismal regeneration and a very high doctrine of the Real Presence in the Eucharist were proclaimed; auricular confession was claimed to be a neglected but genuinely Anglican doctrine and practice. To say the least, in terms of the traditions of the English Church since the sixteenth century these doctrines were either novel or controversial. So they were opposed in sermons, pamphlets and treatises, as usual with varying degrees of skill and learning.

It has been noted in the historical survey how ecclesiological differences between Tractarians and Evangelicals surfaced in terms of different attitudes adopted by each side to specific matters. For example, in the activity to promote the Jerusalem Bishopric and in the subsequent support for Bishop Gobat, Evangelicals worked from a view of the Church which presumed that German Lutheran ministers were truly ordained to the ministry of the Church of Christ and which suspected that the Greek Churches were apostate. Tractarians regarded the apostolic succession of bishops as fundamental and ordination as valid only if conducted by such a bishop; for them, therefore, the Lutherans were not valid ministers and the Greek Churches, having the succession of bishops, were true Churches. Then the passionate controversy surrounding the views of Charles Gorham highlighted not only different approaches to the understanding of what God does in infant baptism but also different views as to the part the state should play in deciding for the Church what was true doctrine. Evangelicals were happy to see the state having a part but the Tractarians believed that doctrinal matters should be left to bishops and church synods.

In the pages which follow an attempt will be made to present those aspects of the doctrines of Church, ministry and sacraments as held by Evangelicals which were directly challenged in the controversy between the two parties. Put another way, as in the two previous chapters, an attempt will be made to explain how Evangelicals responded out of their own tradition to central questions raised by the Tractarian literature. These questions were: What is the relation of the invisible Church and the visible churches? Is episcopacy of the *esse* of the *bene esse* of the visible churches? What are the effects of infant baptism?

and, In what sense is Christ present in the Eucharist? First of
all, however, a brief description of the literature to be used will
be given.

2. THE EVANGELICAL LITERATURE

Strictly speaking only two treatises by Evangelicals on the doctrine of the Church were published between 1833 and 1856.
The first, popular in style and betraying a sermonic origin,
came from the pen of Hugh McNeile and had the title, *The
Church and the Churches; or, The Church of God in Christ and the
Churches of Christ militant here on earth* (1846). It followed his
earlier volume defending Church Establishments. Its title reveals his full commitment to the Protestant distinction between the invisible and visible aspects of the Church. Much of
his argument was directed against what he took to be the traditional Tridentine doctrine of Rome in which there is a close
identification of the visible Church, with the Pope as Head,
and the mystical Body of Christ with Christ as Head. He did,
however, take Tractarian views into account for he saw Tractarianism as a half-way house between the Protestant Church
of England and the Church of Rome. One of his major worries
was that the Tractarian clergy were driving many faithful Protestant laity from the established Church towards congregational independency; another worry was that the British
Roman Catholics, strengthened by secessions from the Church
of England, were making significant numerical advances. So,
perhaps more to strengthen his brethren than to convert either
Tractarian or Roman Catholic, he wrote his book. First, he
dealt with the object of faith described in the creed as 'One-
Holy, Catholic and Apostolic Church'. In four chapters he ex,
plained that this Church was in fact the invisible Church composed of all elect believers of all times and places. Its unity was
in the union of Christ by the one Spirit; its holiness was that
offered and provided in the work of the Holy Spirit; its catholicity was in virtue of the fact that the elect came from every
tribe and nation, and its apostolicity was in the doctrine of the
apostles by which the elect came to their salvation. In a further
chapter he dealt with the visible churches composed of the elect

and the reprobate, and followed this with chapters on Baptism, the Lord's Supper and the Ministry. While far from being a good book it does provide very useful information as to the views of one of the most popular of Evangelical preachers and presumably, therefore, reflects the views of many of his hearers. Eugene Stock, the historian of the Church Missionary Society, believed that McNeile was 'unquestionably the greatest Evangelical preacher and speaker in the Church of England' during the century.

In contrast Edward Arthur Litton's *The Church of Christ, in Its Idea, Attributes and Ministry* (1851) is an academic treatise, aimed primarily at Roman Catholic doctrine but including what he called 'Catholic, or Church, or Sacramental' principles which were rife in the Church of England in 1851. In his terminology he entered a contest between what he saw as an Evangelical and an Ecclesiastical Christianity, a contest which he believed was as old as the Gospel itself; and, as he told readers in the Preface, 'the ground assumed throughout is that of Evangelical Protestantism, the Protestantism of Luther, Calvin and our own Reformers, as distinguished from the political, eclectic and rationalistic systems which at different times have taken its place'. The arrangement of the work may be briefly described. In the first book an attempt was made to fix the true idea of the Church, that is to determine whether it was as the Romanist claimed an external institution or as Protestants claimed a society which has its true being or 'differentia' within. The second book is devoted to the consideration of the predicates or attributes of the Church as expressed in the Catholic Creeds and in the rival confessions of faith. The third book contains an exposition of the difference between the Roman Church and the Church of England on the subject of the ministry. In each area Litton attempted first to determine from the authentic documents of each party what was the real point at issue and then to examine to which side truth inclined. Unlike many of his contemporaries Litton read German and so his discussion of the topics was informed by his reading of works by Möhler and De Maistre on the Roman side and by Baur, Neander and Nitzsch on the Protestant side. Since Litton was, next to Goode, the most learned of Evangelical theologians, his work is valuable as a sophisticated presentation of a controversial doctrine. One weakness of it was that it assumed that the Protestant doctrine from the Anglican side was uniform, an assumption which Dr Woodhouse has shown cannot be maintained.[1]

Turning to the doctrines of Baptism and the Lord's Supper we find that the scene is dominated by important treatises from William Goode. During the Gorham controversy he published his *The Doctrine of the Church of England as to the effects of Baptism in the case of Infants* (1849). With the help of testimonies from divines of the sixteenth century he attempted to show what was the general doctrine of the Articles of Religion and Prayer Book. Then with testimonies from divines of later centuries he showed that the belief that spiritual regeneration always and invariably occurs in the baptism of infants had little or no support in the major Anglican traditions. Though the greater part of the book is taken up with extracts from the writings of bishops and divines there is interpretative comment which is perceptive. In his conclusions Goode anticipated not only the findings of the Judicial Committee of the Privy Council which were announced in 1850 but also the valuable study of J. B. Mozley entitled *A Review of the Baptismal Controversy* (1862).

Goode's large work, *The Nature of Christ's Presence in the Eucharist* (2 vols, 1856) is likewise dominated by quotations and was directed against the views of Denison, Wilberforce and Pusey.[2] This time the quotations came from both the Fathers and Anglican divines. They were followed in each case with careful comment and the whole purpose was to show that the Tractarian doctrine had certainly no justification in the Anglican tradition and only minimal justification in the patristic tradition. It has been claimed by W. H. MacKean that no opponent of the new doctrine was 'so learned and deeply read as William Goode' who not only covered a massive field but who showed 'a greater discrimination' than the Tractarians in sifting the complex evidence.[3]

Of popular sermons and pamphlets in these areas there was no shortage, especially on the topic of baptism. In view of the existence of the major books described above only minimal use will be made of the more popular literature. In particular the printed sermons of Hugh Stowell of Manchester entitled

Tractarianism Tested by Holy Scripture (2 vols, 1845–6) and which represent perhaps the most balanced, popular critique of Tractarianism, and those of Christopher Benson, Master of the Temple, entitled *Discourses upon Tradition and Episcopacy* (1839), which are profound in their simplicity, will be quoted.

3. WHAT IS THE RELATION OF THE INVISIBLE CHURCH AND THE VISIBLE CHURCHES?

To speak of the One, Holy, Catholic Church as invisible and churches as visible was fundamental to Victorian Evangelicalism, be it Anglican or Nonconformist. The invisible Church was taken to be the true Church of Christ and members of this Church, together with false professors of Christianity, were to be found in visible (parish) congregations. By this division Evangelicals believed that they were able to surmount the problems raised for them by the worldliness or even apostasy of both large churches and individual churchmen as well as by the existence of Protestant denominations and sects outside the State Churches of Europe. Also they felt able to support the printing and distribution of the Scriptures by the Bible Societies without reference to any specific ecclesiastical control. Evangelicals were confident that their doctrine faithfully expounded the insights and basic teaching of Holy Scripture and the Reformers.[4] So it is not surprising that in 1853 Goode claimed that the theological differences between Tractarianism and Evangelical Protestantism could be traced to different estimates of the relationship of the invisibility and visibility of the Church of Christ:

> Both the Roman and Tractarian systems are founded upon one and the same fundamental error; namely, that the true Church of Christ must be a body of individuals united together by external and visible bonds of union and communion, under the government of those ordained in succession from the Apostles as their bishops and pastors. From this primary false principle springs an abundant harvest of errors. Truth is sacrificed to unity. The 'priesthood' are exalted to a place not belonging to them, and the ministry of service is turned

into a ministry of *lordly government*. Usurped power is sustained by the expedients to which usurpers are wont to resort, fictions and delusions of every kind calculated to place the minds of men under their yoke. And the spiritual kingdom of Christ, of which hearts are the subjects, and His word and the unseen influences of His Spirit the ruling and directing authorities, is turned into an earthly kingdom, whose subjects are all those who submit themselves to certain human authorities and hold themselves bound by certain human laws.[5]

Therefore true Protestants put the spiritual kingdom of Christ first.

Initial Protestant theological reflection in the sixteenth century concerning the Church gladly took over the division into visible and invisible which was to be found in the writings of Augustine of Hippo.[6] For polemical reasons this way of looking at the subject appeared useful and so it was developed in the Reformed, Lutheran and Anglican traditions. However, while it appears specifically in the Reformed and Lutheran Confessions of Faith, it is not explicitly found in the Thirty-Nine Articles.[7] Article xix reads:

> The visible Church of Christ is a congregation of faithful men, in the which the pure Word of God is preached and the Sacraments be duly administered according to Christ's ordinance in all those things that of necessity are requisite to the same.
>
> As the Church of Jerusalem, Alexandria and Antioch have erred; so also the Church of Rome hath erred, not only in their living and manner of Ceremonies, but also in matters of Faith.

The roots of this Article are in the Augsburg Confession but the latter does not use the word 'visible'. It is possible to argue that this Article and others take for granted the doctrine of the invisible Church, a doctrine which is presupposed in the post-Communion prayer and the collect for All Saints' Day in the Prayer Book. Litton and other Evangelicals proceeded on the assumption that Article xix had to be interpreted by means of *Nowell's Catechism* (1570) and the Continental Confessions of Faith of the same period.[8]

On this basis Litton was able to provide a clear summary of the Protestant position on the invisibility of the Church in these words:

> The one true Church, the holy Catholic Church of the Creed, is not a body of mixed composition, comprehending within its pale both the evil and the good: it is the community of those who, wherever they may be, are in living union with Christ by faith, and partake of the sanctifying influences of His Spirit. Properly, it comprises, besides its members now upon earth, all who shall ultimately be saved. In its more confined acceptation, the phrase denotes the body of true believers existing at any given time in the world.
>
> The true Church is so far invisible as that it is not yet manifested in its corporate capacity; or, in other words; there is no one society, or visible corporation upon earth, of which it can be said that it is the mystical Body of Christ. Hence, of course, the Head of this Body is not visible.

Of the visible churches Litton wrote:

> Particular churches, otherwise unconnected societies, are one by reason of their common relation to, and connexion with, the one true Church or mystical Body of Christ. The outward notes of this connexion, and therefore of a true visible Church, are, the pure preaching of the Word (in fundamentals at least), and the administration of the Sacraments 'according to Christ's ordinance in all those things that of necessity are requisite to the same'. These are the two indispensable notes of true Church: to them may be added, though it stands not in the same order of necessity, the exercise of discipline.
>
> Although visible Churches are, according to the idea, 'congregations of the saints', i.e. really sanctified persons, and must be regarded as such if they are to have the name of Churches, yet they are never really so; in point of fact, they are always mixed communities, comprising hypocrites and nominal Christians, as well as true believers, a perfect separation between whom is, in the present life, impossible and is reserved to the Second Coming of Christ to judgment. Hence the aggregate of visible Christian Churches throughout the

world is not exactly identical with the true Church, which . . . consists only of the living members of Christ.

This way of understanding the doctrine of the Church became fairly common in Anglican theology and clearly surfaced in the controversy with Rome. For example, in the collection of controversial divinity of the seventeenth century known as *Bishop Gibson's Preservative Against Popery* it is both presupposed and argued explicitly.[9]

There is another way of understanding Article xix and that is to insist on the 'remarkable' fact that there is no reference whatever to the invisible Church in the whole Thirty-Nine Articles. It is possible to identify in the Prayer Book, the Ordinal and the Canons of 1604, a way of stating the relation of the invisibility and visibility of the Church which, while not being Roman, is neither Lutheran nor Reformed.[10] This alternative viewpoint works from a much closer identification of the visible and invisible seeing the two as two sides of one coin, or, as it were, of existing close together in parallel lines. So viewed from above the Church is the mystical Body of Christ (invisible from below) and viewed from below is the One, Holy, Catholic and Apostolic Church (divided into national Churches and other groupings). Such a way of stating the relation of the two does not necessarily imply that every baptised member of the visible churches is a member of the mystical Body of Christ, but it does affirm that much more of the New Testament teaching about the Church applies to the visible, continuing, historical, mixed churches than much sixteenth-century Protestant theology allowed. Perhaps in the Service of Infant Baptism this close relation of the mystical and the visible is clearly seen:

> We receive this Child into the congregation of Christ's flock . . . Seeing this Child is regenerate, and grafted into the body of Christ's Church . . . We yield Thee hearty thanks, most merciful Father, that it hath pleased Thee to regenerate this Infant with thy holy Spirit, to receive him for thine own Child by adoption and incorporate him into thy holy Church.

Apparently here it is understood that the child becomes a member of the Body of Christ and of the visible church where the baptism takes place. While this way of understanding the

Anglican doctrine appears to go more naturally with a high view of the historical episcopate and threefold ministry, many of those who were committed to it did nevertheless find room in their definitions of the visible Church for the Reformed and Lutheran Churches.[11]

Tractarianism is best seen as a development of this second way of understanding the Anglican tradition. Tractarians certainly did not deny that the Church could be, and indeed should be, described as both visible and invisible. Several of the early *Tracts* made use of this distinction and in some of the parochial sermons of Newman the relation of the two aspects of the Church is expressed in a beautiful way. There seems to be little doubt that for Newman the mystical Body was the primary concept but but he held that this divine, invisible reality was to be closely identified with the visible, historical, episcopal communion, as one superior reality hovering over and encircling another inferior reality.[12] Furthermore, William Palmer's *Treatise on the Church of Christ* (1838), which was highly respected by Tractarians, likewise accepted the distinction but, in a more scholastic fashion than Newman, saw a close relationship between the visible Catholic Church and the mystical Body of Christ. For this reason he was criticised by both McNeile and Litton.[13] What the Tractarians appear to have done, and to have done the more after *Tract 90*, was to insist that the mystical Body of Christ can be encountered and entered only through the sacraments of the visible, episcopal Churches, which alone make up the One, Holy, Catholic and Apostolic Church. Robert Wilberforce expressed this new emphasis when he wrote:

> For that which joins men to Christ's mystical Body, the Church, is their union with His man's nature; and their means of union with His man's nature is bestowed in His Church or Body mystical. This will become more evident when it is shown that the Sacraments, which are the means of binding us to the mystical Body of Christ, derive their efficacy from the influence of His body natural. And hence the impossibility of answering a question which is sometimes asked, whether men are joined to Christ by being joined to

His Church or joined to His Church by being joined to Him
... The two relations hang inseparably together. By the
mystical Body of Christ is meant the whole family of those
who by the Holy Ghost are united in Church ordinances to
His man's nature. Our real union with each is what gives us a
part in the other.[14]

To the ear of the Evangelical these statements sounded like a
claim that Christ was being replaced by Episcopal Church and
Sacraments.[15]

In 1843 Goode regretted that this development of the doctrine of the Church was taking place within Tractarian thinking; he also regretted that it was being justified by reference to
earlier Anglican divines. It was his conviction that Tractarians
were confusing two different questions by making them identical
questions. 'What constitutes a man a member of the visible
Church?' was being equated with 'What unites a man to
Christ and constitutes him a member of his body?' Because they
were treating the two different questions as the same question
the Tractarians were equating entry into the invisible Church
with entry into the visible parish congregation. As he was very
much aware that High Church divines had taken great care in
the controversy with Roman Catholicism to show that the Roman
claim of the identification of the Roman Church with the
mystical Body of Christ was untenable, Goode re-published short
treatises by Thomas Jackson (1579–1640) and Robert Sanderson
(1587–1663), both authors whom Tractarians esteemed.[16] In
a long introduction he showed that Jackson, especially, though
he had a high view of the visible churches ruled by bishops,
did nevertheless teach that it was possible to be a member
of the mystical Body of Christ without being a member of an
episcopal communion. More importantly, Jackson taught that
spiritual union with Christ and membership of his Body by the
grace of adoption was primary and was attainable without
necessary recourse to the sacraments administered by an episcopally ordained priest; the One, Holy Catholic and Apostolic
Church was the mystical Body of Christ. Therefore, instead
of following the Anglican fathers it was the case, Goode believed, that 'the attention of the Tractarian is directed to the

G

determination of the nature and constitution of the visible Church as it existed in primitive times and, having laid down an exclusive rule of Church government and discipline, he affirms that those who only have submitted to this form Christ's Body and are united to Him and His Church'. Litton agreed and argued that Tractarians put themselves into an intellectually embarrassing position when they rejected both the Romanist doctrine of the universal Church under a visible head and the Protestant doctrine of the priority of the invisible Church under an invisible Head. Their *via media* was a 'no man's land'.

While Goode appears to have been ready to develop a doctrine of the Church based on the writings of both Elizabethan and Caroline divines, Litton appears to have believed that the Protestant Confessions of Faith of the sixteenth century had said all that was necessary – at least in terms of principles if not of terminology. McNeile's position, though not precisely stated, appears to have been that of Litton except that he took great care to emphasise the idea of predestination as central to the understanding of the invisible Church.

On the basis of the biblical evidence (mostly Pauline) which he examined Litton expressed the opinion that

> The expression Catholic Church may be, as it is commonly in the Fathers, very fitly used to denote the whole or the totality of the churches which make up, at any given time, visible Christendom; but all, save Romanists, hold that the aspect which visible Christendom is ordinarily to present is that, not of one visibly organised society, but of a collection of societies, founded on certain common principles: the Catholic Church in this sense being nothing but an aggregate of local Christian societies, distinct from and independent of each other. But there is something more than this involved in the figurative terms 'Body of Christ' or 'spiritual house' by which the Church . . . is commonly described.[17]

The something more was the mystical Body of Christ, the invisible Church which is an object of faith in the creed. Of this Communion he claimed that 'as the characteristic of the mystical Body of Christ is organic unity under one Head, so the component members of it are not churches but individuals'. Then from such passages as Ephesians 4.15–16, 2.20–2 and Colossians 2.19 he claimed to deduce that:

> The union of the members with the Head here described is such, that the vital energy which animates the whole Body flows directly, and by virtue of real incorporation from the Head into each member; a kind of union of which, as it is evident, a society, as such, is incapable. Between a local church, or collection of such churches, and Christ there is no vital, organic connexion such as exists between the branches of a tree and the tree itself; it is individual believers who are in Christ, as the branches are in the vine; it is into individuals and not merely into communities as such that the influences of the Spirit are derived from the Head.

He reinforced this last point when he wrote that local churches may only be said to have Christ as their Head in a mediate sense, the reason being that 'the societies are churches of Christ but it is the individuals who compose them that are (if they be in truth what they profess to be) members of Christ's Body'.[18]

For McNeile, as was noted above, predestination was the key to the understanding of the reality of the invisible Church. To have clear views of the Church of God in Christ was to see the Church as composed of four classes of people.[19] The first consisted of those who 'have fallen asleep in Jesus' and 'whose spirits . . . are present with the Lord in joy and felicity'. Then on earth there are those 'who are quickened into spiritual life by divine grace . . . and who walk by faith and not by sight'. Also on earth are those who, being fore-ordained by God unto salvation, are still in sin and await the work of the Holy Spirit in their hearts, producing repentance and faith. Finally, there are those yet to be born into the world who are elect according to the foreknowledge of God and who will be regenerated by the Spirit after their earthly birth.

McNeile, apparently, had no problems with the word 'invisible' but Litton did. He believed that 'it gave occasion to the papal theologians to charge their adversaries sometimes with reducing the Church to a platonic republic, having no actual existence, and sometimes with making two distinct Churches – a visible and invisible one'. Therefore he suggested that the

'Reformers would have better expressed their meaning and avoided the risk of misrepresentation had they, instead of saying that the true Church is invisible, simply affirmed that that which constitutes the true being of the Church is invisible'.[20] That which was the true being of the Church was expressed in the heart of the doctrine of justification by faith, that is the grace of God and the living faith of men, both unseen but both real. This vital union of individuals to Christ, at present an object of faith expressed in the creed as belief in the One Catholic Church, will at the end of the age become an object of sight, but until that glorious moment 'it is as regards its proper organic unity, or its corporate capacity, invisible'. This explanation does not, of course, change the basic position; it only clarifies further the nature of the mystical Body of Christ.

Happily, some recent Protestant theology has attempted to avoid what in Litton and others appears to be a dualistic (the marked separation of the invisible Church from the visible churches) and individualistic (the insistence that the relation of Christ to a congregation is only in terms of relations with individuals) approach. Karl Barth, for example, has condemned what he calls an ecclesiastical docetism and has emphasised that the one Church is both invisible and visible. There is not some invisible Church different from the visible churches; rather, by the eye of faith the Christian sees the invisible Church in and through the visible churches.[21]

4. IS THE EPISCOPACY OF THE 'ESSE' OR THE 'BENE ESSE' OF THE CHURCH?

Tractarians did not doubt that the historical episcopate was of the 'esse' of the Church. In their view this was needed in order to guarantee the orders of presbyters, who in turn administered valid sacraments of efficacious grace, especially the Eucharist by which spiritual union with Christ was achieved and sustained. Writing in 1839 when the *Tracts* were still regularly appearing Benson could state with some justice:

I cannot but think that the doctrines laid down in the *Tracts for the Times* though they neither deny salvation to Presbyterians as individuals, nor *expressly* unchurch the Presbyterian communities, do still imply that there is no ground for believing, but rather every reason to disbelieve the validity of any of their ministrations. And if so, I apprehend, a Presbyterian would not be able to see much difference between the two views.[22]

What was implicit in 1839 was made explicit in the next two decades.

Looking at the relation of the invisible and visible aspects of the Church and at the purpose and efficacy of the sacraments from a different perspective, the Evangelicals viewed episcopacy as of the 'bene esse' of the Church. For example, Bishop Daniel Wilson made the following positive affirmation in 1843:

> Our episcopal form of Church government affords us the best means under God of preserving the faith. Had Protestant Germany retained her Episcopacy the Neology of the last hundred years might possibly have been averted. Had Reformed France kept her Episcopacy the Arianism of the eighteenth century might never have prevailed. Had Geneva preserved the primitive order of church government she might never have apostosized from the principles of her great founder. If the Church of England is to be saved peaceably and in an orderly manner it is her bishops who under God must save her.[23]

He saw Tractarianism and Latitudinarianism as the threats. Ironically it was the same order of bishops whom Tractarians elevated to whom Wilson looked for the removal of Tractarianism from the Church. *Tract 10* had claimed that 'he that despiseth the Bishops despiseth the Apostles', but there was point to Archbishop Whateley's oft-quoted comment that 'by none is a professed veneration for the episcopal office carried to a more extravagant height than by some who . . . set at nought with the greatest contumely every Bishop who ventures to disagree with them'.[24]

The majority of Evangelicals, including those whom Conybeare called the 'Recordites', appear to have believed that the episcopal form of government was instituted by the apostles and was the polity God intended should be the norm in the visible churches. McNeile, Stowell and Seeley (Recordites?), Benson and Litton all took for granted that in his consecrating of Timothy and Titus, the apostle Paul was creating the distinction between a bishop and a presbyter. Litton wrote:

> Since it is an historical fact that towards the close of the apostolic age the ministry is found to have assumed the episcopal form, and that to the bishop was reserved the right of ordaining, the ministerial commission must, of course, have descended in the line of the episcopate. The fact, therefore, that the ministerial commission, beginning with the apostles, was perpetuated in the episcopate as its regular channel for more than 1500 years after the commencement of the Church is undeniable.[25]

One author who did not believe that the distinction between bishop and presbyter was created in the apostolic period was Charles Bowdler, but he did allow that it began and became the norm in the period immediately following the apostolic times. Opposing the high claims of Tractarians he agreed that 'the worth of episcopacy is readily granted' and proceeded:

> High antiquity, everything short of apostolic origin and appointment is conceded to it, with all of privilege and authority that can be asked for it on that account. What is denied to it is heavenly birth; its asserted institution by our Lord or his apostles; and the consequent claim to that exclusive purity which belongs to any stream whose fountain is divine.[26]

In this last denial he spoke for Evangelicals as a whole who did not believe that any special grace was communicated in the succession of bishops; for them grace was related to the truth of the Gospel and the power of the Spirit while the succession related to the areas of good order and historical continuity.

All Evangelicals appear to have believed that while much could be said in terms of the superiority of the episcopal form of Church government, it could not be said to belong to the centre of the Gospel, or the centre of the Christian Faith. Hugh Stowell claimed:

> We find enough in apostolic precedent, in primitive usage, and in universal order to warrant, nay, we conceive to en-

force our conscientious adhesion to an episcopal church, where the church maintains the truth; but we do not find anything which authorizes us to demand the same adhesion at the hands of others, on peril of their souls. Repentance, faith, obedience – these are clearly constituted conditions of acceptance with God, but not so the possession of an episcopal ministry. And shall we presume to be more exclusive than God, or to make the strait gate narrower than He has made it? Can we hold that episcopacy is necessary to the prosperity without holding that it is essential to the existence of a church?[27]

And Christopher Benson likewise claimed:

Nowhere in the Gospel is a perfect uniformity of ecclesiastical polity so indispensably required as to make it meet for any Christian to pass an absolute sentence of excommunication upon a brother who differs from himself. To his own master he standeth or falleth and our duty lies rather in persuading him to agreement than in urging condemnation because he disagrees with ourselves.[28]

Or, in a brief sentence of Seeley, the Church of England 'carefully abstains from making episcopacy an indispensable requisite in a Christian Church'.[29] Evangelicals were confident that the majority of evidence from Anglican tradition was in favour of the position to which they were committed. To show that even High Church divines held to it Goode printed a letter of Bishop Cosin (1594–1672), containing acceptance of the orders of foreign pastors, in the volume in which were Jackson and Sanderson's treatises.[30]

The spiritual and moral reasons why Evangelicals could not deny the validity of the ministry of Lutherans, Presbyterians and Nonconformists is well expressed in the words of Stowell:

Much as we prize uniformity, how much more ought we to prize living union with Christ. The former without the latter is the shell without the kernel, the body without the soul. Show us the image of our Saviour, in lowliness, in meekness, in patience, in love, in spirituality of mind, in holiness of character, in all the fruits of the Spirit – and if we love the original we cannot but love the likeness. We shall love it when set in alloyed metal, though we may love it better when set in the fine gold of the sanctuary. We are bound to love the pious dissenter *as a brother*, we are not bound to love him *as a dissenter*. His dissent we deplore; his holiness we love.[31]

If pious Dissenters were in spiritual union with the same living Lord by the same Holy Spirit then they could not be treated as heathen and their ministers could not be treated as mere laymen. And if this were true of separatists from the Church of England how much more was it true of the State Churches of Europe and of Scotland. It is significant that Dr Darwell Stone, a noted Anglo-Catholic historian, was obliged to admit that any appeal to the sixteenth and seventeenth centuries in terms of the Anglican tradition is a broken reed for anything except the practical requirement of episcopal ordination in the Church of England.[32] And this was a position which Goode clearly argued in 1852 in his controversy with Chancellor Harington.

5. WHAT ARE THE SPIRITUAL EFFECTS OF INFANT BAPTISM?

This was the vital question at the heart of the Gorham controversy. The Bishop of Exeter, supported by Tractarians, insisted that there was only *one* way to interpret Scripture and the Anglican formularies and that was by stating that regeneration always occurs in baptism conducted within the episcopal communion in services taken by ordained clergy. By regeneration they meant the infusion of grace into the soul, which in turn included the forgiveness of original sin and incorporation into the mystical Body of Christ. This, of course, was not very far removed from the Roman position of the *ex opere operato* nature of baptism, a point which Phillpotts actually conceded.[33] It could claim support from antiquity and from strands of the Anglican tradition.[34]

It was noted in the description of the historical development of the controversy that the topic of baptismal regeneration early became a major focus of attention so that there was at no time after 1838 a shortage of pamphlets, printed sermons and magazine articles on the subject. Such stalwarts as T. T. Biddulph, the leader of Bristol Evangelicalism, and Henry Budd, the passionate advocate of the writings of the English Reformers, reprinted their earlier books with suitable prefaces related to Tractarianism. The *Record* claimed that 'the subject of infant regeneration must be considered the theological turning point of this age in the Church'. This was written on 6 May, 1844. A year earlier another Evangelical had written: 'It is idle to deny, or to undervalue, the strength of the testimony on which the doctrine of baptismal regeneration is founded. In Scripture, in the writings of the early Christians, in the standards of our own Church and in the works of our own Reformers, we constantly find baptism spoken of in a tone quite irreconcileable with the hasty dismissal of the subject by which many modern writers attempt to settle the question.'[35]

Though Evangelicals to a man opposed the dogmatism of Phillpotts and his supporters they did not agree among themselves as to the doctrine of infant baptism. Before attempting to summarize Goode's response it will be useful to note the different approaches to this sacrament which, according to S. C. Wilks, appear to have been held within Evangelicalism as legitimate interpretations of the Thirty-Nine Articles and the Book of Common Prayer.[36] These approaches are to be seen as being rooted in one or more of the tributaries of the Anglican tradition but as having solidified in the controversy over baptism which followed Bishop Mant's controversial *Tracts on Regeneration and Conversion*, based on his earlier Bampton Lectures on the same topic. They were published by the SPCK in 1815 and thus had the appearance of being 'official' Church teaching. In them Mant argued that regeneration, the infusion of grace, always occurs at baptism and that if the child who receives this grace is brought up in a Christian environment then he or she will not need to be converted later but will grow into the faith and obedience of Christ; however, if the grace is lost then there will be need for a fresh turning to God in repentance and faith, that is, a conversion experience. A lot of Evangelicals disagreed with him and so there was a protracted debate involving Biddulph, Daniel Wilson, Charles Simeon, John W. Cunningham and others.[37]

In 1844 Wilks claimed that Evangelical views could be divided into four types. First of all there were those who, following the Augustinian footsteps of Archbishop Ussher, affirmed that all who are regenerated are regenerated in or at baptism.[38] Baptism was thus seen as the 'instrument' of regeneration, as taught in Article XXVII ('. . . . as by an instrument, they that receive baptism are grafted into the Church'). To quote Wilks: 'They would not consider that an unbaptized adult though [seemingly] in a state of repentance, faith and holiness was regenerate if the sacrament had not yet been administered to him; and they would consider that an adult who had been baptized in infancy, but had lived an ungodly life, without any indication of renewal of heart, if he was at length led to repentance and faith was not then regenerated; but, that he had been regenerated in baptism, though until now the seed sown did not give signs of vegetation'. Regeneration is here understood in terms of the implantation by the Holy Spirit of the principle of new life in the soul. This approach, a modification of that found in the Lutheran formularies, connects regeneration with both divine election and with baptism so that all who are elect according to the foreknowledge of God are regenerated in baptism, being born 'of water and of the Spirit'. It was taken for granted that the children of Christians who were brought to baptism were of the elect and would be brought up in the nurture and admonition of the Lord so that the seed of heavenly life would blossom into full Christian commitment.

Secondly, there were those who, influenced by Henry Budd, and including Edward Bickersteth and Hugh McNeile, also closely connected baptism with both regeneration and eternal election.[39] They claimed that on the analogy of the baptism of adult believers regeneration (again understood as the implantation of eternal life and incorporation into the mystical Body of Christ) occurred prior to baptism in response to the prayer of God's people (the prayer beginning 'Almighty, everliving God . . .) in order that baptism could be a full sign of an inward spiritual change and a seal of God's gracious promises towards the child. Again it is presumed that a baptised child, brought up in a Christian home and the visible Church, will come personally to profess the faith which is already his.

Thirdly, there were those who understood regeneration as being synonymous with conversion and as being impossible without being accompanied by repentance towards God, saving faith in Jesus Christ and the visible fruit of the Spirit in the life. Biddulph, Wilson and M'Ilvaine, with perhaps the majority of Evangelicals held one or other form of this approach.[40] They could not allow that divine life implanted in infancy at baptism could take ten, fifteen or twenty years to manifest itself in a conversion experience. For them regeneration had to be a visible change of character and attitude. The baptism of infants was approached through a simple covenant theology; the promises of salvation were declared and a sign and seal of them given because of the belief in the faithfulness of God to honour his covenant-promise which is 'to you and to your children' (Acts 2.39). Thus baptism involved no immediate, inward change but the confirmation of God's covenant promise that he would, when the child reached an age of discretion, work salvation in the life. This covenant approach was possible for both Calvinists and Arminians, for Biddulph as well as for Heurtley; it popularised the familiar idea of 'charitable supposition' in Evangelical vocabulary. That is, it was charitably supposed that the parents and sponsors of the child who made the profession of faith were truly Christians and that their child was therefore an heir of the promises of God in the Gospel. It perhaps needs to be added that a covenant theology was also behind the first two views described above, but in their case the grace of the covenant was immediately given, not held over until later years.

Fourthly, there were those who made a distinction between ecclesiastical (or sacramental) and spiritual regeneration. Henry Ryder, the first Evangelical bishop, felt obliged to do this and wrote of ecclesiastical regeneration:

I would . . . wish generally to restrict the term to the baptismal privileges and considering them as comprehending, not only external admission into the visible church – not only a covenanted title to the pardon and peace of the Gospel but even a degree of spiritual aid vouchsafed and ready to offer itself to our acceptance or rejection, at the dawn of reason.[41]

The strength of this approach was that it did take seriously the fact that in the service of the Prayer Book the child is actually pronounced regenerate. Its weakness was that it used regeneration in two ways, reserving full or true regeneration until conversion later in life.

With this sketch of Evangelical views completed, the contribution of Goode can now be examined. Goode's primary aim, a negative one, was to prove that the Church of England does not teach that all infants who are baptised are necessarily regenerated, that is made members of the mystical Body of Christ. In pursuing this aim it was not his purpose to attempt to prove that spiritual regeneration never took place in baptism, for he obviously believed that in some, perhaps many, cases it did occur. Rather he opposed the view which claimed that wherever an episcopally ordained clergyman baptises a child and uses the service of the Prayer Book that child is born into the kingdom of God and adopted into his heavenly family. Conceding that some roots for this view could be found in divines of the Laudian school and more recently in the *Tracts* of Mant he was quite sure that the major strands of the Anglican tradition did not support it, even though a full-blown *ex opere operato* doctrine could be found in Tridentine Catholicism and earlier Western theology. What he found through his historical researches was that the Church of England allowed not one but a cluster of views concerning the effects of infant baptism. And he believed this to be a wise position in view of the nature of the case:

> It must be carefully remembered, that as the doctrine of Infant Baptism is deduced inferentially, and by analogical reasoning, from statements of scripture applying more expressly to the case of adult baptism, so the doctrine of the *effects* of infant baptism can be obtained only in the same way. Now as we deduce without difficulty, in one case, the *fact* that baptism is to be administered; so, in the other, we equally without doubt, deduce the fact that there is, *under corresponding circumstances*, a blessing given to the child similar to that given to the adult.[42]

But what were the corresponding circumstances? It appears that they were the suppositions that the infant in question was from a Christian home and would, when it reached the age of responsibility, personally appropriate the faith into which it had been baptised.

From this basis Goode allowed that there were several legitimate interpretations of Article XXVII and the services of the Prayer Book. It was possible to follow the learned Dr Jackson and distinguish between a measure of regeneration suitable to a child, that is a regeneration which removes the guilt of original sin and ensures that a child dying in infancy will go to heaven, and a fuller measure of regeneration later in life which is related to the exercise of repentance, faith and love.[43] Then it was possible to link the efficacy of baptism to divine election so that baptism becomes the instrument by which the elect child is incorporated by a spiritual birth into the mystical Body of Christ. The first two Evangelical views described above may be seen as subdivisions of this general position.

Also, it could be held, as Bishop Hooper appears to have taught, that the efficacy of baptism depended upon the prevision or foreknowledge by God of future faith and repentance in the child in a subsequent period of life.[44] Therefore, as Goode commented,

> In such cases, it may be fairly held that the guilt of original sin being removed from the child baptised, as the child of a believer (the vicarious faith of the parent uniting with baptism to produce this result), it is in *contemplation* of its subsequent faith and repentance, *then promised for it*, made a member of the true Church of Christ, and so regenerate.[45]

The best way to illustrate this position, thought Goode, was by the example of an estate purchased by trustees for a minor on the condition (promised by them on his behalf) that when he came of age he would pay a certain amount of money before taking up the full possession of the estate. Here the estate is his, but only his hypothetically until he pays the money; likewise faith and repentance being foreseen by God in the child the covenant made in baptism is valid and effectual and therefore the child is assumed by the Church to be a member of the mystical Body of Christ. The third Evangelical view described above was of this type, though in the majority of nineteenth-century expositions it did not appear to have the certainty of the future regeneration which is found in Hooper's writings. A further position was admissible, said Goode, and that was the position of Luther which stated that as faith and repentance is required in an adult so likewise, in proportion, were they required of infants in order to the full blessing of the ordinance. This faith of the infant could be described as true faith or as the seed or principle of faith. In his *Larger Catechism* Luther wrote that infants are brought to baptism '*hac spe atque animo, quod certo credant*'. This approach was held by Lancelot Ridley, whom Cranmer made one of the six preachers of Canterbury in 1551.[46]

So Goode was prepared to defend any doctrine which came within the areas delineated by these four general positions as being in harmony with the principles of the Articles and Prayer Book. However, he was of the opinion that the separation of ecclesiastical and spiritual regeneration, favoured by Bishop Ryder, was an unacceptable way to interpret the Anglican formularies. Where Phillpotts and the Tractarians were wrong was in their supposition 'that because they are ministers of Christ, and that certain ministrations were appointed for certain ends, therefore those ministrations must always be effectual to the accomplishment of those ends'. Goode conceded that this view was logical but its 'fallacy lies in arguing from a general statement, where conditions are tacitly implied, to particular cases in which those conditions are not fulfilled'.

Goode's personal position was a positive one:

Baptism is the formal act of incorporation into Christ's Body, the Church; not merely the visible Church, but (when God acts in the ordinance) the true Church, the mystical Body of Christ. And therefore it may justly be said, that, where it is efficacious, that we are regenerated by it. For whereas, before, we were only the children of Adam, and so of wrath; we are hereby made children of grace, members of Christ. But it must be remembered that as in the natural birth, there was life previously; so in the spiritual new birth, life, a living principle of faith must have been implanted to make the birth by baptism effectual to the production of a being spiritually alive.[47]

Here he is taking what may be described as a Lutheran view and he was quite convinced that in the Service for the Baptism of Infants the blessing prayed for, and the blessing given, were nothing less than true spiritual regeneration and incorporation into the mystical Body of Christ.

It would appear that because of the intensity of feeling raised by the Gorham controversy there developed in Evangelicalism such a fear of baptismal regeneration *ex opere operato* that gradually all views involving full baptismal regeneration were given up and thus part of Evangelical belief later in the century was the denial of baptismal regeneration.

6. IN WHAT SENSE IS CHRIST PRESENT IN THE EUCHARIST?

In the century which preceded the Oxford Movement there were three major doctrines of the Eucharist found in the Church of England, usually described as the Virtualist, the Memorialist and the Receptionist. To understand both the Tractarian developed doctrine and the Evangelical response it is necessary to understand these three positions. Often associated with John Johnson (1662–1725) of Cranbrook, author of *The Unbloody Sacrifice*, was the Virtualist teaching;[48] this was characterised by Tractarians as the doctrine of the real absence, a significant comment when it is recalled that Non-Jurors held to this doctrine. The bread and wine, once set apart by consecration, become means by which the grace of God is conveyed to the recipients. The presence of Christ is not actually in them but they are more than mere figurative or representative symbols. Though they are not actually the body and blood of Christ they are so in virtue, power and effect through the power of the Holy Spirit. That is, by the grace and power of God, the symbols of bread and wine are instrumentally efficacious and thus 'virtue' or true grace is conveyed by them. One notable teacher of this doctrine in the nineteenth century was Alexander Knox of Ireland, who insisted that the consecrated symbols were actually vehicles through which the blessings of God were conveyed.[49]

The memorialist view is associated primarily with the name of Bishop Benjamin Hoadly (1676–1761) whose treatise on the Eucharist was entitled *A Plain Account of the Nature and End of the Sacrament of the Lord's Supper*. Removing much of the mystery from the sacrament, and probably reacting against transubstantiation, he insisted that Christ was present only in the same way that he was in all worship and fellowship; the purpose of the sacrament was to commemorate, not to partake of or in the the benefits of Christ's death. Seen as memorials of the body and blood of Christ, the taking of bread and wine leads God's people to such good thoughts, resolutions and practices as will strengthen their faith and their Christian witness. Hoadly's view was acceptable to those of a latitudinarian frame of mind and according to the Tractarians the low views of this sacrament in the first third of the nineteenth century could be traced to his influence.

The classic exposition of the Receptionist position is in the book, *A Review of the Doctrine of the Eucharist* by Daniel Waterland (1683–1740). Probably the most widespread doctrine of the Eucharist in England it was held by High Churchmen and Evangelicals and is clearly expressed in the eucharistic hymns of Charles Wesley. Mackean neatly summarises it as follows:

> The bread and wine by consecration are set apart for a new and holy use but they remain bread and wine. The presence or gift is not in the elements nor associated with them. But Christ is present wherever two or three are gathered together in His name; and as the faithful communcant takes part in the sacred service of remembrance, and receives the appointed symbols of Christ's body and blood, his faith opens the door by which the presence of Christ enters the soul. The whole service as well as the reception of the symbols is the means whereby the communicant realises Christ's presence and receives His gifts and is united with Him; the elements are efficacious signs that strengthen his faith and love. Christ can be said to be specially present because He is specially remembered.

Mackean adds that the expression 'the real presence' can be used in this way of understanding the Eucharist and then the idea is usually of Christ as the unseen Giver, who presides at the sacred meal.[50]

While the Tractarian doctrine of the Eucharist could be said to have had its roots in both the Virtualist and Receptionist schemes and to have been a reaction against the Memorialist, it was also a doctrine which reached its mature expression only after 1845. Though earlier expositions were rightly criticised as containing novel emphases as far as the Anglican tradition was concerned, they were not precise formulations and so were open to a variety of interpretations – Pusey's University Sermon of 1843, for example. The later developed teaching of Pusey, Wilberforce and Denison was different from the earlier in that its essential points were clear to both friend and foe. With such studies as those of Mackean and Alf Härdelin we do have available sound expositions of this developed Tractarian doctrine, the very teaching which was challenged by Goode in 1856 and by John Harrison and T. S. L. Vogan in 1871.[51]

To attempt to summarise the Tractarian position is a big undertaking but Goode made the attempt as follows:

> The doctrine of Archdeacon Denison and Dr Pusey . . . is that, in the Lord's Supper, the Bread and Wine are so influenced and operated on by the act of consecration, that though bread and wine remain, yet there is by consecration a real though spiritual presence of the Body and Blood of Christ so united to the Bread and Wine as to form with them one compound whole; and hence that the Body and Blood of Christ are received by *all* the communicants whatever their state of mind may be. Whether they are present by transfusion or conjunction, they do not clearly state – and the difference is unimportant except as affecting the terms used – but it is maintained that that which the communicant puts into his mouth consists of two parts, one bread and wine, the other the Body and Blood of Christ present in a spiritual and supernatural manner in conjunction with the bread and wine.[52]

The position of Wilberforce was similar but not exactly the

same in that he spoke of 'the essential or substantial presence of Christ's body' in the consecrated bread, and wrote: 'Christ is present Himself, and not merely by His influence, effects, and operation; by that essence, and in that substance which belongs to Him as the true Head of mankind. And therefore He is really present; and gives His body to be the *res sacramenti*, or thing signified.' Wilberforce also held that the process by which Christ's body and blood act upon the receiver is spiritual and not physical. Only through the soul did the body and blood of Christ act upon man and for this action he saw faith as essential if the *res sacramenti* was to be the spiritual nourishment of the soul. So though the body and blood of Christ are received by the mouth they do not affect the body except through the soul and the soul cannot profit by their nourishment unless it is alive through faith.[53]

In his preliminary comments on the Tractarian doctrine Goode pointed out that there was little difference between the position of Pusey and Denison and that of the Lutheran theologian, Johann Gerhard (1582–1637).[54] Though Denison had denied that his doctrine was close to that of consubstantiation, he was, maintained Goode, totally ignorant of the writings of Lutheran divines and so unable to judge the matter. Pusey, who did not make such disclaimers, was unwilling to admit the similarity of his position to that of Lutheranism but his early studies in Germany and his long friendship with Professor F. A. G. Tholuck of Halle pointed in this direction.[55] Of Wilberforce, Goode was unable to say that he had adopted fully the doctrine of transubstantiation but he did claim that the former Archdeacon had come sufficiently near to it for it to be said that the only difference between his doctrine and that of Rome was a matter of words. It was not an accident, Goode claimed, that the *Dublin Review* and the *Rambler* were able to welcome Wilberforce's book on the Eucharist as containing doctrine which they could recognise as being substantially that of their own Church.[56]

Before noticing some of the theological, philosophical and historical objections raised by Goode there are two preliminary points which he made and are worth mentioning.[57] First of all he contended that Tractarians had confounded two entirely distinct assertions: they equated the doctrine of 'the Real Presence' with their own 'doctrine of the Real Presence in the consecrated elements' and gave the impression that only they who believed the latter believed the former. This was not acceptable when the Articles of the Church taught the doctrine of the Real Presence not actually in or with the consecrated bread and wine but perceived and received by faith after a heavenly and spiritual manner. Secondly, he pointed out that Tractarian authors had made 'a remarkable blunder' in using a quotation from an advertisement in the first *Book of Homilies* (1547). The advertisement of the printer included the words, 'due receiving of His Blessed Body and Blood, under the form of bread and wine', which, on the surface, appeared to agree with or to confirm the doctrine of Pusey, Wilberforce and Denison. When the second *Book of Homilies* was added, in which was contained a homily against transubstantiation and related doctrines, certain printers continued to print the old advertisement, though it had never been a part of the actual first *Book of Homilies*. Instead of recognising that the words had no authority, at least two Tractarians quoted them as if they were an account of the teaching of the Church.[58]

Following an examination of what he considered bad exegesis of Holy Scripture by the three Tractarians he was opposing, Goode put forward ten objections to the Tractarian doctrine and eight 'sophisms and fallacies' by which the doctrine was maintained. There is space here only to note brief examples. Two of the objections can, however, be taken together.[59] They are:

1. The doctrine in question is opposed to the testimony of Scripture as to Christ's departure from the world, ascension, and session at the right hand of the Father until the end of the world.
2. That Christ's body, being a human body, cannot be present in more than one place at one and the same time.

The three Tractarians had claimed that while Christ with his glorified human nature was localised in heaven, the same human nature, through its unique relation with the divine nature was, in the Spirit and by the love and omnipotence of

God, present in or with the elements of bread and wine in the Eucharist.[60] Admitting that truly God can do anything, Goode maintained that his omnipotence does not involve contradictions. The Tractarian position contained three contradictions. It was claimed that one finite, created body, remaining one, should at one and the same time exist in different places in two totally different forms – one material the other immaterial, one tangible the other intangible, one passible the other impassible; that is, should in fact be two bodies. Secondly, with specific reference to the Body of Christ eaten in the Eucharist, it was maintained that a finite, created body was in many different places at the same time and under different circumstances. Thirdly, it involved the self-contradiction that a body remaining a body should nevertheless be without any of those properties which are the distinguishing characteristics of a body, that is be a body but not yet a body but a spirit, at one and the same time. As Goode surveyed his opponents' books he could not but remark that the arguments used by learned divines and bishops of the Church of England against the confusion of thought concerning the Body of Christ involved in the two theories of consubstantiation and transubstantiation applied equally well against the general position of the Tractarians.[61]

An example of a sophism was:

> The charge of Zwinglianism or Calvinism against all who interpret the words of institution figuratively; and the calumny that a denial of the real bodily presence in the elements involves the assertion that the consecrated bread and wine are in all cases mere naked and inoperative signs.

To show that many learned Anglicans, especially authors favoured by Tractarians, interpreted the words 'This is my body' figuratively, Goode quoted from their works. After making the point that 'all who do not hold a real corporeal or bodily presence must maintain that the words of institution were spoken in a figurative sense' he went on to show how the doctrine of the Church of England differed from Zwinglianism (another term for Memorialism). 'Our Church', he wrote, 'does not hold that the consecrated elements are inoperative signs, to the reception of which by the faithful no particular blessing is, by promise, attached; but, that they are effective instruments, in the case of all faithful recipients, for bringing the communicant into a state of spiritual union and communion with Christ, and causing him to enjoy the blessings which such an union brings with it.'

Having discussed the Tractarian doctrine with the aid of theology, history and philosophy, Goode applied himself to the question whether the early Fathers taught such an objective presence of the Body and Blood of Christ, in, with, or under the consecrated bread and wine, or under their forms, as to make with them one conjoined whole, so that the Body and Blood were substantially, though in a spiritual and immaterial form, received into the mouths of the communicants. This massive enquiry took nearly four hundred pages and that which he believed he found to be the truth of the matter he expressed in two brief paragraphs.

> First, that the Fathers, generally, did not hold, that the real Body and Blood of Christ, in any form, are so joined to the consecrated bread and wine, or so exist under their forms, that they are received into the mouths of the communicants; but that the mode of reception is spiritual, that is, by the soul or spirit, the sole mean by which they are received being faith.

> Secondly, that the Fathers generally held that the wicked, who have no faith, do not eat and drink the real Body and Blood of Christ; but only the Sacramental Body and Blood of Christ, that is the sacred symbols and representatives of them.

One of his major complaints against the way in which Wilberforce and Pusey interpreted the Fathers was that they did not take sufficient account of the simple fact that 'signs are commonly called by the Fathers by the names of the things signified'. Other complaints he made included the point that they did not always take into account that the Fathers were not obliged to use precise language in areas where later controversy was to show the need for precision, and the further point that there is a love in the Fathers for mystifying the doctrines and rites of the Faith, a tendency to be explained in terms of their education in pagan philosophy.

Goode's second volume is given over to an examination of the teaching of the formularies and writings of divines of the Church of England. The joint testimony of the latter who included men from the sixteenth, seventeenth and eighteenth centuries, mostly High Churchmen, was, he believed, to show an unqualified rejection of the doctrine of the real presence of the substance of the Body and Blood of Christ, even in a supernatural mode of existence, or in a spiritual and immaterial form, in or under the consecrated bread and wine, or under their forms. Goode's own understanding of the doctrine of the Church of England was what was described above as the Receptionist position, although he did not outlaw the Virtualist position. He obviously believed that the Memorialist position was inadequate.

To summarise the Evangelical response to the Tractarian doctrine of the presence of Christ in the Eucharist it may be said that it was argued that there is no foundation for the doctrine either in the Fathers or in Anglican divinity; the only foundations for it were in the Roman doctrine of transubstantiation and the Lutheran doctrine of consubstantiation. It was, therefore, a major innovation in the doctrinal tradition of the Church of England.

Few scholars today would question Goode's conclusions about the teaching of Anglican divines from the sixteenth to the eighteenth centuries. Few also would question that in the Fathers of the first three centuries there is no doctrine of the Real Presence which approaches that of Pusey and Wilberforce. The early Fathers are realist in their interpretation, taking the consecrated bread and wine to be what they were designated to be, the Saviour's body and blood. However, the later Fathers of the fourth and fifth centuries begin to show a tendency to explain the identity not in realist terms but as being the result of an actual change or conversion in the bread and wine. This probably means that Goode overstated his case.

CONCLUSION

From the vantage point of the late twentieth century perhaps what is most impressive about the controversy between the Tractarians and Evangelicals is the great area of agreement which existed between the two parties. They were agreed on the ①divine inspiration of Holy Scripture②the catholic doctrines of the Holy Trinity and the Person of Christ③the need to pursue holiness both in the visible Church and in the individual life, ④the blessed hope of the Second Coming of Christ⑤the resurrection of the dead⑥and the life everlasting. Yet, in the early years of Queen Victoria's reign these large areas of agreement were not regarded as significant; what mattered were the differences ①concerning the place of tradition②the authority of the ordained ministry③the nature and efficacy of the sacraments,④and the place of ritual and ceremonial in worship. To Evangelicals the Tractarian doctrine and ethos appeared as a disguised or dressed up Romanism and as such was bitterly attacked. To Tractarians the Evangelical doctrine and ethos appeared as an incomplete religion, lacking the depth of catholic principles.

The way in which a theological controversy develops is influenced as much by its social and religious context as by the personalities involved. Thus, as was noted above, the Evangelical response to Tractarianism was affected by the presence within and around Evangelicalism of strong feelings about the preservation of Protestantism in Great Britain and its constitution. Novel doctrines were examined in the light of the teaching of Rome. This consciousness of a Protestant heritage, however, had also been fed into the Evangelical ethos from other sources as well – for example, the contest over Mant's tracts on baptism, the heightened sense of prophecy as a means of interpreting the signs of the times, the calls from Henry Budd and his friends to read the Reformers' works, the controversy with Irvingism and the defence of the Establishment against attacks from Dissenters.

What, then, were the general effects of this controversy on

Evangelicalism? First of all it can be said that the controversy helped to increase and to cement party feeling within Evangelicalism and probably also within the Church of England. It is common knowledge that whenever a cause is under attack those whose position is threatened feel a common responsibility and loyalty one to another. They feel the need to stand together to oppose what they fear or dislike. The years from 1833 to 1856 witnessed the creation of several distinctly Evangelical societies and organisations, the Church Extension Fund and the Church of England Education Society for example, founded in direct opposition to similar institutions which it was believed were infected with Tractarianism. These new organisations, together with older ones such as the Church Missionary Society, and not forgetting the Protestant societies of older or more recent vintage, gave a further definite identity to Evangelicalism in the Church. The Gorham case also served to isolate the sympathetic High Churchman (Conybeare's 'Anglican') from Evangelicals and make the noble ideal of the Evangelical High Churchmen or the High Church Evangelical a nearly impossible goal. Nevertheless, and this may seem paradoxical, Evangelicals remained, in general, individualists at heart and were never organised solely under one banner. Instead they gave their allegiance to one or more societies which were Evangelical.

Another result of the controversy was the claim, be it implicit or explicit, that Evangelical theology and the theology of the Reformation were to all intent and purpose the same. As the Reformers were invoked as authorities in the attempts to put down Tractarianism, and as the Parker Society faithfully published the works of sixteenth-century divines to strengthen Victorian Protestantism a confidence arose in Evangelicalism that its theology rested on secure grounds, those of Scripture and the Reformation. Certainly in such areas as that of justification by faith there appears to be no significant difference between the Reformers and Victorian Evangelicals but the same cannot be said of other areas, the sacrament of baptism and the exercise of private judgment for example. Henry Budd believed that too many of his Evangelical brethren did not understand or appreciate the teaching of the Reformers and thus he spoke somewhat harshly of 'modern Evangelism' meaning the Anglican

Evangelicalism of 1840.[1] William Goode, hardly a 'modern Evangelist' of Budd's definition, was so influenced by what we now know to be latitudinarian interpretations of the Reformation that he believed that the doctrine of private judgment was an essential principle of the Reformers, and this claim became a standard Evangelical presupposition. The basic point here is that the belief that their theology was identical with that of the divines of the sixteenth century gave a false confidence to Evangelicalism and blinded later Evangelicals to the differences between the Reformers and themselves in various points of doctrine, making the renewal of Evangelical theology difficult.

A sad aspect of the controversy was the generally negative attitude that it bred among the average clergy and laity towards the early Fathers and to the usefulness of tradition. This mentality is well expressed in the comment of the *Record* that the expository commentaries of Prebendary Horne were of more value than the whole works of the Fathers in giving to people the message of the Gospel of Christ. Twenty years later J. C. Ryle could speak of the Fathers being greatly 'overrated as commentators and expositors'. In the period after 1856 a few Evangelicals were first-rate patristic scholars, a good example being Professor Heurtley, but in general the Fathers and tradition were not given a fair hearing or reading in Evangelicalism. Instead the idea of *sola scriptura* with private judgment and related to *sola fide* was much emphasised. In practice this meant for ordinary laity the daily reading of the Bible with the help of popular expository aids and its effect was to assist the general process of individualism in religious faith and practice.

Then also it must be admitted that this controversy produced an unhealthy antagonism towards innovations in ceremonial, ritual and architecture. Again the pendulum of reaction swung too far. In its extreme form this antagonism insisted on pursuing relentlessly through the courts those priests who introduced ritual which was not permitted by the canons and rubrics, and in refusing to co-operate with Anglo-Catholics and ritualists; in a less extreme form it meant that the wearing of the surplice when preaching, or the use of choirs in robes and surplices, or even a weekly communion service were seen as capitulating to Tractarian notions. Therefore possibilities of improving the sacramental, aesthetic, ceremonial and musical side of Evangelical worship were either lost or restrained. The mentality was encouraged that to change is necessarily to change for the worse and so services and ceremonial and ritual tended to stay as they were in 1840 or 1845. To what extent preaching, and the contents of sermons, changed through this controversy admits of no easy answer and requires more research.

However, though the negative effects of the controversy cannot be overlooked for they seriously influenced the face and the development of Victorian Evangelicalism, it must also be stated, and stated firmly, that the Evangelicals, by the position they took up, did help preserve for the Church of England aspects of her Protestant heritage which could easily have been lost. Tractarians, often with only minimal knowledge of earlier Anglican divinity (a fact which Goode rightly was often pointing out), made a series of claims concerning the pedigree of their doctrines – of the episcopate and the sacraments, for example – which could have been uncritically and generally adopted in the Church had not Evangelicals (sometimes assisted by High and Broad Churchmen) reminded the whole Church that the Tractarians were essentially innovators and that their historical claims were all too often ill-founded. Of course it cannot be denied that the influence of Tractarianism on the thought and practice of both the Church of England and the Anglican Communion has been immense. It would probably have been much greater had not the Evangelicals reminded the Church that it had long and strong Protestant roots as well as Catholic ones.

Having claimed this positive role for Evangelicalism in helping to preserve the principles of Protestantism for the Church of England, it must be admitted that nothing positive appears to have been added to Evangelical thought or practice by this controversy. Certainly those Evangelicals of a scholarly persuasion who engaged in research and debate probably clarified and extended their own knowledge of the Church of England and her theology, not to mention that of the Fathers and the Early Church; but, for the majority who had only minimal time for study and reflection, controversy had the effect it appears, of confirming them in the position they already held before the contest began. Indeed, it could be argued that the 'Catholic' as over against the 'Protestant' ingredients of Evangelical faith were minimised, reduced or maimed. While the advantages of the threefold ministry were never questioned the possibility of a doctrine of baptismal regeneration (even in its more Augustinian expression) was apparently soon abandoned after the Gorham controversy; and while the creeds were accepted without question the use of the Fathers who helped to compose them became, as was noted above, minimal or nil. On the other hand, the distinctively Protestant emphases of the priority of the invisible Church and the right of private judgment were probably over-developed.

Perhaps the negative impact of controversy with Tractarians would have been less severe had not a new battle been joined immediately by Evangelicals against those in and outside the Church who were apparently setting aside the authority and inspiration of Holy Scripture in the name of natural science or the latest German 'neological' scholarship. So already forced on the defensive in one major controversy, Evangelicals were kept on the defensive, even driven back more beyond their own lines, by this second controversy which was to last a long time, and for some, has not yet finished. (The Evangelical response to the new ideas on Scripture and science from 1855 onwards has yet to be written.)

There are two questions which must be faced before this work is complete. The first is whether or not the Evangelicals and the Low Churchmen ('heirs of latitudinarianism and minimisers') were originally two separate groups who so came together in their opposition to Tractarianism that after the struggle the Evangelical party had become a fusion of the two. Y. Brilioth, following Elliott Binns and H. A. Wilson, asserts that there was such an alliance for the defence of Protestantism of Evangelicals and Low Churchmen (by which he means Latitudinarians) and that the printed organ of this Low Church Evangelicalism was the *Record*.[2] As it stands this is a false assertion and needs to be modified by the following observations. First of all, the Evangelicals before 1828, the year in which the *Record* began, were not an homogeneous group. They were not all of one theological mould or of one persuasion in the application of theology to life. They included different types of Calvinists and Arminians with various eschatological theories and different degrees of commitment to what may be termed Protestant Constitutionalism. Secondly, the problems raised by Roman Catholicism in Ireland, and the existence of a vigorous Protestantism within the Church of Ireland from 1820, meant the arrival in England of clergy and laity who, though firmly committed to Evangelical Protestantism, were nevertheless also much committed to the overthrow of Popery and certainly committed to opposition to all concessions being made towards it or its priests. These men, with their English supporters, gladly co-operated with Dissenters and Scottish Presbyterians in societies and organisations whose purpose was to defend or to propagate Protestant principles and whose headquarters were usually at Exeter Hall. They were called 'Low Churchmen' because the doctrine of the historical episcopate was low in their order of priorities of theological doctrines. They did not deny it but rather made little of it because of its asssociation with Roman Catholicism and because it was a barrier between them and Protestant Nonconformists. This vigorous Protestantism, which believed passionately in the need to convert men to God through Christ, was fully supported by the editorial policy of the *Record*. In Conybeare's language they were 'Recordites'.[3] Thirdly, Evangelicals opposed the appointment of Dr Hampden as Regius Professor at Oxford because of his supposed latitudinarian tendencies; but a decade later the *Record* supported him when Tractarians tried to prevent his consecration as Bishop of Hereford. This support was based on the belief that in his years at Oxford as Professor he had faithfully maintained Protestant doctrine against all Tractarian innovations. In fact this case is a good illustration of the way in which Evangelicals co-operated with liberal thinkers. When the latter served the cause of Protestantism then the Evangelicals were glad to praise them, but they did not support them when they set themselves up as critics of the Bible. As the new Broad Church party took form in the late 1840s the Evangelicals had little or no sympathy with it for on the crucial doctrine of the inspiration of Scripture they found the Broad Churchmen were lacking. Therefore the truth would seem to be that the only fusion which took place was a fusion of elements which were there in Evangelical Protestantism in 1833. That is, the tough negative aspect of Protestantism, consisting of opposition to popery, especially in Ireland, made a great noise as the 1830s turned into the 1840s because more Evangelicals felt the need to move in this direction, joining themselves together in such societies as the Protestant Association. The Low Churchmen were in fact none other than right-wing Evangelical churchmen who worked with Dissenters and who made little of the value of the historical episcopate.

The second question is to what extent Tractarianism can be said to be the continuation of, or the fulfilment of, the earlier Evangelical Revival and Evangelical Movement. J. H. Overton claimed that the Tractarian 'Revival was not the antagonist but the supplement of the Evangelical Revival which preceded it' and, in stating this he was following others, Gladstone for example.[4] Looking at this question from an Evangelical viewpoint, the relation could probably be expressed as follows. The Tractarian could only legitimately be regarded as the fulfilment of the Evangelical Revival had it taken up the central Evangelical emphases – the sole authority of Scripture as the Word of God and justification by grace through personal faith – and set them in a dynamic, ecclesiological framework. In other words, had the Tractarians produced a high doctrine of the visible Church as the Body of Christ in the here and now, of the ordained ministry as the servant of Christ, of the sacraments as vital vehicles of grace, at the heart of which doctrines were the basic Evangelical emphases, then there would be a strong case for asserting that Tractarianism was the completion of Evangelicalism. As it was, the Tractarians virtually denied the Evangelical emphases by their sacramental theology. To reject Overton's claim is not to deny that there were similar emphases in each movement – the quest for personal holiness and the desire to propagate the faith in city parish and heathen land – but it is to insist that the foundations of the two systems were not the same. Both held to the doctrines of the creed but in terms of their differing systems what mattered was that for Evangelicals the individual sinner approached God directly through Jesus Christ the Mediator, in faith and prayer, while for Tractarians this direct route through Jesus Christ involved a detour through the visible Church with her apostolic ministry and efficacious sacraments. Thus for an Evangelical to become a Tractarian, be he a Newman, a Manning or a Wilberforce, there had to be a basic change of theological reference in the doctrines of salvation and ecclesiology. The move from an Evangelical position to a Tractarian was not a simple expansion of a previously held faith and it was not a logical development of principles and views already held, but it was a basic change of reference in the account of how a holy and loving God grants salvation to a needy sinner. A careful study of the spiritual and theological pilgrimages of the converts from Evangelicalism to Tractarianism (and, in some cases, to Rome) should confirm this claim.[5]

We may end this book with a quotation from Bishop H. C. G. Moule, an Evangelical leader at the close of the nineteenth century. His evaluation of the impact of Tractarianism on the Church of England was a wise one:

> With all readiness I admit that this epoch and its results brought contributions of good to English Christianity. An exaggeration is sometimes used to correct its opposite, and the extreme prominence given by the Tractarians to the sacraments and to the corporate idea and to the greatness of worship had a work to do in that way and did it. But this cannot overcome in me the conviction that the root principles of the Oxford Movement were widely other than those of the Reformation, and out of scale with the authentic theology of the Scriptures. I do not wonder then that from nearly the first the new teaching was regarded with suspicion, and that earnest efforts were made to counteract it.[6]

It was the contribution of the Evangelicals to ensure that the Church retained that which the Tractarians overlooked and denied, the Protestant character of her theology.

NOTES

ABBREVIATIONS

Chadwick   Owen Chadwick, *The Victorian Church* (2 vols, 1971–2)
CEQR   *Church of England Quarterly Review*
CG   *Christian Guardian*
CLM   *Christian Lady's Magazine*
CMR   *Churchman's Monthly Review*
CO   *Christian Observer*
DNB   *Dictionary of National Biography*
JEH   *Journal of Ecclesiastical History*
Liddon   H. P. Liddon, *Life of Edward Bouverie Pusey* (4 vols, 1894)
Mozley   Anne Mozley, *Letters and Correspondence of John Henry Newman during his Life in the English Church* (2 vols, 1891)
R   *Record*

INTRODUCTION (pp. 1 to 9)

1. Hampden, *A Lecture on Tradition* (1839); and Powell, *Tradition Unveiled* (1839).

2. Faussett, *The Revival of Popery* (1838).

3. For these and other Oxford Evangelicals see J. S. Reynolds, *The Evangelicals at Oxford, 1735–1871* (1953).

4. These figures are based on the following sources: *Christian Observer* (1809), pp. 173–4; W. E. Gladstone, *Gleanings of Past Years, 1843–1879* (1879), vii, pp. 209 ff.; James Grant, *Travels in Town* (1839); ii, p. 105; Robert Vaughan, *Religious Parties in England* (1839), p. 109; the *Eclectic Review*, v (1839), p. 139; and W. J. Conybeare, *Essays Ecclesiastic and Social* (1855), Essay 2.

5. Mark Pattison, *Essays* (1889), ii, p. 269; and R. W. Church, *The Oxford Movement* (1892), pp. 12–16.

6. Mozley, ii, pp. 62, 97 and 210; Newman, *Apologia Pro Vita Sua* (ed. M. J. Svaglic, Oxford, 1967), p. 66.

7. C. P. S. Clarke, *The Oxford Movement and After* (1932), chap. 7.

8. B. E. Hardman, 'The Evangelical Party in the Church of England, 1855–1865' (Cambridge University PhD thesis, 1964), chap. 2.

9. Two unpublished theses do in fact offer some help. I. S. Rennie, 'Evangelicalism and English Public Life, 1823–1850' (Toronto University PhD thesis, 1962) is brief but solid. A. R. Acheson, 'The Evangelicals in the Church of Ireland 1784–1859' (The Queen's University, Belfast, PhD thesis, 1967) is useful since in this period the Church of Ireland was joined to that of England.

10. See further Conybeare, op. cit., pp. 74 ff. 'Recordite' came from the *Record* newspaper.

11. For more details of this later period see Anne Bentley, 'The Transformation of the Evangelical Party in the Church of England in the Later Nineteenth Century' (Durham University PhD thesis, 1971).

12. See further L. P. Fox, 'The work of T. T. Biddulph, with special reference to his influence on the Evangelical Movement in the West of England' (Cambridge University PhD thesis, 1953).

13. Mrs Oliphant, *The Life of Edward Irving* (1862), ii, p. 45.

14. Mrs A. H. Corsbie, *A Biographical Sketch of Alexander Haldane* (1882). This is an expansion of the obituary which appeared in the *Record* on 28 July, 1882.

15. Acheson, op. cit., p. 175.

16. Charlotte Elizabeth was her pen name. She appears in the *DNB* as C. E. Tonna.

17. For a helpful description of the literary and social work of C. Elizabeth see A. G. Newell, 'Studies in Evangelical Popular Prose Literature: its rise and decline' (Liverpool University PhD thesis, 1976), chap. 9.

CHAPTER ONE (pp. 13 to 45)

1. See further R. W. Church, *The Oxford Movement, 1833–1845* (1892); and Y. Brilioth, *The Anglican Revival: Studies in the Oxford Movement* (1933).

2. W. Palmer, *A Narrative of Events connected with the publication of the Tracts for the Times* (1883 ed.), p. 49.

3. Palmer, op. cit., p. 59.

4. Bodleian MS St Edmund Hall, 67/9, Vol. 9. Henceforth cited as 'Diary'.

5. The correspondence is printed in W. Tuckwell, *Reminiscences of Oxford* (1901), pp. 279–81.

6. Marsh had been at St Edmund Hall. In 1843 he wrote: 'I am weeping over the Tractarians. I corresponded with some of their leaders at one time.' C. M. Marsh, *The Life of William Marsh* (1868), p. 155.

7. In late January 1834 Pusey wrote: 'I am very sorry to hear that Girdlestone has been writing to the *Christian Observer* or connecting himself with it. I fear also that he has been writing without sufficient knowledge or thought of the source of our commission.' Liddon, 1, p. 278. (The original letter is in the Pusey correspondence in Pusey House, Oxford.) It is probable that the letter of Girdlestone is that printed in the *CO* in February 1834 for which see below.

8. Mozley, ii, pp. 11–12.

9. See further H. H. Rowden, 'Secession from the Established Church in the early Nineteenth Century', *Vox Evangelica*, iii (1962), pp. 76 ff. Cf. also the comments of E. A. Knox, *The Tractarian Movement* (1933), p. 365.

10. For proof that Newman was this Churchman see Mozley, i, pp. 435–6 and ii, p. 7. For Newman's earlier relations with Evangelicals in Oxford

see T. C. F. Stunt, 'J. H. Newman and the Evangelicals', *JEH*, xxi (1970), pp. 65 ff.

11. Mozley, ii, p. 7.

12. *CG* (1834), p. 25 refers briefly to two of the *Tracts*. In 1838 there were short reviews of the first four volumes of *Tracts*: *CG* (1838), pp. 185–92, 345–51 and 484–92.

13. *CO* (1837), p. 115.

14. *CO* (1834), pp. 88 and 186.

15. *CO* (1834), p. 324.

16. David Newsome, *Parting of Friends* (1966), pp. 14–15. One group of men who were sure about the nature of the teaching of the *Tracts* was that which met at the home of Henry Blunt in Chelsea. Wilks wrote: 'Shortly after the commencement of the Tracts there was a meeting of Reverend brethren at the house of Mr Blunt, then Rector of Chelsea, and it was intended to make a vigorous and united Anti-Tract effort; but the proceeding was abandoned in deference to the opinions and wishes of some in authority, who thought that such an association would be objectionable and inflame the wounds of the Church.' *CO* (1847), p. 142.

17. G. H. Sumner, *Life of C. R. Sumner* (1876), pp. 243–4; Y. Brilioth, *Three Lectures on Evangelicalism and the Oxford Movement* (1934), p. 28, and D. Voll, *Catholic Evangelicalism* (1963), pp. 4 ff. oversimplifies the relation between Evangelicals and Tractarians.

18. Hill, 'Diary', Vol. 9, 6 April, 1835 etc.

19. The extant correspondence is among the Pusey MS Letters in Pusey House; it is not mentioned by Liddon.

20. Bodleian MS Eng. Lett. e. 144 f. 233. Pusey to T. G. Tyndale.

21. Hill, 'Diary', Vol. 9, 21 and 22 April, 1835.

22. Newman, *Apologia* (ed. M. J. Svaglic), p. 66.

23. *CO* (1838), pp. 821–2. Liddon mentions the active role of R. L. Cotton of Worcester, J. Hill of St Edmund Hall and B. P. Symons of Wadham in opposition to Hampden's appointment. Liddon, i, pp. 374–5.

24. Liddon, ii, pp. 9–10. The late Fr Stephen Dessain assured me that the clergyman was John Steele of Christ Church, Macclesfield.

25. This theme is developed by D. W. F. Forrester, 'The Intellectual Development of E. B. Pusey' (Oxford University DPhil thesis, 1967), Chap. 9.

26. The comments of Maurice and Rose are taken from Liddon, i, p. 350. For the reaction of Thomas Arnold see A. P. Stanley, *The Life . . . of Thomas Arnold* (1844) ii, p. 43.

27. T. R. Birks, *A Memoir of Edward Bickersteth* (1853), ii, p. 81.

28. This has now been printed as *J. H. Newman and the Abbé Jager: A Controversy on Scripture and Tradition, 1834–5* (ed. L. Allen, 1975).

29. G. Battiscombe, *John Keble* (1963), p. 193.

30. His cousin, Daniel Wilson, also thought so: see his episcopal *Charge* (1838). Further response came from G. S. Faber in *Justification* (2nd ed., 1838), appendix.

31. *CO* (1837), p. 121.

H

32. *CO* (1838), p. 312.

33. E. S. Purcell, *Life of Cardinal Manning* (1895), i, pp. 131 ff.; and *R*, 11 November, 1838, a letter from F. K. of Cheltenham to the editor.

34. W. S. Bricknell, *The Judgment of the Bishops on Tractarian Theology* (1845), pp. 178 ff. and 627 ff.

35. *Letters and Memoir of W. A. Shirley* (ed. T. Hill, 1849), p. 275.

36. *CLM*, xiii (1840), pp. 565–6.

37. *CMR* (1842), p. 506.

38. *R*, 10 October, 1839.

39. *R*, 16 May, 1839. T. H. Horne, *An Introduction to the Holy Scriptures* (7th ed., 1834).

40. 'Newman to Pusey' MS Letters, i (1823–40) in Pusey House, dated 10 January, 1837.

41. Liddon, ii, p. 12.

42. Liddon, *Walter K. Hamilton, Bishop of Salisbury* (1869), pp. 12–13. On 7 December, 1838 Samuel Wilberforce told Dr Hook that Hamilton's 'Church views enlarge and clear themselves most hopefully', A. R. Ashwell, *Life of Samuel Wilberforce* (1880), i, p. 131.

43. Mozley, ii, p. 222.

44. The book against Knox was *The Primitive Doctrine of Justification* (1837). Appendix five of the second edition (1838) refers to his correspondence with Newman, some of which is still to be found in the Oratory, Birmingham. The late Fr S. Dessain kindly showed me all the letters of Faber some of which related to his nephew, F. W. Faber, who with Newman joined the Church of Rome.

45. *CLM*, xv (1841), pp. 460–2.

46. *CO* (1841), pp. 160 ff.; and *Churchman*, iv (1841), p. 411.

47. Liddon, ii, pp. 12–13.

48. A correspondent of C. S. Bird gave this information. Bird, *Sketches from the Life of C. S. Bird* (1864), p. 164.

49. *British Magazine*, xii (1837), pp. 637 ff.; and Liddon, ii, pp. 14–16.

50. See further W. R. W. Stephens, *The Life and Letters of W. F. Hook* (1878), i, chap. 5, and Liddon, ii, pp. 40–3.

51. For Newman on Reserve see R. C. Selby, *The Principle of Reserve in the writings of John Henry Cardinal Newman* (Oxford, 1975), and David Newsome, 'Newman and the Oxford Movement' in *The Victorian Crisis of Faith* (ed. A. Symondson, 1970), pp. 79 ff. For Keble's views see B. W. Martin, *John Keble. Priest, Professor and Poet* (1976), pp. 135–54.

52. Townsend, *Sermons . . . with Two Charges* (1849), p. 455.

53. Bird, *Sketches from the Life of C. S. Bird*, p. 170. The title of the booklet was *The Oxford Tract System considered with reference to the principle of Reserve in preaching* (1838).

54. Taylor, *Ancient Christianity*, i, pp. 464 ff.; Stowell, *Tractarianism Tested by Holy Scripture* (1845), i, sermons 6 and 7; Faber, *Justification* (1838), appendix 9, and J. T. O'Brien, *Charge* (1843).

55. W. J. Baker, 'Hurrell Froude and the Reformers', *JEH*, xxi, 3 (1970), pp. 243 ff.

56. For the relationship of Golightly and Newman see R. W. Greaves, 'Golightly and Newman, 1824–1845', *JEH*, ix (1958) pp. 209–28.

57. *CO* (1837), pp. 495–9. S. R. Maitland subjected the volumes of Foxe to criticism in the *British Magazine*, xii (1837).

58. Liddon, ii, pp. 64 ff.

59. The prospectus, *Memorial of Cranmer, Latymer and Ridley*, is in the Bodleian Library. Liddon, ii, pp. 64 ff. gives details of Tractarian attitudes.

60. Hill, 'Diary', Vol. 12 has eleven references to meetings between 29 December, 1838 and 25 March, 1840. The Note-Book of Golightly containing the list of subscriptions is in Wadham College Library.

61. For Scott's comments see his *Personal and Professional Recollections* (1879), pp. 89 ff. He admitted that as yet he had not been awakened to true (Gothic) church architecture and so there were defects in the design of the aisle.

62. Cf. Robert Vaughan, *Religious Parties in England* (1839), pp. 108–9 who writes of a great improvement in spirituality of members of the old High and Dry Churchmen.

63. *CEQR*, x (1841), p. 257.

64. Lambeth MS 1805, f. 229, Faber to Golightly.

65. Budd, *Infant Baptism, the means of National Regeneration* (1827), pp. 426 ff. L. Elliott-Binns is wrong to assert (in *The Evangelical Movement*, 1928, p. 83) that Evangelicals first began appealing to the Reformers in order to refute the Tractarians. Cf. John Walsh, 'The Yorkshire Evangelicals in the Eighteenth Century' (Cambridge University PhD thesis, 1956), p. 28.

66. *CLM*, x (1838), p. 471.

67. There were further publications from both Golightly and Miller. This led to a correspondence between them. See Lambeth MS 1808 ff. 86 ff.

68. Fry, *The Listener in Oxford* (1840), p. 173. Her married name was Wilson.

CHAPTER TWO (pp. 46 to 77)

1. Church, *Oxford Movement*, p. 296.

2. J. F. White, *The Cambridge Movement: the Ecclesiologists and the Gothic Revival* (Cambridge, 1962).

3. Lough, *The Influence of John Mason Neale* (1962), chap. 4.

4. W. Perry, *The Oxford Movement in Scotland* (Cambridge, 1933). Apparently only one Scottish Episcopal priest wrote against Tractarianism in this period: C. P. Miles of St Jude's, Glasgow, in *The Voice of the Glorious Reformation* (1844).

5. For fiction see J. E. Baker, *The Novel and the Oxford Movement* (New York, 1965).

6. H. P. Thompson, *Into All Lands* (1951), pp. 113–14; and H. J. Burgess and P. A. Welsby, *A Short History of the National Society, 1811–1961* (1961), pp. 24 ff.

7. See the interesting comments in R. Ornsby, *Memoirs of James Robert Hope-Scott of Abbotsford* (1884), i, pp. 267–8.

8. *Apologia* (ed. M. J. Svoglic), pp. 78 ff.

9. Church, *Oxford Movement*, pp. 286-7.

10. F. Close is reported to have stated: 'When I first read No. 90 I did not then know the author; but I said then, and I repeat here, not with any personal reference to the author, that I should be sorry to trust the author of that Tract with my purse.' *Cheltenham Examiner*, 1 March, 1843, quoted by Church, op. cit., p. 299.

11. *Two Letters Concerning No. 90* (printed for private distribution only), 1841. Griffiths' letter is the second, dated 5 April, 1841.

12. Liddon, ii, pp. 170 ff.

13. C. Elizabeth, *A Peep into Number Ninety* (1841); J. Jordan, *The Crisis Come, being Remarks on Mr. Newman's Letter to Dr. Jelf and on Tract 90* (1841).

14. C. Elizabeth, op. cit., p. 34.

15. *CLM*, x (1838), p. 374; *R*, 22 March and 12 April, 1841.

16. Oakeley's work was *The Subject of Tract XC historically examined* (1845), and was specifically related to the case of W. G. Ward, for which see below. When Pusey republished *Tract 90* in 1865 Goode reissued his work against Oakeley.

17. Goode, *Tract XC*, pp. 5-6.

18. Bricknell, *Resignation and Lay Communion* (1841), pp. 26-9. Bricknell's strong Protestantism is seen also in his *Preaching, its warrant, subject and effects considered with reference to the 'Tracts for the Times'* (1841).

19. Bricknell, '*Is there not a Cause?*'. *A Letter to the Rev. E. B. Pusey . . . occasioned by his circular in support of the Rev. Isaac Williams* (1841), p. 6.

20. *CO* (1841), pp. 756-7; Liddon, ii, pp. 260-1.

21. E. Hodder, *The Life . . . of the Seventh Earl of Shaftesbury* (1886), i, pp. 386 ff.

22. Bricknell, '*Is there not a Cause?*' (1841), and '*Horae Canonicae*' . . . *A Second Letter to . . . E. B. Pusey* (1841), pp. 4-5.

23. 'Diary', Vol. 13, 20 January, 1842.

24. *CO* (1842), p. 127.

25. Garbett, *Prophet, Priest and King* (1842), ii, pp. 502-3.

26. Golightly, *Facts and Documents* (1859), p. 11.

27. 'Golightly Correspondence'. Lambeth MSS 1804-11.

28. See further *Correspondence illustrative of the Actual State of Oxford with reference to Tractarianism* (1842), and W. Palmer, *A Letter to . . . C. P. Golightly* (1842).

29. Lambeth MS 1808, ff. 218-30.

30. Liddon, ii, p. 306.

31. *The Plea of the Six Doctors Examined* (1843), p. 8; *R*, 5 June, 1843.

32. Lambeth MS 1804, f. 34.

33. Lambeth MS 1806, f. 108.

34. Dr B. Godwin of New Road Chapel published *An Examination . . . of Dr. Pusey's Sermon* (1843) while Garbett published *A Review of Dr. Pusey's Sermon* (1843).

35. The full text in *CMR* (1843), p. 680, and *R*, 30 November, 1843.

36. *CMR* (1844), p. 539.

37. Hill, 'Diary', Vol. 14, 25 June, 1844.

38. Griffiths, *Letters with a few remarks concerning rumours which have lately been in circulation* (1844).

39. Hill, 'Diary', Vol. 15, 7 and 8 October, 1844.

40. Liddon, ii, p. 413.

41. Liddon, ii, p. 415.

42. *CMR* (1844), p. 630.

43. T. Hill, *Letters . . . of W. A. Shirley* (1849), pp. 392 ff.

44. *CO* (1845), pp. 120–1.

45. The memorial is printed in the last two editions of Bricknell's *Oxford, Tract 90 . . .* (1845).

46. 'Diary', Vol. 15, 13 February, 1845.

47. He told Golightly this on 13 January, 1846. Lambeth MS 1807, f. 31.

48. J. B. A. Kessler, *A Study of the Evangelical Alliance in Great Britain* (Goes, Netherlands, 1968), pp. 1 ff.

49. *English Churchman*, 5 October, 1843. For a similar address from Bolton-le-Moors to Bishop Sumner see *R*, 23 November, 1843.

50. James Bateman, a layman from Cheshire, used Elliott's work extensively in his *Tractarianism as described in Prophecy* (1845).

51. There is a useful chapter on the prophetic background in S. C. Orchard, 'English Evangelical Eschatology, 1790–1850' (Cambridge University PhD thesis, 1968), chap. 6.

52. *R*, 7 October, 1841. See further R. W. Greaves, 'The Jerusalem Bishopric', *English Historical Review*, xliv (1949), and P. J. Welsh, 'Anglican Churchmen and the Establishment of the Jerusalem Bishopric', *JEH*, viii (1957).

53. E. Hodder, *Life of Shaftesbury*, i, p. 396.

54. To those listed by Liddon, ii, pp. 279 ff. may be added two Evangelical replies: W. Atwell (Curate of St Mark's, Dublin), *Dr Pusey Answered* (1842); and J. Davies (Rector of Gateshead), *The Present Crisis of the Church* (1842).

55. *British Critic*, xxxi (1842), p. 246.

56. Lord Selborne, *Memorials, Family and Personal* (1896), i, p. 210.

57. The question of post-baptismal sin had been brought into public debate again by the publication of a sermon by Charles Wordsworth entitled *Evangelical Repentance* (1841). See the critical review in *CMR* (1842), pp. 40–53.

58. *CLM*, xx (1843), pp. 269–72.

59. *CMR* (1843), p. 883.

60. E. J. Boyce, *A Memorial of the Cambridge Camden Society* (1888), p. 21.

61. On 23 January, 1845 the Fund had reached £11,000 and the Council had declared that new churches would be vested in Evangelical trustees. *R*, 23 January, 1845.

62. Close, *Restoration of Churches is the Restoration of Popery* (1844), p. 4.

63. *R*, 31 March, 1845; White, *Cambridge Movement*, pp. 139–44.

64. *CMR* (1844), pp. 295–6.

65. See further B. F. L. Clarke, *Church Builders in the Nineteenth Century*

(new ed. 1969) for a discussion of various attitudes to architecture in the nineteenth century.

66. *CO* (1845), p. 54.

67. See further P. J. Welch, 'Bishop Blomfield and the Development of Tractarianism in London', *Church Quarterly Review*, clv (1954).

68. A. Blomfield, *A Memoir of C. J. Blomfield* (1863), ii, pp. 47, 55–6.

69. See further Chadwick, i, pp. 218–20. For the foundation of the Episcopal Free Church in Exeter which occurred in 1844 see *R*, 19 September, 1844, and the anonymous *A History of the Free Church of England* (1960).

70. *CMR* (1844), p. 826.

71. *CO* (1845), p. 54.

72. C. Benson, *Rubrics and Canons of the Church of England considered* (1845); and Goode, *A Letter to a Lay Friend on the State of the Church and the course which the present crisis demands* (1845).

73. *R*, 8 February, 1844; and *CO* (1844), pp. 559 ff.

74. Bird, *A Second Plea*, p. 101. For Ward's view of development see W. Ward, *W. G. Ward and the Oxford Movement*, pp. 226 ff.

75. Bird told Golightly this in a letter of 25 May, 1843. Lambeth MS 1804 f. 41.

76. *CO* (1844), p. 181.

77. Bird, *Second Plea*, p. 99.

78. *CMR* (1843), pp. 244–5.

79. J. R. Hope Scott believed Golightly was an Evangelical: R. Ornsby, *Memoirs of James Robert Hope-Scott*, i, p. 267. A lifelong friend of Golightly, E. M. Goulbourn, commented as follows on Thomas Mozley's description of Golightly (in *Reminiscences chiefly of Oriel College* (1882), ii, pp. 109–11):

'I hardly think he puts Golightly's ecclesiastical temperature as "High" as it really was. A distinction has been drawn between a High Church Evangelical and an Evangelical High Churchman to this effect – that in the first, Evangelicalism is the basis of the man's religious mind, and the High Churchism is super-induced, and the growth of a later age; in the second, the views are fundamentally High Church and the Evangelicalism is the colour subsequently given to them. To this latter class rather than the former I should say that Golightly belonged, though I doubt not that the controversy with the Tractarian school in which his better years were spent, drove him into a more pronounced Low Church attitude than was strictly congenial with his nature.' *Reminiscences of Charles P. Golightly* (1886), p. 13.

80. 'The Principal Clergy of London classified according to their opinions on the great Church Questions of the day' (1844). Bodleian MS. Add. C. 290.

CHAPTER THREE (pp. 78 to 109)

1. Conybeare, *Essays*, pp. 57 ff.

2. A. M. Allchin, *The Silent Rebellion: Anglican Religious Communities, 1845–1900* (1958).

3. B. Heeney, *Mission to the Middle Classes. The Woodard Schools, 1848–1891* (1969); and L. James, *A Forgotten Genius. Sewell of St Columba's and Radley*, n.d.

4. Liddon, iii, pp. 278–80.

5. Beresford Hope had much influence in the religious policy of the *Morning Chronicle*. According to the *Record*, 8 March, 1852, the average sales of the *MC* dropped from 4,692 in 1845 to 2,915 in 1850.

6. *R*, 14 January, 1857. The proprieter of the Union was F. G. Lee for whom see H. R. T. Brandreth, *Dr Lee of Lambeth* (1851).

7. *CO* (1945), preface, p. iii. In April 1844 an article had appeared entitled 'The National Society for Education and the Tractarians', claiming that Tractarianism was strong in the training schools in London.

8. In 1843 long-standing Evangelical subscribers and supporters of the SPG, such men as Josiah Pratt and Edward Bickersteth, were attempting to get assurances from the Secretary of the SPG that Tractarian personnel would not be used as missionaries. J. and J. H. Pratt, *Memoir of Josiah Pratt*, pp. 360–8; T. R. Birks, *Memoir of Edward Bickersteth*, ii, pp. 223 ff.; *R*, 9 and 23 February, 2 March, 29 April, 4 May, 1843. In the 'Reports of Association Secretaries, 1840–1848' (*CMS* Archives, ref. H/H7 A1) there are many references to Tractarianism in parishes and some references to Tractarian support for the SPG. On the latter point see the boxes labelled CH 21 and 25 in the SPG archives; they deal with Tractarianism in the Society. Mr Brian Stanley kindly brought the latter to my attention.

9. The other three were Francis Wilson, incumbent of Armitage, author of *No Peace with Tractarianism* (1850); R. J. M'Ghee, the Irish Protestant activist, who challenged Gresley to a debate in Brighton on Auricular Confession to which Gresley responded in print with *A Letter of Confession* (1851); and E. B. Elliott, the commentator on the Apocalypse, who sent a letter to Gresley entitled *The Delusion of the Tractarian Clergy as to the validity of their ministerial Orders* (1856).

10. *CMR* (1846), p. 230.

11. *R*, 26 March, 1846.

12. The controversy between Gresley and Close continued with each man producing two more tracts. There are some provocative comments on the exchange in *Oxford and Cambridge Review*, xvii (December 1846), article 1.

13. The letters were reprinted in the *Record* on 6 and 17 November, 1845. Two of the contributors to the *Review*, George Rawlinson and S. J. Rigaud, both of Exeter College, wrote to Golightly denying any intention to Romanise. Lambeth MS 1809, ff. 3–6 and 31–4.

14. Lambeth MS 1804, f. 45.

15. Lambeth MS 1804, f. 108.

16. Of the four letters one related to the Stone Altar case, two to F. Oakley and the Court of Arches, and one to Newman. The last is reprinted in Browne, *Annals of the Tractarian Movement* (1861), pp. 120–4.

17. The original draft of this letter is in Lambeth MS 1809, f. 108.

18. Lambeth MS 1806, ff. 110–12.

19. Lambeth MS 1809, f. 110. This is the original to which reference is made by Symons in his letter to Pusey printed in Liddon, iii, p. 56. The

letters of Golightly to Symons and Symons to Golightly were printed in the first issue of the *Guardian* on 21 January, 1846.

20. See the review in *CMR* (1846), pp. 165–84.

21. 'Diary', Vol. 16, 17 May, 1847.

22. Hill, *Letters . . . of W. A. Shirley*, pp. 426 ff. They were published as *The Supremacy of Scripture* (1848).

23. Chadwick, i, chap. 4; J. C. S. Nias, *Gorham and the Bishop of Exeter* (1951); G. C. B. Davies, *Henry Phillpotts, Bishop of Exeter* (1954); and Liddon, iii, pp. 201 ff.

24. For Hatchard see A. L. Humphreys, *Piccadilly Bookmen. Memorials of the House of Hatchard* (1893), and for Maskell see *DNB*.

25. Maskell, *Letter to . . . Dr Pusey on his receiving persons in Auricular Confession* (1850).

26. *Memoir of the late Rev. James Scholefield* (1855), p. 186.

27. R. I. Wilberforce replied with *The Doctrine of Holy Baptism* (1849).

28. *CO* (1849), pp. 809–56.

29. *R.*, 25 July, 1850.

30. Purcell, *Life of Cardinal Manning*, i, pp. 540–1.

31. McNeile, *'Baptism doth Save'. A Letter to . . . the Bishop of Exeter* (1850).

32. *The Royal Supremacy discussed in correspondence between Archdeacon Wilberforce and the Rev. Dr McNeile* (1850), p. 27.

33. Goode, *Reply to the Letter and Declaration respecting the Royal Supremacy* (1850).

34. *R*, 16 September, 1850. See also 14 October and 14 November for letters of Manning, Wilberforce, Goode and McNeile.

35. *CG* (1851), pp. 23–8, 64–8 and 118–22. For Walter see *DNB*.

36. Two pamphlets appeared against Wilson's, *The Church of England in Danger: A Letter to the Vicar of Islington* by one of his parishioners (1850), and William Scott, *A Letter to the Rev Daniel Wilson* (1850).

37. *CG* (1851), pp. 318 ff.; and *R*, 2 September, 1850.

38. C.A. is possibly the Rev A. Cooper of St Mark's, Audley St., London.

39. See further P. Toon and M. Smout, *J. C. Ryle: Evangelical Bishop* (1976), p. 36.

40. *CO* (1852), p. 767.

41. Hodder, *Life of Shaftesbury*, ii, p. 407.

42. This petition is described in the *Record* of 12 December, 1850 and is printed in Phillpotts, *A Pastoral Letter* (2nd ed., 1851), pp. 119–22.

43. *R*, 12 December, 1850.

44. W. Goode, *Address delivered at a Public Meeting . . .* (1850), p. 16.

45. Hill, 'Diary', Vol. 18, 8 January, 1851 has a description of the meeting.

46. According to Dr J. E. Orr there was a revival in 1859–60 within the Church of England. Orr, *The Second Evangelical Awakening in Britain* (1949). This is rightly challenged by B. E. Hardman, *The Evangelical Party in the C. of E., 1855–1865*, pp. 296 ff.

47. The *Annual Reports* of the Institute for 1847–58 are in the Islington Public Library.

48. *R*, 14 April, 1851 where the correspondence is printed.

49. On 11 March, 1846 the *Guardian* had called him 'a fanatic partisan' for Protestantism.

50. For a previous Letter of D'Aubigné to Sumner see *R*, 12 March, 1846.

51. For the correspondence see Browne, *Annals of the Tractarian Movement*, pp. 230 ff. For comments see *CO* (1851), pp. 730–2, and *R*, 8 September, 1851.

52. Goode, *A Reply to Archdeacon Churton and Chancellor Harington* (1852), p. 31.

53. Goode, *A Letter to the Bishop of Exeter* (1850), p. 2. In this he had shown that in 1833 Phillpotts had a friendly and sympathetic attitude to Dissenters.

54. *R*, 8, 11, 15 and 18 June, 1846; *Guardian*, 15 April and 10 June, 1846.

55. *R*, 19 and 22 September, 13, 17 and 20 October, 1853; *CO* (1853), pp. 843 ff.

56. For the text of the letter see Browne, op. cit., pp. 320–1.

57. Chadwick, i, pp. 491–5; and Hardman, op. cit., pp. 125–43.

58. G. A. Denison, *Notes on My Life* (1879), p. 222; and Liddon, iii, p. 427. The official magazine of the Evangelical Alliance, the monthly *Evangelical Christendom*, has no report of this supposed official action. The accusation probably arose because of the readiness of some Nonconformists to give money to support the prosecution of Denison. In fact, Archdeacon Henry Law, who was closely connected with the prosecution, later claimed that Goode was constantly urging Ditcher, the Evangelical neighbour of Denison, to continue with the legal proceedings – see *Gloucestershire Chronicle* (1885), p. 246.

59. *CO* (1853), p. 144.

60. Goode, *The Nature of Christ's Presence in the Eucharist* (1856), p. 3.

61. *Guardian*, 29 November, 1854, 20 August, 1856.

62. *CO* (1853), pp. 593–4.

63. At least two other Evangelical authors wrote against Wilberforce's views. Robert Maguire (Rector of St Olave's, Southwark), *Transubstantiation a Tractarian Doctrine* (1854), and James Taylor (Headmaster of the Free Grammar School, Wakefield, Yorkshire), *An Appeal to the Archbishop of York on the uncondemned heresies of Archdeacon Wilberforce . . .* (1854).

64. For the development of Wilberforce's thinking see David Newsome, *Parting of Friends* (1966), pp. 370 ff.

65. *R*, 26 January, 12 and 23 February, 1852.

66. *R*, 4, 11 and 14 December, 1857. A. G. Lough, *J. M. Neale* (1975), pp. 106 ff.

67. *R*, 11 June, 1853. See further Heeney, *Mission to the Middle Classes*, pp. 78–81 and 184. For letters to Golightly from Sussex Protestant clergy about these schools see Lambeth MS 1806, ff. 12–16 (from J. M. Grubb) and 1807, ff. 91–5 (from T. A. Holland).

68. *R*, 14 January, 1856. Prominent supporters included Shaftesbury, Isaac Taylor, Robert Bickersteth and Sir Culling Eardley. See Hardman, op. cit., pp. 157 ff.

69. *CO* (1854), p. 650. *R*, 7 and 9 July, 1856. See also James Bateman,

The Tractarian Tendency of Diocesan Theological Colleges (1853). Believing that the colleges at Wells and Chichester were under Tractarian control, Bateman opposed the scheme for a college at Lichfield.

70. See further F. W. B. Bullock, *A History of Training for the Ministry . . . 1800-1874* (St Leonards-on-Sea, 1955).

71. Chadwick, ii, pp. 308 ff. N. Dimock, *The Doctrine of the Sacraments* (1871); and J. Harrison, *An Answer to Dr Pusey's Challenge Respecting the Doctrine of the Real Presence* (2 vols, 1871).

CHAPTER FOUR (pp. 113 to 140)

1. C. Wordsworth, *Miscellanies, Literary and Religious* (1879), i, pp. 76 and 82.

2. For some account of the Evangelical response to the *Essay* see P. Toon, 'Newman's Essay on Development Revisited', *The Churchman*, 89 (1975), pp. 47-57.

3. *CO* (1838), p. 263.

4. This information is taken from W. S. Bricknell, *The Judgment of the Bishops upon Tractarian Theology* (1845), p. 173. Tractarians did not share the high opinions of Hawkins and Gilbert. See the review in *British Critic*, xxxi (1842), pp. 98-104.

5. Goode, *Divine Rule*, i, 36-7.

6. The whole work was anonymous but the title page did state it was by 'the author of *Spiritual Despotism*' which itself was anonymous. However, reviewers announced that Taylor was the author and in his *Four Lectures of Spiritual Christiantiy* (1841), pp. 202-3 he admitted to being the author.

7. James Beaven, *A Calm Exposure . . .* (1840), and W. J. Edge, *An Earnest Appeal . . .* (1840) were critical replies; the reviewer in the *Churchman's Monthly Magazine* was shocked by the *Supplement* of 1843 – *CMM* (1844), pp. 71-84, 129-42 and 259-73. In contrast, the reviewer in *CMR* (1842), pp. 506-33, and (1844), pp. 81-91 was full of praise.

8. Similar sentiments are found in his Introductory Essay to the *Life of Martin Luther* by G. Pfizer (translated by T. S. Williams, 1840). See the review of this book in *CO* (1840), pp. 498-510. Taylor, like Harnack, was fond of the young Luther's theology (A. Harnack, *Outlines of the History of Dogma*, 1893, Bk. III, Chap. IV).

9. Taylor, *Ancient Christianity*, i, 'Letter to T. B. Monsell', p. viii. On p. 70 he named the historians as Mosheim, Milner and Neander.

10. Taylor, op. cit., ii, pp. 18-19.

11. Taylor, op. cit., ii, p. 75.

12. Ibid., p. 365.

13. The question as to whether the Reformers did use a book or books of quotations from the Fathers is interesting. See further P. Polman, *L'élément historique dans la controverse religieuse du XVIe siècle* (Gembloun, 1932).

14. *CMR* (1844), p. 81.

15. Newman, *The Prophetical Office* (1837), pp. 270, 296, 297.

16. Goode, op. cit., i, pp. 108-13. (Irenaeus, *Adversus Haereses*, Bk. 1,

c. 10 and Bk. III, c. 4; Tertullian, *De Praescriptione haereticorum*, c. 13; *Adversus Praxeas*, c. 2.) Cf. Fitzgerald, *Holy Scripture*, pp. 86 ff. for similar comment.

17. Goode, op. cit., pp. 116–39. The articles were Christ's descent into hell and the communion of saints. For a modern discussion of this problem see J. N. D. Kelly, *Early Christian Creeds* (1960).

18. Shirley, *The Supremacy of Scripture* (1847), p. 19. The quotation is from Manning, *Rule of Faith* (1838), p. 76.

19. e. g. Garbett, *Christ as Prophet, Priest and King* (1842), ii, pp. 78 ff.

20. Goode, op. cit., i, p. 193.

21. Ibid., p. 344.

22. Wilson, *The Sufficiency of Holy Scripture* (1841), p. 29.

23. Ibid., pp. 36 and 43. Similar points are made by Benson, *Discourse upon Tradition* (2nd ed., 1839), pp. 14–17. E.g. he wrote: 'The word of God is comparatively small in extent and conveys its fulness of wisdom with a pregnant brevity which neither absorbs our whole time nor overloads the memory. The Fathers are voluminous, and it is admitted that it would require a whole life to read them in order to see how far they agree or differ' (p. 16). Note also the comment of Garbett, op. cit., ii, p. 97: 'the Fathers whose multitudinous works took the illustrious Ussher eighteen years to peruse and with which not more than *half a dozen* theologians at any one time can really have anything like a thorough acquaintance'.

24. Goode, op. cit., ii, p. 61.

25. For the Protestant background see H. D. McDonald, *Ideas of Revelation. An Historical Study, 1700–1860* (1959), especially chapter 8.

26. Goode, op. cit., ii, p. 181.

27. Ibid., p. 457.

28. Horsley, *Sermons* (1829), ii, pp. 373–5. I have been unable to determine the origin of the term 'standard divines' but it appears to have been a term to describe leading bishops and theologians, mostly High Churchmen, who were neither Puritans nor Non-Jurors and who were orthodox in the faith.

29. Goode, op. cit., iii, p. 314.

30. Garbett, op. cit., ii, p. 104.

31. Taylor, *Ancient Christianity*, i, p. 47.

32. Goode, op. cit., ii, pp. 202 ff. Garbett, op. cit., ii, p. 77 also mentioned these items, while Taylor, op. cit., i, p. 51 referred only to the Lord's Day. Faber, *Primitive Doctrine of Justification* (2nd ed., 1838), pp. 359 ff., specifically mentions the Lord's Day and infant baptism.

33. Garbett, op. cit., ii, pp. 74 ff. Goode, op. cit., i, p. 214 wrote: 'I admit fully that our Church has . . . sanctioned the principle, that nothing is to be admitted as a fundamental point of faith that has not some support in the patristical testimony of the first five or six centuries; a rule which (especially at the time when it was first made) was a prudent precaution against the novelties of enthusiasm and Popery.'

34. Faber, op. cit., p. 359.

35. The authority of this Canon was the source of discussion in the pages

of the *Christian Observer* (1837), pp. 687–8, and (1838), pp. 43, 51 ff. and 121 ff.

36. Faber, op. cit., p. 365.

37. See, for example, *Christian Examiner* (Dublin, 1837), pp. 933 ff.

38. Faber, *The Difficulties of Romanism* (1826); Trevern, *Answer to the 'Difficulties of Romanism'* (trans. by F. C. Husenbeth, 1828), pp. 130–80; Faber, *The Testimony of Primitive Antiquity . . . in reply to 'An Answer . . .'* (1828).

39. Faber, *Apostolicity of Trinitarianism* (1832), i, pp. 206 ff.

40. Faber, *Primitive Doctrine of Justification* (2nd ed., 1838), pp. 441 ff.

41. Bird, *The Oxford Tract System considered with reference to . . . Reserve* (1838).

42. Taylor, op. cit., i, pp. 464 ff.

43. Stowell, *Tractarianism Tested by Holy Scripture* (1845), i, pp. 305–9.

44. Townsend, *Sermons . . . with Two Charges* (1849), p. 454.

45. In Newman's *Prophetical Office of the Church* (1837), chapters 5, 6 and 7 are on this topic and he also published an essay in the *British Critic* (1841) entitled 'Private Judgment'.

46. *The Prophetical Office*, pp. 325 and 174.

47. Goode, op. cit., i, preface to second edition, p. xlii.

48. Goode himself (ii, pp. 121–4) quoted at length from a work by W. Clagett *Of the Authority of Councils . . .* (1689). This was reprinted in Bishop Gibson's *Preservative against Popery*, in which are several pieces on private judgment – e.g. by Kidder, Bishop of Bath and Wells.

49. Goode, op. cit., ii, p. 61.

50. Fitzgerald, *Holy Scripture*, pp. 168–9.

51. Ibid., p. 172; Wilson, op. cit., p. 21 has a similar argument. The Reformers believed that the perspicuity of Scripture extended rather wider than some of their nineteenth-century followers could allow. Divisions within Protestantism and controversy with Rome had narrowed the area in which the Scriptures were thought to be clear to all honest seekers after truth.

52. I rely here primarily on the articles by H. A. Oberman, 'Quo Vadis? Tradition from Irenaeus to Humani Generis', *Scottish Journal of Theology*, xvi (1963), pp. 225–55, and A. N. S. Lane, 'Scripture, Tradition and Church: An Historical Survey', *Vox Evangelica* (ed. D. Guthrie), ix (1975), pp. 37–55.

53. Goode, op. cit., i, preface to the first edition, p. xx.

54. Goode took up this matter in i, pp. 72–5. *In Lectures on the Prophetical Office*, p. 388, Newman had taken the phrase 'the evangelical tradition' to mean 'the tradition of the Church' when in fact it meant the teaching of the gospels.

55. Goode, op. cit., i, preface to the first edition, p. xxii.

56. E.g. see S. L. Greenslade, 'The Authority of Tradition of the Early Church in Early Anglican Thought', and G. V. Bennett, 'Patristic Tradition in Anglican Thought, 1660–1900' in *Oecumenica* (1971/2) which is entitled *Tradition im Luthertum und Anglikanismus*.

57. E.g. see G. W. H. Lampe, 'The Early Church' in *Scripture and Tradition Essays by F. W. Dillistone et al.* (1955), pp. 21–52, and R. P. C. Hanson, *Tradition in the Early Church* (1962).

58. See B. M. G. Reardon, *From Coleridge to Gore* (1971), chapter xiii, and the literature cited there.

59. J. C. Ryle wrote that 'the Fathers appear to me greatly overrated as commentators and expositors' in *Expository Thoughts on the Gospel of St. John* (1864), preface.

60. See Ryle's chapter on 'Private Judgment' in his oft-reprinted *Knots Untied,* where duties are not mentioned. Yet in 1845 Hugh Stowell, *Tractarianism tested by Holy Scripture,* Sermon I did emphasise the duties.

CHAPTER FIVE (pp. 141 to 170)

1. While the statement is probably from a second generation Lutheran theologian, Luther himself said something similar in his comments on Gal. 1.3 in his *Commentary on Galatians* (1535).

2. *British Critic,* xxxiv (1843), p. 33.

3. Faber wrote against Knox's views as they were stated in his *Remains* (4 vols, 1834–7). Knox had made use of the admission by Milner that from early times until the Reformation there had been no clear teaching on Justification by Faith in the Church. For Milner's approach to history, see John Walsh, 'Joseph Milner's Evangelical Church History' *JEH,* (1959), pp. 174 ff. Knox refers to Milner in *Remains,* i, 256 ff., and iv, 252.

4. Already in 1833 James Thomas O'Brien of Trinity College, Dublin, had published what became a standard Protestant work on Justification: *An Attempt to Explain the Doctrine of Justification by Faith Only* (1833). See further E. R. Norman (ed.), *Anti-Catholicism in Victorian England* (1968) and note the reprint in 1848 of Gibson's *Preservative against Popery,* by the British Reformation Society.

5. T. L. Sheridan, 'Newman and Justification. A Study in the Development of a Theology', a thesis submitted to the Faculty of Theology of the Institut Catholique de Paris (1965). See also David Newsome, 'Justification and Sanctification: Newman and the Evangelicals', *Journal of Theological Studies,* n.s. xv (1964), pp. 32 ff.

6. See further C. S. Dessain, 'Cardinal Newman and the Eastern Tradition', *The Downside Review,* 94, No. 315 (1976), pp. 83 ff.

7. W. Ward, *Life of Newman* (1912), i, p. 432; and Faber, *The Primitive Doctrine of Justification* (2nd ed., 1838), p. 410. Newman himself believed the Lectures to be one of the five constructive books he produced in his lifetime. Ward, *Life,* ii, p. 262.

8. Appendices v and vi, pp. 393 ff. and 408 ff.

9. Faber, op. cit., pp. 425–7.

10. See further W. S. Bricknell, *The Judgment of the Bishops upon Tractarian Theology* (1845), chapter XIII. Nonconformists also joined in the controversy: for example, James Bennett, a Secretary of the London Missionary Society, published *Justification as Revealed in Scripture* (1840).

11. C. F. Allison, *The Rise of Moralism* (1966), pp. 63 ff.

12. Faber, *Provincial Letters* (1842), preface.

13. Sumner had previously published expositions of Matthew, Luke, John and Acts. The Hon and Rev A. P. Perceval published *A Letter to the Right Rev. John Bird, Lord Bishop of Chester: with remarks on his late Charge, more especially as relates to the Doctrine of Justification* (1841). The points he made were that the bishop did not mention the relation of baptism and justification and did not say enough about repentance and justification.

14. *Charge* (1841), p. 22.

15. In the *British Critic*, lxvii (1843), pp. 63 ff. there is a review of the book and on p. 74 there is an attempt to summarise the differences between the systems of Sumner and Newman. The publication of the *Tract* by the SPCK led to a minor controversy. William Scott in *An Appeal to the Members of the SPCK* criticised Sumner's doctrine while R. Burgess, the Evangelical rector of Upper Chelsea, defended it in *Observations on 'An Appeal'*. See further *Churchman's Monthly Review* (1844), pp. 298 ff. Sumner himself defended the relation of justification by faith and holy living in *Christian Charity the Test of Christian Faith* (1843), a sermon preached in Liverpool on 2 November, 1843.

16. See further William Carus, *Memorials of the Rt Rev Charles Petit McIlvaine* (1882). Carus was also the biographer of Charles Simeon, and the latter's successor at Trinity Church, Cambridge.

17. A reply to the bishop came from Vanburgh Livingston in *An Inquiry into the merits of the Reformed Doctrine of Imputation* (New York, 1843).

18. Carus, op. cit., p. 129.

19. The address was published as *The Chief Dangers of the Church in these Times* (New York and London, 1843).

20. For an exposition of Newman's doctrine see Sheridan, op. cit., chap. ix. See also C. S. Dessain, 'The biblical basis of Newman's ecumenical theology', in *The Rediscovery of Newman: An Oxford Symposium* (ed. J. Coulson and A. M. Allchin, 1967), pp. 100 ff. Hans Küng, *Justification* (1964), pp. 202-3 refers to Newman with admiration.

21. *British Critic*, xxviii (1840), No. 56, p. 42, cited by M'Ilvaine, *Oxford Divinity*, p. 40.

22. Knox, *Remains*, ii, p. 60, cited by M'Ilvaine, op. cit., p. 42.

23. Faber, *Primitive Doctrine of Justification* (2nd ed., 1838), p. xx.

24. M'Ilvaine, *Oxford Divinity*, pp. 126-32.

25. For useful articles on 'habitus' as used in medieval theology see C. A. Dubray, 'Habit', *The Catholic Encyclopedia* (1910), vii, p. 102, and R. J. Tapia, 'Habit (in Theology)', *New Catholic Encyclopedia* (1967), vi, pp. 884-5.

26. Garbett, *Jesus Christ as Prophet, Priest and King*, i, pp. 460-2.

27. There is no biography of him in English. For his doctrine of justification see M. J. Arntzen, *Mysticke rechtvaardigingsleer. Een bijdrage ter beoordeling van de theologie van Andreas Osiander* (Kampen, 1956).

28. See further Franz Lau and Ernst Bizer, *A History of the Reformation in Germany to 1555* (1969), pp. 230-1, and Émile G. Léonard, *A History of Protestantism, Vol. I. The Reformation* (1965), pp. 93 and 150-1. Osiander's

teaching is condemned in the Formula of Concord, Art. III and by Calvin in *Institutes*, Bk. 3, Ch. 11, sec. 5–12.

29. *Lectures*, p. 426. Newman probably knew Osiander's teaching through the description of it in Scott's *Continuation of Milner's History*, ii, p. 116.

30. Laurence, *Visitation of the Saxon Reformed Church* (1839), p. 189.

31. Garbett, op. cit., i, p. 459; and M'Ilvaine, op. cit., pp. 99–100.

32. Heurtley, *Justification* (2nd ed., 1849), pp. 88 and 342.

33. Faber, op. cit., pp. xx–xxi, quoted by M'Ilvaine, op. cit., pp. 44–45.

34. Garbett, op. cit., i, pp. 374–5.

35. Newman, *Lectures*, pp. 259, 293 and 303.

36. Faber, *Primitive Doctrine of Justification* (1838), p. 418. 'Cruden' is *Cruden's Concordance*.

37. M'Ilvaine, op. cit., pp. 185 ff.

38. Garbett, op. cit., i, p. 395.

39. Heurtley, op. cit., p. 227.

40. Ibid., pp. 254–5. Bishop Burnet defined baptism thus: 'Baptism is a federal admission into Christianity: in which, on God's part, all the blessings of the Gospel are made over to the Baptised; and, on the other hand, the person baptised takes on him, by a solemn profession and vow, to observe and adhere to the Christian Religion.' *Thirty-Nine Articles*, comment on Article XXVII.

41. M'Ilvaine, op. cit., p. 413.

42. Heurtley, op. cit., pp. 258–9.

43. M'Ilvaine, op. cit., pp. 420–1, 433–4.

44. Heurtley, op. cit., pp. 268–70.

45. Ibid., p. 281.

46. M'Ilvaine, op. cit., p. 374.

47. Garbett, op. cit., pp. 445–7; Sumner, *Charge*, pp. 23–4, and *Practical Exposition*, pp. xxvii–xxix.

48. He was unjustly accused of Novatianism. For the way in which Clement, Origen and Tertullian faced the problem of the forgiveness of post-baptismal sins see Maurice Wiles, 'One Baptism for the Remission of Sins', *Church Quarterly Review*, clxv, 1964, pp. 59 ff. For the role of penitence in the history of the Church see P. E. McKeever, 'Sacrament of Penance', *New Catholic Encyclopedia* (1967), xi, pp. 73–83 and the literature there listed.

49. Pusey, *Letter*, p. 93. See also the whole section, pp. 81–96.

50. Ward's comments appear in the review of Heurtley's *The Union of Christ and His People* (1842), and in the *British Critic*, xxxi (1842), pp. 449–452.

51. Heurtley, op. cit., p. 330.

52. For both Shaftesbury and Haldane see Hodder, op. cit., ii, pp. 400 ff.

53. There are useful summaries of the teaching of Knox, Erskine, Campbell and Maurice in B. M. G. Reardon, *From Coleridge to Gore* (1971).

54. See further on this point O. Pfleiderer, *The Development of Theology in Germany since Kant and its Progress in Great Britain since 1825* (1890), p. 382.

55. See e.g. J. A. Ziesler, *The Meaning of Righteousness in Paul* (Cambridge,

1972) and the review by G. B. Caird in *Journal of Theological Studies*, xxiv (1973), pp. 555 ff. Ziesler consciously attempts to weave together Protestant and Catholic understanding.

CHAPTER SIX (pp. 171 to 202)

1. H. F. Woodhouse, *The Doctrine of the Church in Anglican Theology, 1547–1603* (1954), pp. 43 ff.

2. Two years later Goode published *A Supplement to His work on the Eucharist; containing Two Letters of Bishop Geste . . . illustrating the history and meaning of the twenty-eighth and twenty-ninth Articles; together with a Reply to Dr Pusey's Answer . . .* (1858). Pusey's work was *The Real Presence . . .* (1857). Liddon, iii, pp. 438 ff.

3. MacKean, *The Eucharistic Doctrine of the Oxford Movement* (1933), pp. 194–5.

4. It is perhaps worth making the point that the issue as to whether an Anglican should join the Evangelical Alliance had nothing to do with the priority of the invisible Church. Rather it had to do with the claim of the national Church over against Nonconformity.

5. Goode, *Rule of Faith* (2nd ed.), i, p. 444.

6. See further Woodhouse, op. cit., p. 52, and Litton, *Church of Christ* (1851), p. 319.

7. See e.g. *First Helvetic Confession* (1536), sec. 15, and *Augsburg Confession* (1530), art. 3.

8. Litton, op. cit., pp. 48 ff. For the same viewpoint see J. D. MacBride, *Lectures on the Articles of the United Church of England and Ireland* (1853), pp. 345 ff.

9. See e.g. the treatises by Freeman, Sherlock and others collected in vols. iii, iv and xiv of the edition of 1848, edited by John Cumming. To assert that the doctrine was common in controversial literature is not to assert that it is not to be found in earlier Anglican divinity – see e.g. Hooker, *Ecclesiastical Polity*, bk. 3, chap. 1, sec. 1–3, and Field, *Of the Church*, bk. 1, chap. 10.

10. See further Leonard Hodgson, *The Doctrine of the Church as held and taught in the Church of England* (1948).

11. See further N. Sykes, *Old Priest and New Presbyter* (1956), pp. 85 ff., and F. L. Cross and P. E. More, *Anglicanism* (1951), sec. 10.

12. O. Chadwick, *The Mind of the Oxford Movement* (1960), pp. 138–40; and Y. Brilioth, *The Anglican Revival* (1933), pp. 260 ff.

13. Litton, op. cit., pp. 304–5; and McNeile, *The Church and Churches* (2nd ed., 1846), p. 88.

14. Wilberforce, *Doctrine of Incarnation* (4th ed., 1852), p. 255.

15. C. S. Bird made this criticism in *The Sacraments and Priestly System Examined* (1854).

16. *Two Treatises on the Church* (ed. W. Goode, 1843).

17. Litton, op. cit., pp. 310–11.

18. Ibid., p. 313.

19. McNeile, op. cit., pp. 61–2.

20. Litton, op. cit., p. 322.

21. Barth, *Church Dogmatics IV. Doctrine of Reconciliation, I.* (1956).

22. C. Benson, *Discourses upon Tradition and Episcopacy* (2nd ed., 1839), p. 107.

23. Wilson, *Charge* (1843), p. 33.

24. Whately, *Kingdom of Christ*, essay 2, sec. 42.

25. Litton, op. cit., p. 577.

26. C. Bowdler, *Two Letters on Apostolic Episcopal Succession and Tradition* (1841), p. 74.

27. Stowell, *Tractarianism tested by Holy Scripture* (1845), i, p. 162.

28. Benson, op. cit., p. 95.

29. Seeley, *Essays* (1840), p. 228.

30. The letter was from Cosin for a Mr Cordel. The article in *DNB* on Cosin comments on his sympathetic approach to the orders of foreign Protestants.

31. Stowell, op. cit., i, p. 260.

32. Stone as cited by N. Sykes, *Old Priest and New Presbyter*, p. 211.

33. Phillpotts, *Charge* (3rd ed., 1849), p. 11.

34. J. B. Mozley, *A Review of the Baptismal Controversy* (2nd ed., 1883), pp. 177 ff.

35. *CMR* (1843), p. 367.

36. *CO* (1844), pp. 662–85.

37. See further J. H. Overton, *The English Church in the Nineteenth Century* (1894), pp. 70 ff., and L. P. Fox, 'The work of T. T. Biddulph . . .', pp. 100 ff.

38. For Ussher see R. B. Knox, *James Ussher, Archbishop of Armagh* (Cardiff, 1967), p. 117.

39. Budd, *Infant Baptism* (1841); Bickersteth, *A Treatise on Baptism* (1840). In the light of the Gorham case he probably modified his position. See his letters in the *Record*, December 1849; McNeile, op. cit., pp. 336 ff.

40. Biddulph, *Doctrine of Baptismal Regeneration* (1837); Wilson, *Sermons and Tracts* (1825), i, pp. 53 ff.; and M'Ilvaine, *Oxford Divinity*, pp. 413 ff.

41. Ryder, *Charge* (1816), cited by Wilks in *CO* (1844), p. 682. For Ryder see G. C. B. Davies, *The First Evangelical Bishop* (1957).

42. Goode, *Doctrine of . . . the Effects of Baptism*, p. 9.

43. Jackson, *Works* (1672–3), iii, p. 471, where he is writing on the creed. Bk. xi. c. 17. This view was also shared by Bishop Davenant. Goode, op. cit., pp. 270 ff.

44. Hooper, *Early Writings* (Parker Society), p. 74.

45. Goode, op. cit., p. 15.

46. See further the discussion by W. Niesel, *Reformed Symbolics. A Comparison of Catholicism, Orthodoxy and Protestantism* (1962), chap. 9, and for Luther see James Atkinson, *Martin Luther and the Birth of Protestantism* (1968), pp. 191–2.

47. Goode, op. cit., pp. 21–2.

48. There are older forms of Virtualism – see e.g. Jeremy Taylor, *The*

Real Presence ... *proved* (1654). See further R. T. Beckwith, *Priesthood and Sacraments* (1964), pp. 61 ff.

49. Mackean, op. cit., pp. 6–7.

50. Mackean, op. cit., pp. 11–12.

51. Harrison, *An Answer to Dr Pusey* ... (2 vols, 1871); and Vogan, *The True Doctrine of the Eucharist* (1871).

52. Goode, *The Nature of Christ's Presence* (1856), i, p. 2.

53. Wilberforce, *Doctrine of the Holy Eucharist* (1853), pp. 178 and 404–6.

54. Goode, op. cit., p. 20 citing Gerhard, *Loci Theologici*, Loc. 20. Perhaps a weakness of Härdelin, *The Tractarian Understanding of the Eucharist*, is that he does not take sufficiently seriously the correspondence between Tractarian and developed Lutheran theology of the Eucharist.

55. For the friendship see Liddon, i, pp. 160–2, and ii, pp. 158–60. In Pusey House there are MS letters from Tholuck to Pusey.

56. *Dublin Review* (April 1854), pp. 48–74; and *Rambler* (January 1854), pp. 55–6.

57. Goode, op. cit., pp. 29–47.

58. E.g. Pusey, *The Presence of Christ* ... (1853), pp. 14, 16 and 22, and Wilberforce, *Doctrine of Eucharist* (1853), pp. 130, 165 and 180.

59. Goode, op. cit., pp. 131–73.

60. Pusey, op. cit., pp. 21–3; and Wilberforce, op. cit., pp. 155 ff.

61. In particular he mentioned three bishops – Taylor, Bilson and Morton. The last two were 'two of the most able and learned prelates our Church has ever produced'. Goode, op. cit., p. 172.

CONCLUSION (pp. 203 to 210)

1. Budd, *Infant Baptism* (1840), preface.

2. Brilioth, *Three Lectures on Evangelicalism and the Oxford Movement* (1934), pp. 28–30; D. Voll, *Catholic Evangelicalism*, p. 30 follows Brilioth.

3. After the appearance of Conybeare's article in the *Edinburgh Review* (which was later printed in his *Essays*) the *Record* of 14 November, 1853 reviewed it and took particular exception to the insinuation that 'Record-ites' were antinomian in principle. It was argued that the paper had always insisted that living faith in Christ was vital to Christianity and that this worked itself out in holy living. The assertion that there were Evangelicals to the right of the moderates associated with the *Christian Observer* was not denied.

4. Overton, *The Anglican Revival* (1897), p. 15. W. E. Gladstone, *Gleanings of Past Years, 1843–1879* (1879), vii, pp. 232–5; and R. Wilberforce, *A Charge* (1851), pp. 10–12. See also Voll, op. cit., p. 38, and Newsome, op. cit., p. 14.

5. G. W. E. Russell, *A Short History of the Evangelical Movement* (1915), pp. 90 ff. lists some of the well-known converts.

6. Moule, *The Evangelical School in the Church of England* (1901), pp. 31–2.

SELECT BIBLIOGRAPHY

1. MANUSCRIPT

a. Bodleian Library, Oxford

Add. MS C. 290. 'The Principal Clergy of London classified according to their opinions on the great Church Questions of the Day'. 1844
St Edmund Hall MSS 67/9. 'The Diary of John Hill'
MS Eng. Lett. e. 144, f. 233. Letter of E. B. Pusey to T. G. Tyndale

b. Pusey House, Oxford

'Newman to Pusey. MS Letters (1823–1840)', i. Letter of 10 January, 1837
'Correspondence of Mrs Tyndale with E. B. Pusey'

c. The Oratory, Birmingham

'Correspondence of G. S. Faber with J. H. Newman'

d. Lambeth Palace Library, London

Lambeth MSS 1804–1811. 'The Correspondence of C. P. Golightly'

e. Church Missionary Society Archives, London

'Reports of Association Secretaries, 1840–1848'

2. NEWSPAPERS AND JOURNALS

British Critic
British Magazine
British Protestant
Christian Examiner
Christian Guardian
Christian Lady's Magazine
Christian's Monthly Magazine
Christian Observer
Christian Remembrancer
Church of England Quarterly Review
Churchman
Churchman's Monthly Review
Ecclesiologist
Eclectic Review
Edinburgh Review
English Churchman
Guardian
North British Review
Protestant Magazine
Oxford and Cambridge Review
Record

3. SELECT TRACTARIAN PUBLICATIONS

Allen, L. (ed.), *John Henry Newman and the Abbé Jager: A Controversy on Scripture and Tradition* (Oxford, 1975)
Denison, G. A., *The Real Presence: Three Sermons* (1853)
Denison, G. A., *Notes on My Life* (1879)
Froude, R. H., *Remains* (2 vols, 1838–9, ed. J. H Newman and J Keble)
Gresley, W., *The Real Danger of the Church of England* (1846)
Keble, J., *Primitive Tradition recognised in Holy Scripture* (1836)
Keble, J., *On Eucharistical Adoration* (1857)

Mozley, A. (ed.), *Letters and Correspondence of John Henry Newman* (2 vols, 1891)

Newman, J. H., *The Arians of the Fourth Century* (1833)

Newman, J. H., *The Prophetical Office of the Church* (1837)

Newman, J. H., *Lectures on the Doctrine of Justification* (1838)

Oakeley, F., *The Subject of Tract XC historically examined* (1845)

Pusey, E. B., *A Letter to the Bishop of Oxford* (1839)

Pusey, E. B., *A Letter to the Archbishop of Canterbury* (1842)

Pusey, E. B., *The Holy Eucharist a Comfort to the Penitent* (1843)

Pusey, E. B., *The Presence of Christ in the Holy Eucharist* (1853)

Pusey, E. B., *The Doctrine of the Real Presence* (1855)

Tracts for the Times (1833–1841)

Wilberforce, R. I., *The Doctrine of the Incarnation* (1850)

Wilberforce, R. I., *The Evangelical and Tractarian Movements. A Charge* (1851)

Wilberforce, R. I., *The Doctrine of the Holy Eucharist* (1853)

Wordsworth, Chas., *Evangelical Repentance* (1841)

4. SELECT POST-TRACTARIAN PUBLICATIONS

Newman, J. H., *An Essay on the Development of Christian Doctrine* (1845)

Newman, J. H., *Apologia Pro Vita Sua* (Oxford, 1967, ed. M. J. Svaglic)

5. ANGLICAN EVANGELICAL WRITINGS AGAINST TRACTARIANISM

Atwell, W., *Dr Pusey Answered* (1842)

Bateman, J., *Tractarianism as described in Prophecy* (1845)

Bateman, J., *The Tractarian Tendency of Diocesan Theological Colleges* (1853)

Benson, C., *A Theological Enquiry into the Sacrament of Baptism* (1817 and 1843)

Benson, C., *Discourses on Tradition and Episcopacy* (1839)

Benson, C., *Discourses upon the Power of the Clergy* (1841)

Benson, C., *Rubrics and Canons of the Church of England considered* (1845)

Bickersteth, E., *The Christian Fathers* (1838)

Bickersteth, E., *A Treatise on Baptism* (1840)

Biddulph, T. T., *The Doctrine of Baptismal Regeneration as it has been stated in some recent Tracts* (1837)

Bird, C. S., *The Oxford Tract System . . . with reference to Reserve* (1838)

Bird, C. S., *A Plea for a Reformed Church* (1841)

Bird, C. S., *A Second Plea: A Defence of the Principles of the English Reformation* (1843)

Bird, C. S., *The Danger attending an immediate revival of Convocation* (1852)

Bird, C. S., *The Sacramental and Priestly System Examined: or Strictures on Archdeacon Wilberforce's Works on the Incarnation and Eucharist* (1854)

Bowdler, C., *Two Letters on Apostolic Episcopal Succession and Tradition* (1841)

Bricknell, W. S., *Preaching . . . considered with reference to the 'Tracts'* (1841)

Bricknell, W. S., *'Is there not a cause?' A Letter to . . . E. B. Pusey* (1841)

Bricknell, W. S., *'Horae Canonicae'. A Second letter to . . . E. B. Pusey* (1841)

Bricknell, W. S., *Resignation and Lay Communion . . . a reply to Professor Keble* (1841)

Bricknell, W. S., *Oxford: Tract 90 and Ward's 'Ideal'* (1845)

Bricknell, W. S., *The Judgment of the Bishops upon Tractarian Theology* (1845)
Browne, J. H., *Strictures on some parts of the Oxford Tracts* (1838)
Browne, J. H., *Strictures on some parts of the Oxford Tract System* (1840)
Budd, H., *Infant Baptism* (3rd ed., 1841)
Close, F., *The Written Tradition* (1842)
Close, F., *The Tendency of 'Church Principles'* . . . *to Romanism* (1843)
Close, F., *Church Architecture scripturally considered* (1844)
Close, F., *The Restoration of Churches is the Restoration of Popery* (1845)
Close, F., *An Apology for the Evangelical Party* (1846)
Close, F., *High-Church Education Delusive and Dangerous* (1855)
Cotton, R. L., *Lectures on the Holy Sacrament of the Lord's Supper* (1849)
Croly, D., *An Index to the 'Tracts for the Times'* (1842)
Croly, G., *The Reformation a direct gift of divine Providence* (1839)
Davies, J., *The Standard of Faith* (1841)
Davies, J., *The Present Crisis of the Church* (1842)
Davis, C. H., *Hints and Suggestions on a Revision of the Liturgy* (1851)
Declaration of Ministers and Members of the Church of England respecting several controverted truths (1844)
Elizabeth, C., *A Peep into Number Ninety* (1841)
Elliott, E. B., *The Delusion of the Tractarian Clergy* (1856)
Faber, G. S., *The Primitive Doctrine of Justification* (2nd ed., 1838)
Faber, G. S., *The Primitive Doctrine of Regeneration* (1840)
Faber, G. S., *Provincial Letters* (1842)
Fawcett, J., *Baptism considered in connexion with Regeneration* (1842)
Fitzgerald, W., *Episcopacy, Tradition and the Sacraments considered in reference to the Oxford Tracts* (1839)
Fitzgerald, W., *Holy Scripture the Ultimate Rule of Faith to a Christian Man* (1842)
Fry, C., *The Listener in Oxford* (1840)
Garbett, J., *Christ as Prophet, Priest and King* (2 vols, 1842)
Garbett, J., *A Review of Dr Pusey's Sermon on the Eucharist* (1843)
Garbett, J., *Diocesan Synods and Convocation* (1852)
Goode, W., *Some Difficulties in the late Charge of the Bishop of Oxford* (1842)
Goode, W., *The Case as it is* (1842)
Goode, W., *The Divine Rule of Faith* (3 vols, 1842 and 1853)
Goode, W. (ed.), *Two Treatises on the Church* (1843)
Goode, W., *Altars prohibited by the Church of England* (1844)
Goode, W., *Tract XC historically refuted* (1845)
Goode, W., *A Letter to a Lay Friend on the state of the Church* (1845)
Goode, W., *A Defence of the Thirty-Nine Articles* (1848)
Goode, W., *A Vindication of 'A Defence'* (1848)
Goode, W., *The Doctrine of the Church of England as to the effects of Baptism in the case of Infants* (1849)
Goode, W., *A Reply to the Letter and Declaration respecting the Royal Supremacy* (1850)
Goode, W., *A Letter to the Bishop of Exeter* (1850)
Goode, W., *An Address delivered at a Public Meeting* (1851)

Goode, W., *A Reply to the Bishop of Exeter's Second Arraignment of his Metropolitan* (1852)

Goode, W., *A Reply to Archdeacon Churton and Chancellor Harington* (1852)

Goode, W., *The Case of Archdeacon Wilberforce compared with that of Mr Gorham* (1854)

Goode, W., *The Nature of Christ's Presence in the Eucharist* (2 vols, 1856)

Graham, J., *Essays for Family Reading; intended to counteract the errors of the 'Tracts for the Times'* (1843)

Griffiths, J., *Letters with a few remarks concerning rumours which have lately been in circulation* (1844)

Harrison, J., *Whose are the Fathers?* (1867)

Harrison, J., *An Answer to Dr Pusey's Challenge respecting the doctrine of the Real Presence* (2 vols, 1871)

Heurtley, C. A., *The Union of Christ with His People* (1842)

Heurtley, C. A., *Justification* (1846)

Hill, F. T., *A Letter to the Laity . . . on some points connected with the Tractarian Controversy* (1842)

Hoare, E. N., *The Tendency of the Principles advocated in the 'Tracts for the Times' considered: in Five Letters* (1841)

Hughes, H., *The Voice of the Anglican Church; being the declared opinions of her Bishops on the doctrines of the Oxford Tracts writers* (1843)

Jackson, M., *The Oxford Tracts Unmasked* (1838)

Jordan, J., *A Review of Tradition as taught by . . . the 'Tracts'* (1840)

Jordan, J., *The Crisis Come, being Remarks on Mr Newman's Letter to Dr Jelf and on 'Tract 90'* (1841)

Lee, S., *Remarks on the Sermon of Dr Pusey* (1843)

Litton, E. A., *The Church of Christ* (1851)

MacBride, J. D., *Lectures on the Articles of the United Church of England and Ireland* (1853)

McNeile, H., *The Church and the Churches* (1846)

McNeile, H., *'Baptism doth save'. A Letter to the Bishop of Exeter* (1851)

Maguire, R., *Transubstantiation a Tractarian Doctrine. Suggested by Archdeacon Wilberforce on the Holy Eucharist* (1854)

Maguire, R., *The 'Oxford Movement'; Strictures on the 'Personal Reminiscences' and revelations of Dr Newman, Mr Oakeley and others* (1855)

Marsh, E. G., *The Christian Doctrine of Sanctification* (1848)

Marsh, E. G., *A Letter to R. I. Wilberforce on his Inquiry into the Principles of Church Authority* (1854)

Maurice, P., *The Popery of Oxford confronted, disavowed and repudiated* (1837)

Maurice, P., *A Key to the Popery of Oxford* (1838)

Meller, T. W., *Dr Pusey and the Fathers* (1843)

Miles, C. P., *The Voice of the Glorious Reformation; or an Apology for Evangelical Doctrines of the Anglican Church* (1844)

Miller, J. C. *'Subjection. No; not for an hour'* (1850)

M'Ilvaine, C. P., *Oxford Divinity compared with that of the Romish and Anglican Churches* (1841)

Nevile, C., *A Review of Mr Newman's Lectures on Romanism* (1839)

Noel, B., *The First Five Centuries of the Church; or the Fathers no safe guides* (1839)

Nolan, F., *The Catholic Character of Christianity as recognised by the Reformed Church* (1839)

O'Brien, J. T., *A Charge* (1843)

O'Brien, J. T., *A Charge* (1846)

Pearson, G., *The Doctrine of Tradition as maintained by the Church of England and the Primitive Church* (1838)

Plain Tracts for Critical Times (1838)

Pratt, J., *Perverted Tradition the Bane of the Church* (1839)

Royal Supremacy discussed in a Correspondence between Archdeacon Wilberforce and Dr McNeile (1850)

Scholefield, J., *Scripture Grounds of Union considered* (1841)

Scholefield, J., *The Christian Altar* (1842)

Scholefield, J., *Baptismal Regeneration as maintained by the Church of England* (1849)

[Seeley, R. B.], *Essays on the church* (1833–1841)

Shirley, W. W., *The Supremacy of Holy Scripture* (1847)

Sinclair, J., *Synodal Action in the Church unreasonable and perilous* (1852)

Smith, G. S., *The Tractarian and Evangelical Systems* (1843)

Spooner, W., *A Charge* (1837)

Stowell, H., *Tractarianism Tested by Holy Scripture and the Church of England in a series of sermons* (2 vols, 1845–6)

Sumner, J. B., *A Charge* (1841)

Sumner, J. B., *A Practical Exposition of the Epistle to the Romans . . .* (1843)

Sumner, J. B., *A Tract on Justification* (1843)

Symons, B. P., *The Claims of the Church of England upon her members* (1842)

Tayler, C. B., *Tractarianism not of God* (1844)

Taylor, I., *Ancient Christianity* (2 vols and Supplement, 1840, 1842 and 1844)

Taylor, J., *An Appeal to the Archbishop of York on the uncondemned heresies of Archdeacon Wilberforce's Doctrine of the Holy Eucharist* (1854)

Townsend, G., *The Doctrine of Atonement to be taught without Reserve: A Charge* (1838)

Townsend, G., *Sermons . . . with Two Charges* (1849)

Wilson, D. (Snr.), *The sufficiency of the Scriptures as a Rule of Faith* (1841)

Wilson, D. (Snr.), *A Charge* (1843)

Wilson, D. (Jnr.), *Our Protestant Faith in Danger* (1850)

Wilson, D. (Jnr.), *A Revival of Spiritual Religion the only effectual remedy for the dangers which now threaten the Church of England* (1851)

Wilson, F., *No Peace with Tractarianism* (1850)

Wilson, W., *A Brief Examination of Professor Keble's Visitation Sermon* (1837)

Young, E., *Protestantism or Popery. A Tract for the times showing that the Tractarian Movement is a departure from the principles of the Church of England* (1842)

6. NON-ANGLICAN WRITINGS AGAINST TRACTARIANISM

Alexander, W. L., *Anglo-Catholicism not Apostolical* (Edinburgh, 1843)

Bennett, J., *Justification as Revealed in Scripture in opposition to . . . Mr Newman's Lectures* (1840)

Brown, J., *The Exclusive Claims of Puseyite Episcopalians to the Christian Ministry indefensible* (Edinburgh, 1842)

Buchanan, J., *On the Tracts for the Times* (Edinburgh, 1843)

Bulteel, H. B., *The Oxford Argo . . . by an Oxford divine* (1845)

Candlish, R. S., 'The Progress of Tractarianism', *North British Review* 3 (1845)

Cumming, J., *Tractarianism tried by its own standards* (1842)

Cumming, J., *Popery and Tractarianism* (1843)

Darby, J. N., *Puseyism* (1855)

D'Aubigné, J. H. M., *Geneva and Oxford* (1843)

Godwin, B., *Examination of the Principles . . . of Dr Pusey's Sermon* (1843)

Jackson, T., *A Letter to Dr Pusey, being a vindication of the tenets and character of the Wesleyan Methodists* (1842)

Weaver, R., *A Complete View of Puseyism* (1843)

Yorke, C. J., *The Puseyism of all ages briefly analysed* (1842)

INDEX